Stunning WATERCOLOR SKIES

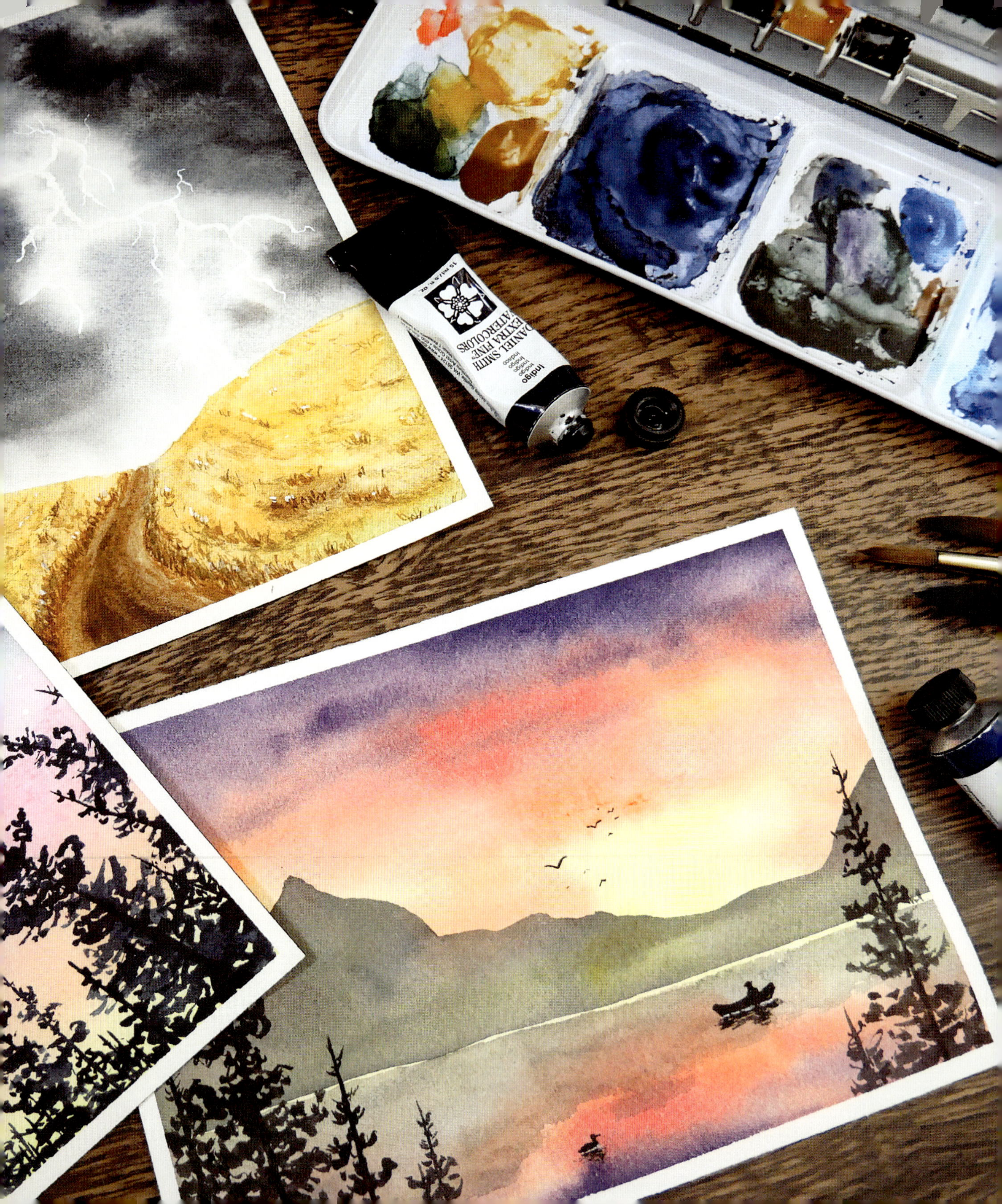
DANIEL SMITH
EXTRA FINE
WATERCOLORS
Indigo

Stunning WATERCOLOR SKIES

Learn to Paint Dramatic, Vibrant Sunsets, Clouds, Storms and Night Sky Landscapes

RACHAEL MAE MOYLES
Creator of Proximae Artistry

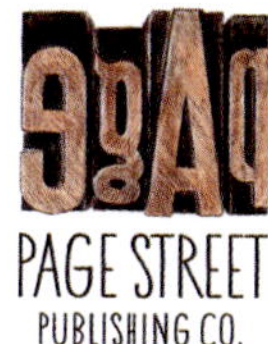

PAGE STREET
PUBLISHING CO.

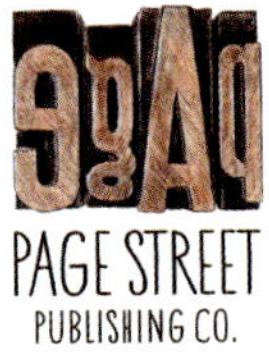

First published in 2023 by
Page Street Publishing Co.
27 Congress Street, Suite 1511
Salem, MA 01970
www.pagestreetpublishing.com

Distributed by Macmillan, sales in Canada by The Canadian Manda Group.

27 26 25 24 23 1 2 3 4 5

ISBN-13: 978-1-64567-902-8
ISBN-10: 1-64567-902-0

Library of Congress Control Number: 2022946411

Cover and book design by Molly Young for Page Street Publishing Co.
Photography by Rachael Mae Moyles

Printed and bound in the United States

Page Street Publishing protects our planet by donating to nonprofits like The Trustees, which focuses on local land conservation.

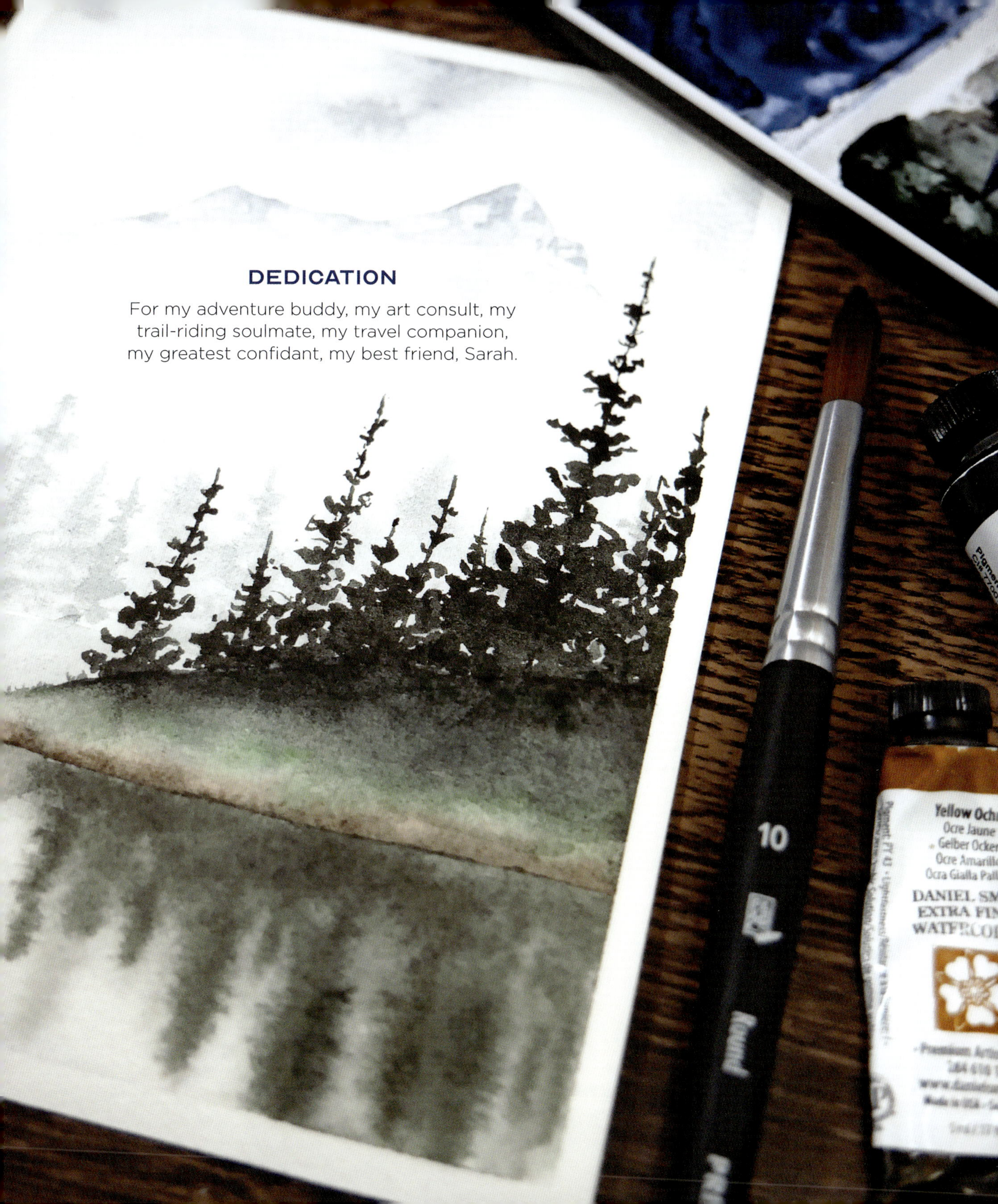

DEDICATION

For my adventure buddy, my art consult, my trail-riding soulmate, my travel companion, my greatest confidant, my best friend, Sarah.

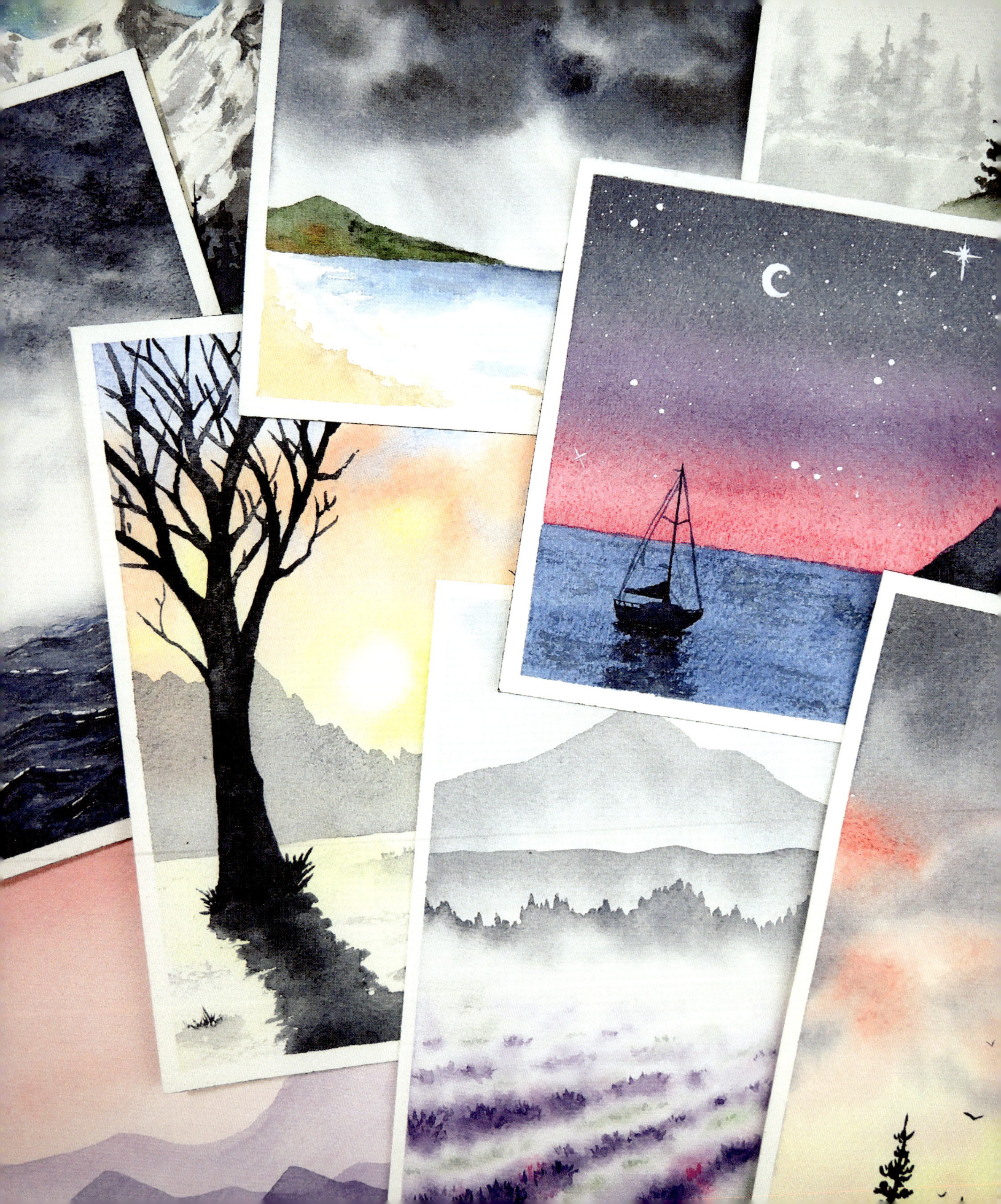

Table of CONTENTS

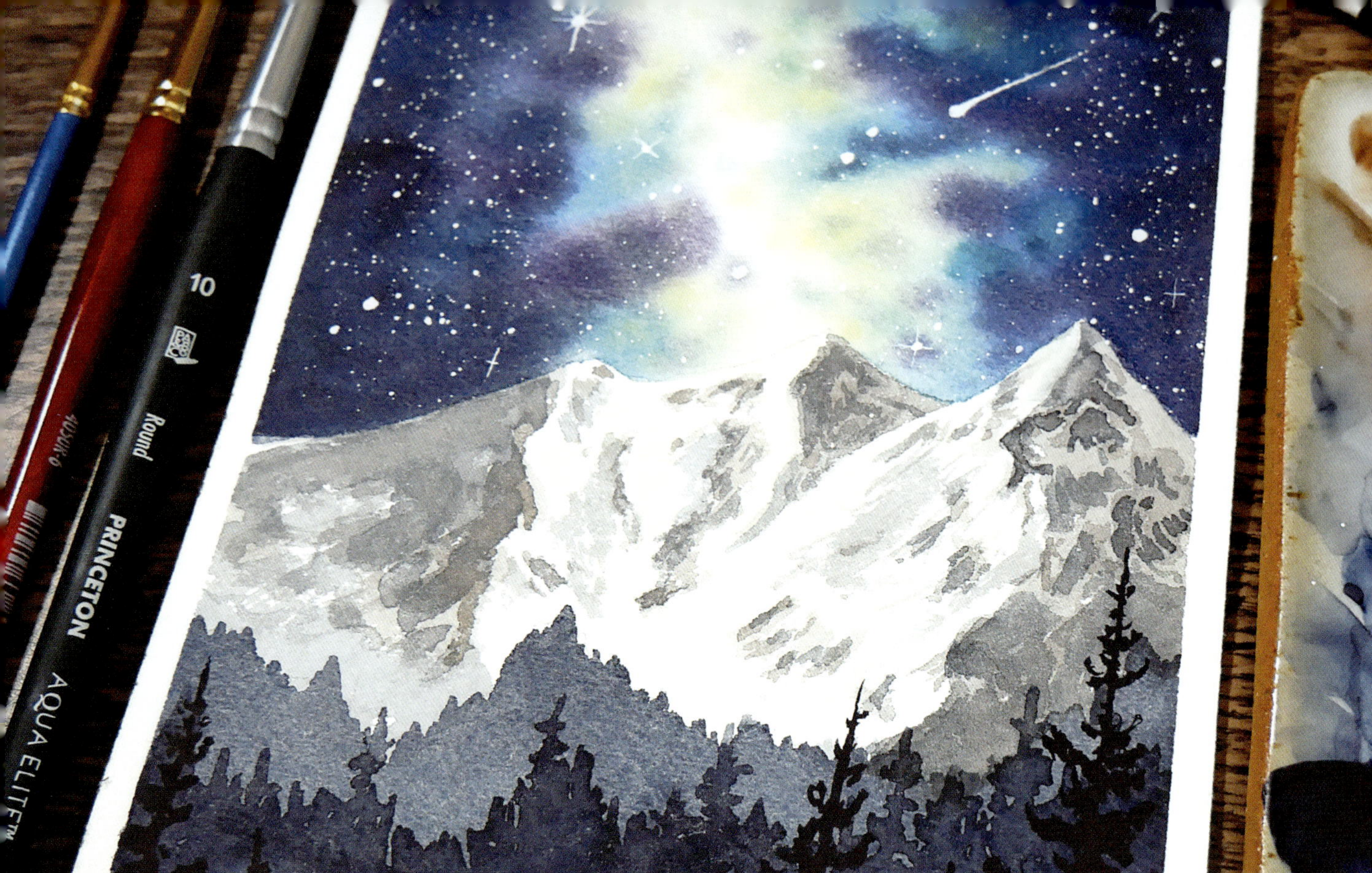

INTRODUCTION

I never thought I could fall in love with watercolors. Like many, my familiarity with the medium didn't extend beyond the dollar store watercolor sets they'd hand out in elementary school art class. Though I never considered myself an "artist" by any means (I was more of a music kid, actually), I still had a decent level of comfort with acrylic painting thanks to art class. Acrylic paints are what you'd think painting would be: straightforward, easy to control, predictable and opaque. You can easily paint over mistakes. Watercolor is not that.

Watercolor painting scared me. The paints moved across the page too quickly, too out of control. I found it difficult to shape both the paint and my thoughts and expectations. Many of my projects involving watercolor paints were quickly abandoned in art class, and I found myself favoring mediums with more predictability. Then, in high school, I abandoned art altogether. I never believed I was good enough. Yet, my desire to be an artist, to be *creative*, never disappeared, but it was buried under ideas of self-doubt.

For me, my *true* watercolor journey all started with a viral video of someone painting a galaxy sky with watercolor paints. Suddenly, my desire for creativity resurfaced. I took in everything about the video: the colors, the ease in which the artist painted, the final product, the *magic*. I was enthralled. And I wanted so very badly to create something similar. Now, as an adult, I had the ability to impulsively drive to the store, purchase watercolor supplies and begin. So, I did just that. I booked it to the nearest Michaels®, forked over money for supplies, returned home and began to paint, trying to replicate what I had seen in that viral video.

It was a disaster.

It looked *nothing* like I'd envisioned. Right then and there, I experienced a flashback only movie characters receive: little elementary school Rachael, dissatisfied yet again with watercolors, abandoning her painting and giving up. But something was different now for me. I spent money on these supplies, it took time and energy to retrieve them and I felt a spark of something: *curiosity*. I was learning. I saw potential. I enjoyed the painting process, and that's what truly mattered. My mother has always told me that "The first step is the most difficult one." And she was right. But now that first step was done, and I wanted to take another. So, I tried again, putting to use the skills I just learned. And you know what? My painting improved.

My watercolor journey had begun in earnest. That same innate chaotic nature of watercolor paints that initially scared me now captivated my attention. Painting with watercolors required me to let go of my desire for control and, instead, flow with the paints. Their vibrancy and ability to dance across the paper quickly drew me into my favorite subject: skies. I have long been fascinated with the sky, always looking up and spending an extra moment of my day to admire its brilliance. The sky is an endless expanse of inspiration, constantly changing, as chaotic and radiant as the paint medium that captured my curiosity.

In this book, we'll explore the many moods of the sky. We'll begin with a review of my favorite supplies and essential watercolor techniques and, from there, we'll expand upon that knowledge and create twenty unique sky landscapes. If you're anything like me, you learn by doing, so within each project, you'll put to practice watercolor skills discussed in earlier sections of the book. Sprinkled throughout the book are some helpful tips that I wish I had known sooner, so keep an eye out for them!

I hope this book can meet you where you are—whether you've never picked up a paintbrush or you've picked up many. I hope it can provide inspiration for you. I hope you, too, will fall in love with watercolors.

I would absolutely love to see your watercolor journey and support you! So, please tag me on Instagram (@proximae.artistry) or on Facebook (Proximae Artistry). Plus, use the hashtag StunningWatercolorSkies so I can see your work!

I, like many, believed that the title of "artist" belonged to someone who spent their life honing their artistic abilities. But that's not true. An artist is someone who's brave. Brave enough to attempt putting a pen to paper, a brush to canvas, a song into the air, you name it. Anyone can be an artist, and anyone can use watercolor paints to capture the magnificence of our sky—including you. All you need to do is take that first step (the hardest one!), then another and another. So, together, let's look up toward the heavens, take a deep breath and then put a paintbrush down to paper.

Rachael Mae Moyle

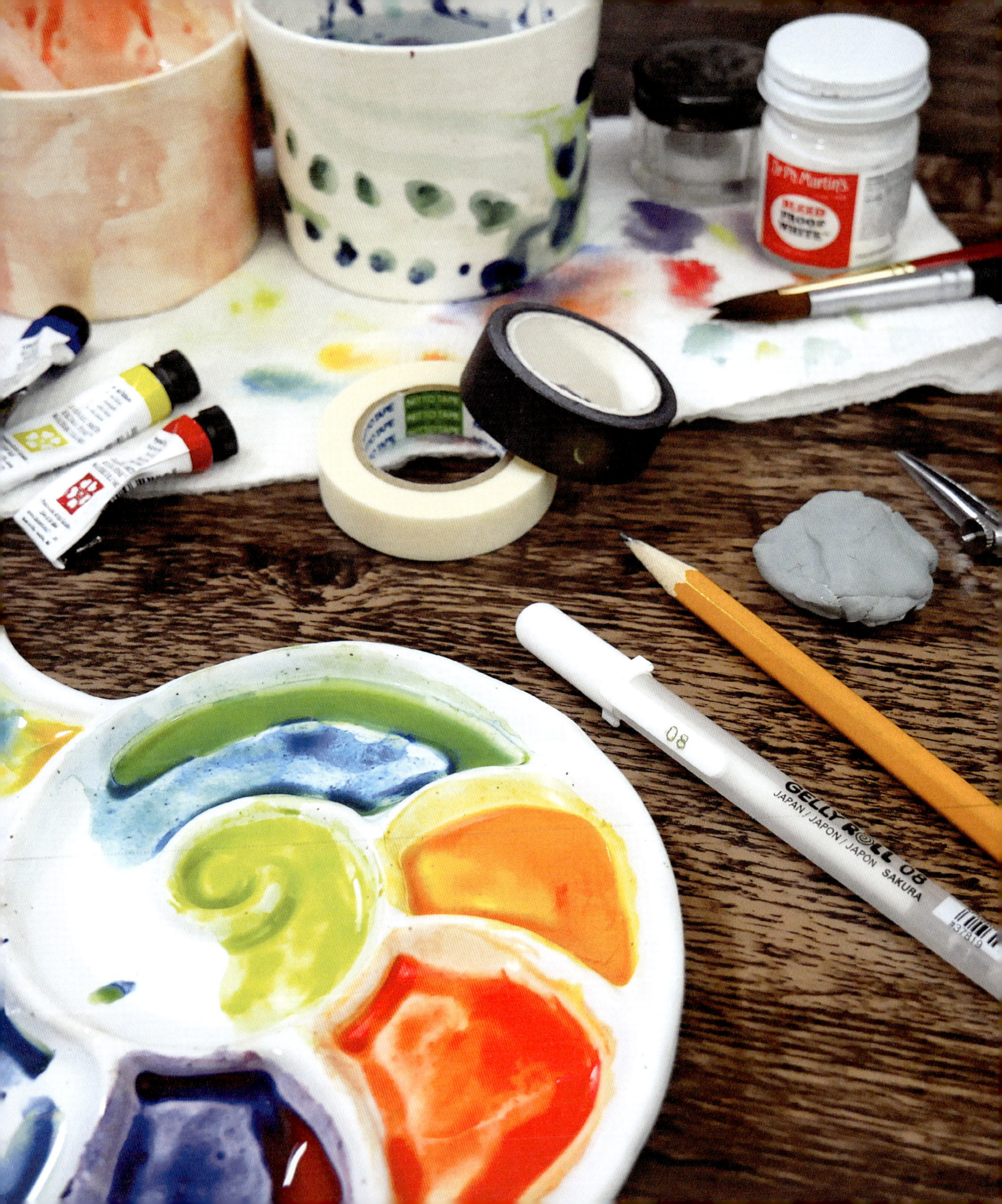
Dr. Ph. Martin's
BLEED PROOF WHITE
08
GELLY ROLL 08
JAPAN / JAPON / JAPON SAKURA

Important SUPPLIES *for* PAINTING BEAUTIFUL SKIES

Remember that story I shared about running to Michaels to purchase watercolor supplies, having no idea what I was doing or where to even start? Turns out, your supplies do matter, and poor-quality paints, paper and brushes will only serve to increase your frustration. I don't want cheap, poor-quality supplies to chase anyone away from the magical world of watercolors. I will always stand by high-quality, artist-grade supplies, but don't worry! There are plenty of budget-friendly options that are perfect for beginners and well-seasoned artists alike.

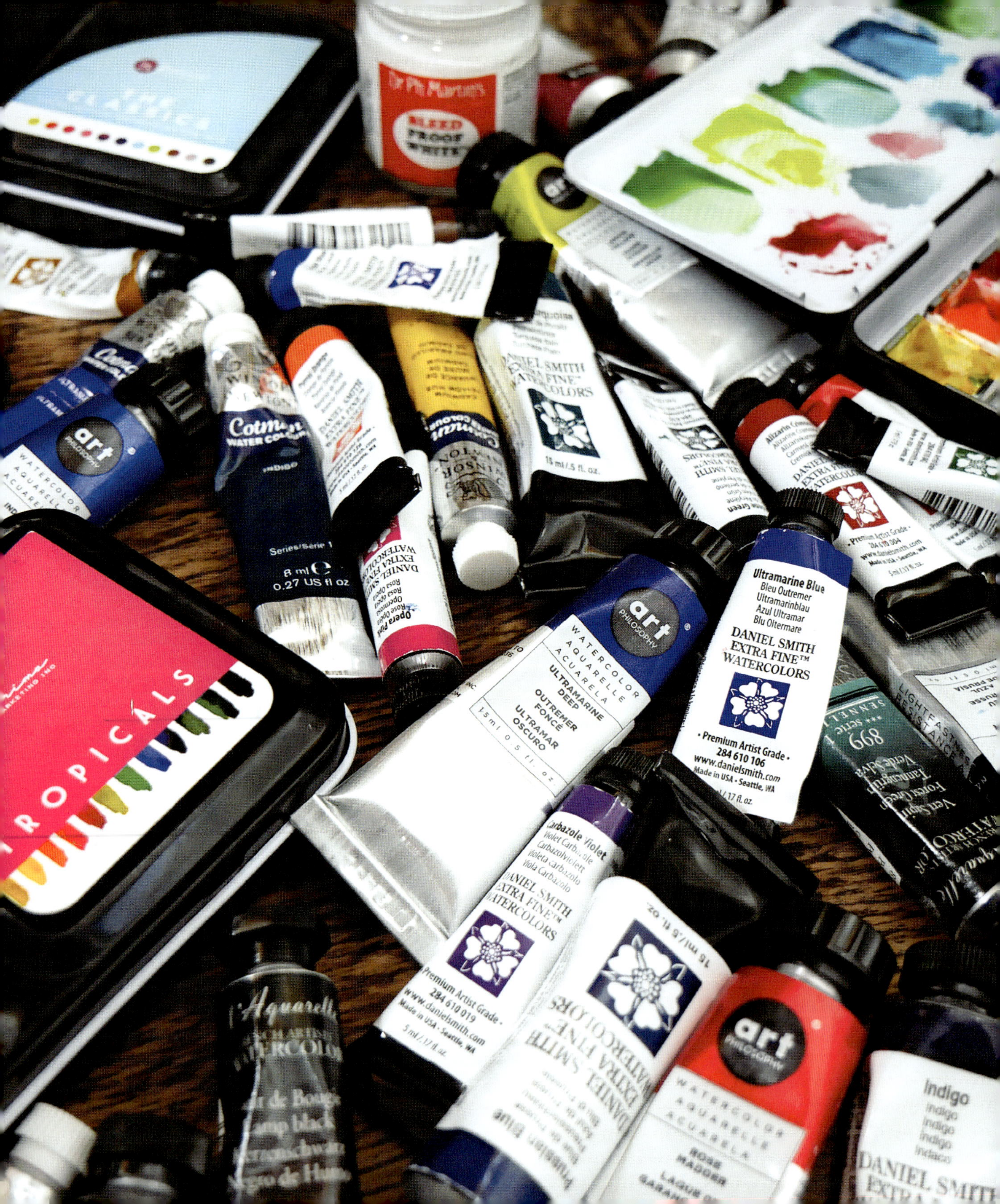
THE CLASSICS
Dr. Ph. Martin's
BLEED PROOF WHITE
Cotman
WATER COLOURS
INDIGO
Series/Série 1
8 ml
0.27 US fl oz
art PHILOSOPHY
WATERCOLOR
AQUARELLE
ACUARELA
ULTRAMARINE DEEP
OUTREMER FONCÉ
ULTRAMAR OSCURO
15 ml 0.5 fl. oz
Ultramarine Blue
Bleu Outremer
Ultramarinblau
Azul Ultramar
Blu Oltermare
DANIEL SMITH
EXTRA FINE™
WATERCOLORS
· Premium Artist Grade ·
284 610 106
www.danielsmith.com
Made in USA · Seattle, WA
TROPICALS
Carbazole Violet
Violet Carbazole
Carbazolviolett
Violeta carbazol
Viola Carbazolo
DANIEL SMITH
EXTRA FINE™
WATERCOLORS
Premium Artist Grade ·
284 610 019
www.danielsmith.com
Made in USA · Seattle, WA
5 ml/.17 fl. oz.
15 ml/.5 fl. oz.
ROSE MADDER
Indigo
Indigo
Indigo
Indigo
Indaco
DANIEL SMITH
EXTRA FINE
Opera Pink
Alizarin Crimson
Lamp black

WATERCOLOR PAINTS

Watercolor paints are made out of two basic components: pigments (where the color comes from) and binders (what holds the pigments in suspension and what allows the paint to bind to the paper surface). Student-grade paints tend to have a higher binder-to-pigment ratio, but they are affordable and perfect for those who are experimenting and learning about watercolor. Artist-grade paints are a bit more expensive (more pigment rather than binders), but because their colors are vibrant, they tend to produce more predictable washes, and they'll withstand the test of time. All of the paints I have listed below will be reliable, so feel free to choose what fits your budget and desires.

Additionally, watercolors come in many forms: tubes, dry pans, bottles and even flat sheets. I find that the highest-quality paints either come in tube form or in dried watercolor pans that are activated with water.

Some of my favorite watercolor sets, ranging from student-grade to artist-grade (in that order), are:

- Winsor & Newton™ Cotman Series (tubes or pans)
- Grumbacher® Academy® Watercolors (tubes)
- Art Philosophy® Watercolor Confections® (tubes or pans)
- Etchr Lab Watercolour 24 Half Pan Set (pans)
- Mijello Mission Gold Artists' Watercolor sets (tubes)
- Sennelier L'Aquarelle Honey-Based Watercolor (tubes)
- Daniel Smith Extra Fine™ Watercolors (tubes)

Like many watercolor artists, my favorite watercolor brand is Daniel Smith. I find their paints are consistently high quality and vibrant. If you can slowly accumulate larger tubes of paint over time, it can be more affordable (this is what I did)! Plus, larger watercolor tubes last a very long time (several years or more).

You are certainly not limited to only these brands, but these are a few of my favorites, and I can confidently recommend them to both beginners and seasoned artists. If you're like me and dislike opening up watercolor tubes every time you paint, you can always squeeze watercolor tubes into empty pans and put them in a palette (you can purchase empty palettes from artist supply stores or online very easily). They also become much more portable this way.

My favorite thing about watercolors? After they dry on your palette, they can be reactivated with water, unlike acrylic paints that dry out and need to be thrown away. Need to step away from your watercolor painting? No worries! You can reactivate the paints on your palette when you return—far less waste that way.

Colors You'll Need for This Book

- Lemon yellow
- Yellow ochre
- Pyrrol orange
- Pyrrol red (or permanent red)
- Rose madder or alizarin crimson
- Hooker's green
- Perylene green
- Phthalo turquoise
- Opera pink
- Carbazole violet
- Payne's gray
- Prussian blue
- Indigo
- Cobalt blue
- Burnt umber

Note: You certainly don't need these exact colors, but this is the palette I used to create all of the paintings in the book. If you wish, you can get away with a smaller palette of a few primaries and mix the rest yourself (see page 28 for more information on color mixing).

WATERCOLOR PAPER

Paper is perhaps the most important supply you'll need for watercolor painting. If you're going to aim to save money on supplies, you can go cheaper on paints and brushes, but I never recommend going cheap on watercolor paper.

I highly recommend using professional-grade watercolor paper, which will perform better than mixed-media paper. Professional-grade paper is made from 100 percent cotton, which absorbs watercolor paint into the fibers and can withstand multiple washes. Student-grade papers are often made of cellulose, wood pulp or a low-cotton blend, which not only has trouble holding up under multiple washes, but will make our paints behave differently. For example, the paints may dry faster, not allowing us to create smooth washes. Additionally, when using paper made from cellulose or wood pulp, the watercolor pigments tend to sit on top of the fibers rather than be absorbed, which will make layering far more difficult (the paints will activate more easily, disturbing previous layers and muddying your colors).

Student-grade paper, however, does have its purpose. I enjoy using it for practice, color swatching, experimenting and more.

Watercolor paper also has certain types: hot-pressed, cold-pressed and rough. This is referring to the "tooth" of the paper and has to do with how the paper is made. Hot-pressed paper is smooth and lacks texture; many artists prefer hot-pressed paper for inks. Cold-pressed paper has a bit more texture and, as such, will be a bit "bumpy" when you run your fingers across it. Rough paper takes that texture a step further and is even more "bump" than cold-pressed. My favored paper type for all my watercolor paintings is cold-pressed. I find it has just the right amount of texture for my liking. The increased texture creates more surface area and allows the paper to stay wet a bit longer than hot-pressed. This extra time allows me to spend more time using the wet-on-wet technique, something we'll discuss on page 20.

In addition to paper types, you'll also encounter different paper weights. For the paintings we'll create in this book, I recommend nothing less than 140-lb (300-gsm) paper. Anything less will not be able to handle the multiple washes we'll be performing and will warp terribly. That being said, any watercolor paper may warp, but paper of lesser weight and quality will always warp more dramatically.

Watercolor paper can come in blocks, in which three of the four sides are glued together, or in separate sheets. For each project, I used separate watercolor sheets and taped them down to my desk surface. The tape will help minimize warping and will create a nice, sharp and clean border around your piece. Additionally, all projects in this book were designed for a 5 x 7–inch (13 x 18–cm) paper for uniformity and because I find that size is large enough to add all the detail I wish, without being so large that it is intimidating.

Watercolor Paper Recommendations (Cold-Pressed and 140lb [300gsm])

Student-Grade

- Canson® XL Paper
- Fabriano® Studio Watercolor Paper
- Blick® Student Watercolor Paper
- Strathmore® 400 Series Paper
- Legion Paper™ Stonehenge Aqua Series

Professional-Grade

- Arches® Watercolor Paper/Blocks
- Bee Paper Company® Paper
- Strathmore® 500 Series Paper
- Arteza® Expert Watercolor Paper Pad
- Fluid™ 100 Artist Watercolor Block

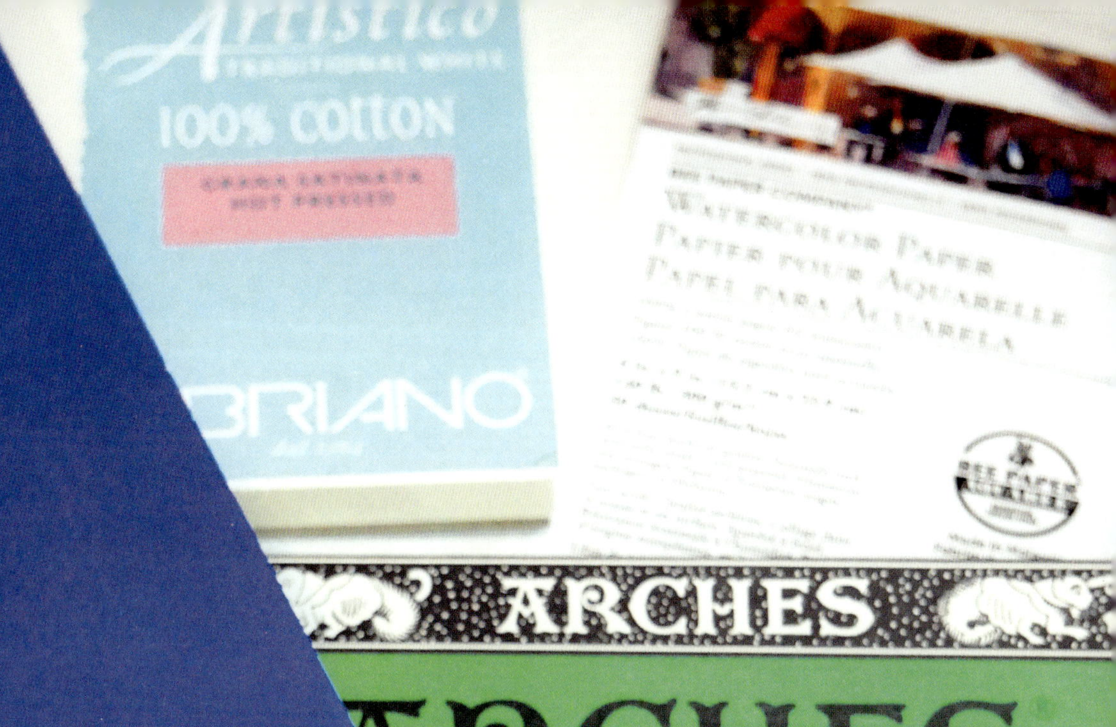

Artistico
100% cotton
BRIANO
Watercolor Paper
Papier pour Aquarelle
Papel para Acuarela
ARCHES
ARCHES
WATERCOLOUR - AC
GRAIN FIN
OLD PRESSED
ANO FINO
m² - 140 lb
cm - 7 in x 10 in
L'AQUARELLE ET LA DÉTREMPE
ERCOLOUR AND WET MEDIA BLOCK
BLOC ACUARELA Y TÉCNICAS HÚMEDIAS
100% COTTON
100% COTON
100% ALGODON
ACID FREE
SANS ACIDE
SIN ACIDO
140 LB
M X 25.40 CM
STONEHENGE
AQUA COLDPRESS

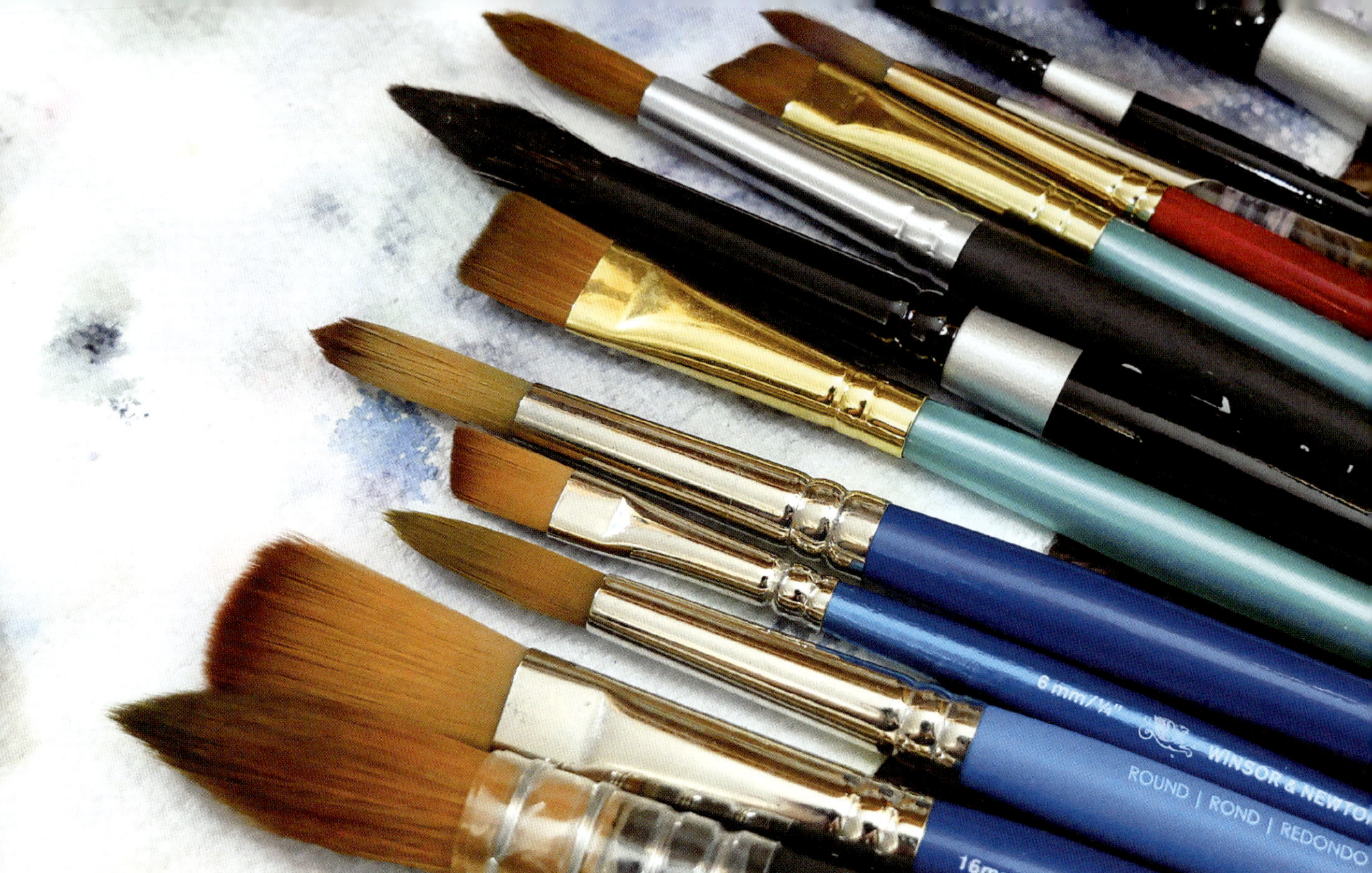

WATERCOLOR BRUSHES

There is almost an overwhelming number of paintbrushes you can buy in a variety of all shapes and sizes. For me, I like to keep things simple. For practically all of my paintings, I use synthetic round-shaped watercolor brushes in sizes 12, 10, 6 and 2. One additional brush I suggest for this book is a ⅜-inch (1-cm) flat or angled brush, as we'll use one in one of the projects. This, however, is optional, and you can certainly use a round brush instead.

That said, it's important to take good care of your brushes so that they'll last a long time. Here are some tips and tricks to do just that:

While you can use mixed-media brushes for watercolors, I recommend using brushes labeled for watercolor use. This is because watercolor brushes are designed for holding larger amounts of water rather than thicker paints like acrylic or oil.

Never leave your brushes in your water dish with their tips pressed against the glass. Doing this for extended amounts of time will warp the tip of your brush and alter its shape.

Always clean your brush after each painting session. Leaving the paint to dry in your brush will damage the bristles. I clean my brushes by holding them under a gentle stream of water and gently rubbing my fingers through the bristles to loosen any remaining pigments.

You can always purchase brush soap. I recommend The Masters® Brush Cleaner, which comes in a plastic tin. Follow the instructions on the package to achieve superclean brushes!

Once you've cleaned your brushes, always allow them to dry on a flat surface before storing them away. If you try to dry them upright, for example, excess water will run down the shaft of your brush, potentially loosening bristles and the ferule (the part of the brush that attaches the bristles to the handle). Drying your brushes upright means you'll be picking brush bristles out of your paintings.

Some of my favorite brush brands, in no particular order, are:

- Princeton Artist Brush Co.® Velvetouch Series
- Princeton Artist Brush Co.® Glacier Series
- Princeton Artist Brush Co.® Neptune Series
- Blick Essentials Series
- Etchr Lab Synthetic Brush Series

OTHER IMPORTANT WATERCOLOR SUPPLIES FOR THIS BOOK

Here are the other supplies you'll need for completing the projects in this book. They are essentials for any watercolor artist!

- A pencil
- A kneaded eraser, which is useful for lifting excess graphite off the paper without leaving eraser shavings
- A ruler for drawing straight lines
- Paper towels or rags for removing excess water and paint from our brushes
- Tissues for lifting paint
- Two cups (480 ml) of water, one for rinsing your brush and the other for getting clean water
- A ceramic or plastic palette for mixing your paints
- A white gel pen
- White gouache or Dr. Ph. Martin's® Bleedproof White™ (an opaque, water-soluble white acrylic ink)
- Masking fluid for keeping sections of your paper white
- Salt for adding texture
- Washi or painter's tape for taping down our watercolor paper and creating clean, crisp borders
    - With all of the projects in this book, I have taped down the edges of my watercolor paper to my desk. I do this to prevent the paper from warping while I'm working and to create sharp, clean edges all of the way around my paper. While this is a personal preference, I highly suggest using washi, painter's or artist's soft tape for beginners as it creates a stable surface on which to paint. It's no fun holding down your paper while also trying to paint, trust me!
- The painter's tape I use in this book is Holbein™ Soft Tape, a painter's tape made specifically for artists. It tapes down paper very well, but it's gentle when removed and won't rip your paper. It's very nice but not completely necessary. Washi and regular painter's tape will also get the job done!
- A drawing compass, bottle cap or another small circular object for drawing perfect circles
- Scrap sheets of watercolor paper
    - I always keep scrap sheets near me at all times. They're great for practicing techniques, testing colors and more.

My favorite place to shop for watercolor supplies is Blick Art Materials. They carry everything you may need, at reasonable prices, and even have a few in-person stores scattered across the United States. Their online store, however, is incredible—you may find many things you didn't know you needed! They also ship internationally. Another great option is Jackson's™ Art Supplies, which is based in the United Kingdom, and they also ship worldwide. Amazon follows, as their prices and art supply availability can vary greatly. Additionally, stores like Michaels or Hobby Lobby® also carry a decent selection of watercolor supplies. However, if you're able, I highly suggest stopping in to your local fine art store. Not only will you be supporting a small business, but many host art demonstrations, in-person classes and more! You will often find a welcoming community at your local fine art store—all the more reason to visit and say hello.

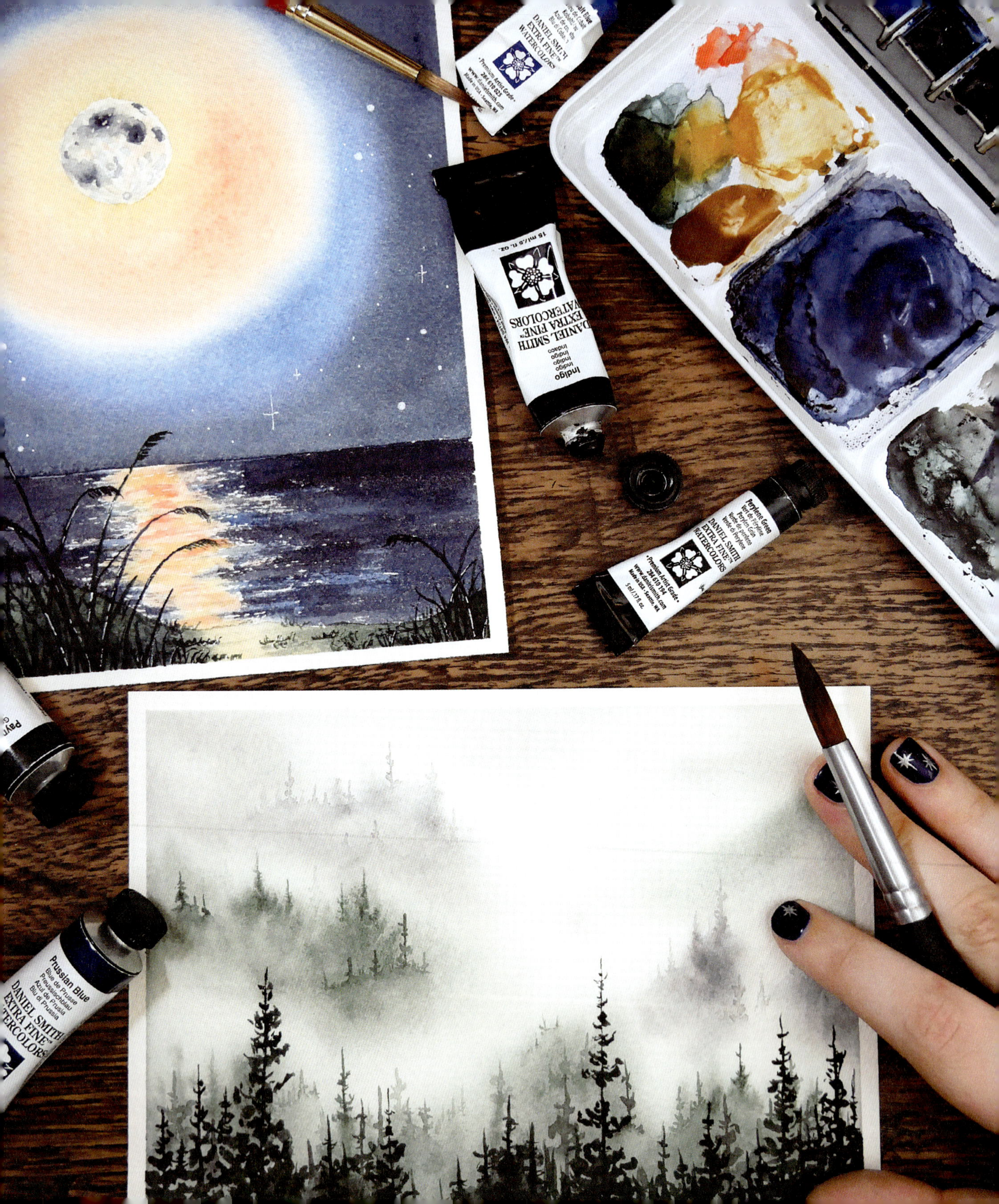
Indigo
DANIEL SMITH
EXTRA FINE
WATERCOLORS
Perylene Green
DANIEL SMITH
EXTRA FINE
WATERCOLORS
Prussian Blue
Bleu de Prusse
Preussischblau
Azul de Prusia
Blu di Prussia
DANIEL SMITH
EXTRA FINE

Watercolor ESSENTIALS *for* BREATHTAKING PAINTINGS

In this section, we'll be going over essential watercolor techniques and know-how that are important for all watercolor artists (beginners and seasoned alike). All watercolor masterpieces are created with the two foundational watercolor techniques: the wet-on-wet technique and the wet-on-dry technique. It is essential that we also cover some fundamentals of color theory, so we'll be touching on both elements in the following sections, as well as an overview on color mixes we'll be using throughout the book.

MUST-HAVE TECHNIQUES

All watercolor masterpieces are created with two foundational watercolor techniques: the wet-on-wet technique and the wet-on-dry technique.

Wet-on-Wet

The wet-on-wet technique is the quintessential, yet unique, aspect of the watercolor medium. Watercolors, obviously, are soluble in water; therefore, they'll spread every which way when applied to wet paper. Due to this unique feature, they're perfect for creating soft blends, translucent washes and, ultimately, vibrant and deep skies.

One of the questions people ask me most frequently is how to "control" the wet-on-wet technique. You don't. You can only guide the paint. To me, that is the most interesting thing about watercolors. In fact, I don't know of any other painting mediums that can perform this magical, chaotic feat in the same way! That said, there are ways to master this technique using the following three ideas below.

To start, the most important tip I can provide to anyone is this: more water = less control. Meaning, the more water you have on your paper, the more your paint will spread and dance across the paper in all directions. If your paper is only just damp, any paint you apply will remain closer to the confines of your brushstroke, leaving blurry edges behind. The more you practice, the better you will be at judging water-to-paint ratios. It's important to note, however, that I caution aspiring artists away from using so much water that it puddles on your paper. Wet watercolor paper should glisten, not puddle. Puddles warp even the strongest watercolor paper, and applying paint to puddles means you'll have *no* control. If you apply too much water, you can always mop it up with some paper towels or a clean rag.

Next, watercolor pigments will always travel to where there's water. If you touch your wet, loaded brush to an area that has not finished drying, those pigments will immediately mix and

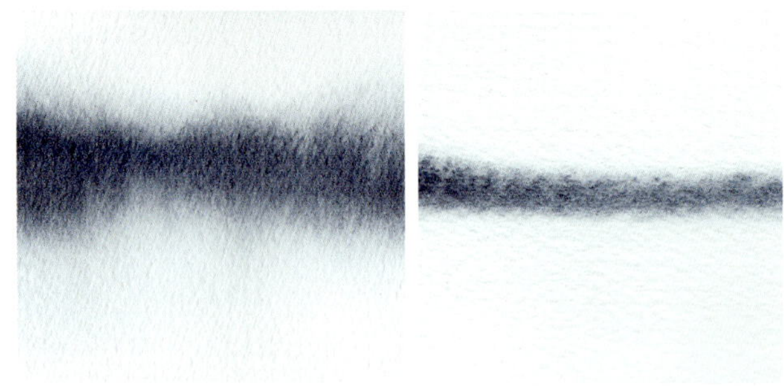

Left: paint applied with a lot of water on the paper. Right: paint applied when paper was damp.

flow into one another. If you don't wish for this to happen, make sure that your previous sections of paint are completely dry before moving on to the next step.

Third, you can utilize a brush moistened with clean water to blend paint already existing on the paper. This is very useful for blending two colors together in a gradient or pushing pigments around to reveal more white space of the paper beneath.

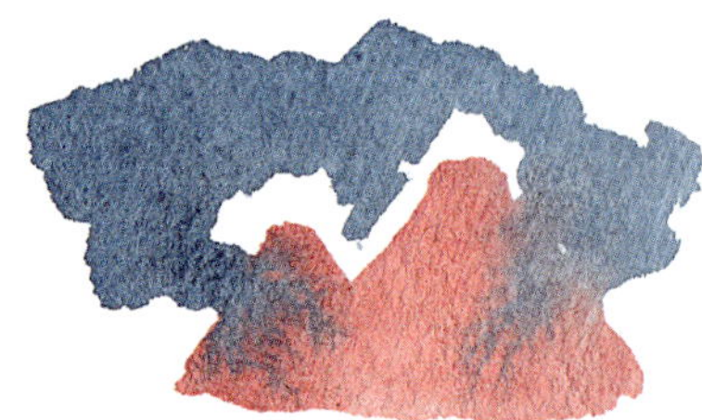

Prussian blue paint was applied to the edge of the pyrrol red paint before it was dry, causing bleeding to occur.

Wet-on-Dry

The wet-on-dry technique is much more straightforward. This technique is simply taking a loaded paintbrush and applying it to dry paper. With this, the paint will stay within the confines of your brushstroke, and the pigment will remain more concentrated since it doesn't have water to carry its flow outward. This technique is used by artists to create details and crisp lines where needed. For example, we'll use this technique a

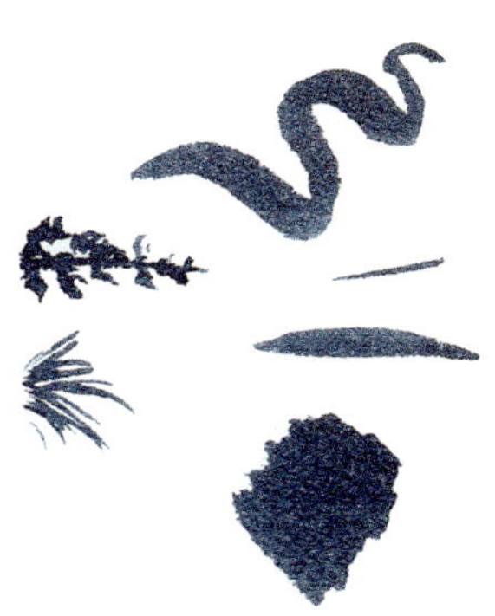

Indigo paint was applied to dry paper, creating shapes with crisp, clean edges.

lot throughout the book to create pine trees and other foreground elements.

All other watercolor techniques build upon these two foundations, and you'll become intimately familiar with them as you progress through the book. Let's also discuss a few more things you may encounter while learning watercolors.

Lifting

Talk to just about any watercolor artist and you'll find that a majority of them (myself included) don't have any white watercolor paint in their palettes. Instead, watercolor artists rely on the white of the paper. So, watercolor artists need to plan ahead for the white parts of their paintings either by painting around a section or by applying masking fluid (we'll talk about this later on page 22).

That said, what happens if you accidentally paint over an area you intended to leave white? That's where the lifting technique comes in! Lifting can be done in two ways: by physically lifting the wet paint off the paper using a Q-tip®, paper towel or tissue, or by using a clean, damp, "thirsty" brush. In order to lift with a brush, you'll need to clean off any pigment within its bristles in clean water, dab it on a paper towel so that it is nearly dry and gently rub the paint you wish to remove with your brush. A "thirsty" brush will actually soak up the wet paint into its bristles, lifting it off the paper. Make sure to then dab your brush on a paper towel before returning to the paper to lift more, otherwise you'll end up reapplying the pigments you just removed.

We'll explore this technique a lot in projects involving clouds.

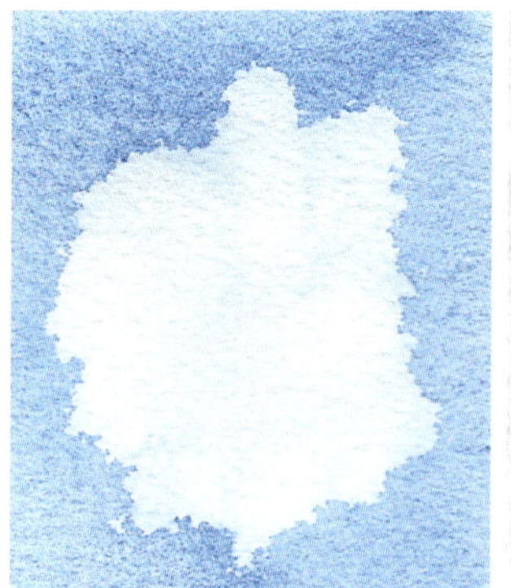

Left: paint lifted with a tissue. Right: paint lifted with a clean, damp brush.

Glazing

In watercolor, "glazing" is simply a fancy term for "layering." The key to watercolor painting is layering. Nearly all watercolor paintings require more than one layer of paint, and it is quite rare to achieve all of what you hope to depict in a single layer, just like how it's difficult to give detailed instructions to someone in a single sentence.

I like to break down layers into two categories: background and foreground. In watercolor, the rule of thumb is to work from the background layer to the foreground. Our job, as artists, is to decide what belongs in each layer and how the combination of our subjects contributes to the whole piece. For a majority of this book, our skies will be the shining stars of each project, and foreground details will mostly serve to "ground" our skies.

Glazing is also another way to "mix" colors without actually mixing the two paints on your palette. Since watercolors are transparent, the pigments of one color will shine through another, effectively combining them, though they were never mixed when wet. For example, when we layer a blue paint on top of an already dried yellow color, we will appear to see green (pictured) and, when we layer the same color, a darker value will appear where they overlap. Due to this, we'll need to be strategic with what colors and color values occupy our background layers.

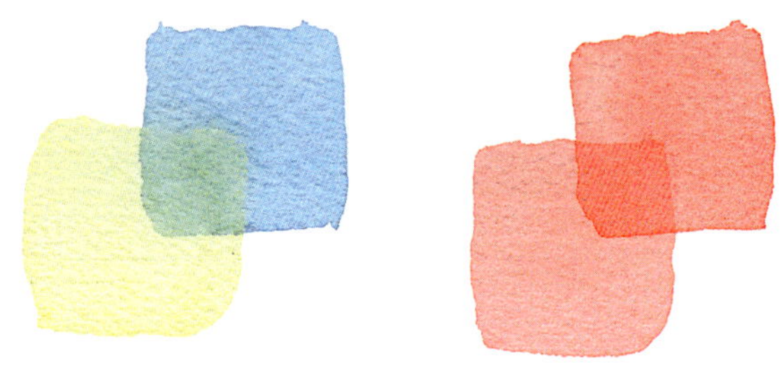

Left: layers of lemon yellow and cobalt blue, overlapping to create green. Right: layers of pyrrol red, overlapping to create a more saturated color.

Watercolor Blooms

A bloom is a flow mark created when water comes into contact with a wash that's in the process of drying. Blooms (also known as backruns or cauliflowers) occur because water always seeks a state of equilibrium (i.e., wet paint will always flow toward a drier area). Blooms occur when there's a significant difference in the degree of wetness on the page. For example, if you add water to a wash that's still wet, the pigments will not move nearly as much as if the wash was almost dry (pictured). Sometimes, blooms can be purposeful, but I often came across them in the beginning stages of my watercolor journey when I made the mistake of attempting to "fix" something in my painting that was already drying.

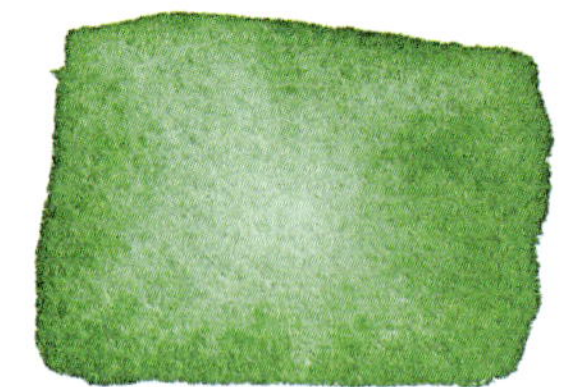

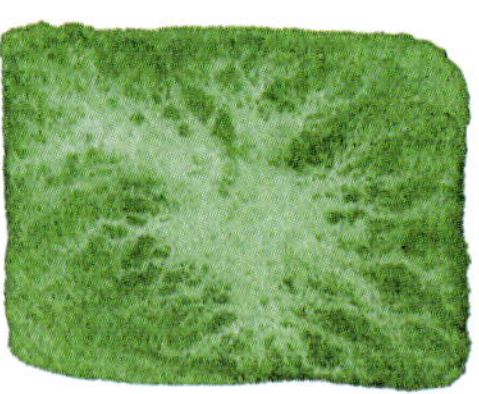

Left: a watercolor bloom that occurred while the paper was still wet. Right: a watercolor bloom that occurred when the paper was nearly dry.

It's vital to pay attention and observe the level of moisture on your paper, as well as the amount of water in your brush. Water control takes practice and a certain level of accepting that mistakes will occur. As a recovering perfectionist, I can tell you that the learning curve is worth it and mistakes are how you learn. Nonetheless, my best piece of advice for you in regard to unintentional watercolor blooms is to wait until your layer is dry before returning to fix mistakes. If your paper/paint is no longer wet enough, STOP and wait for it to dry. You can always add on another layer!

Masking Fluid

Masking fluid is a liquid, latex-based product that's used to preserve areas of the paper so that they remain white.

Masking fluid can be applied in many ways, including with a brush, a ruling pen or a toothpick. Some masking fluid products come with a fine-tip applicator or in a pen so you can simply draw the masking fluid directly onto the paper. I will caution, however, that you should not use a brush you particularly like to apply masking fluid. Masking fluid is the place where brushes go to die. If the masking fluid is allowed to dry in the bristles, it will ruin the brush. Many artists use a supercheap brush they don't care for and specifically dedicate it to masking fluid use, while others may use silicone brushes. Silicone brushes won't be ruined by masking fluid and can easily be cleaned when the masking fluid is dry. If you must use a regular brush, wet it and coat it in some mild soap before you dip it into the masking fluid. The soap will protect the bristles and make it easier to clean off later.

My favorite way to apply masking fluid is with either a ruling pen or a toothpick. A ruling pen allows for more precision and can be easily cleaned, and a toothpick is cheap, effective and a household staple!

To use masking fluid, simply apply it to whatever area on your painting you wish to preserve, and wait for the fluid to dry. Most masking fluids will change color slightly when dry, but you can always lightly touch your finger to an area to test it. Then, simply paint over the area you wish to. When your painting has dried, it's time to remove the masking fluid.

To do so, use a kneaded eraser, a regular eraser, your finger or another dull-sided tool. For example, I use the dull, flat-sided end of one of my favorite brushes. Gently rub whatever tool you're using against the masking fluid, and watch as the medium sticks to itself and peels away.

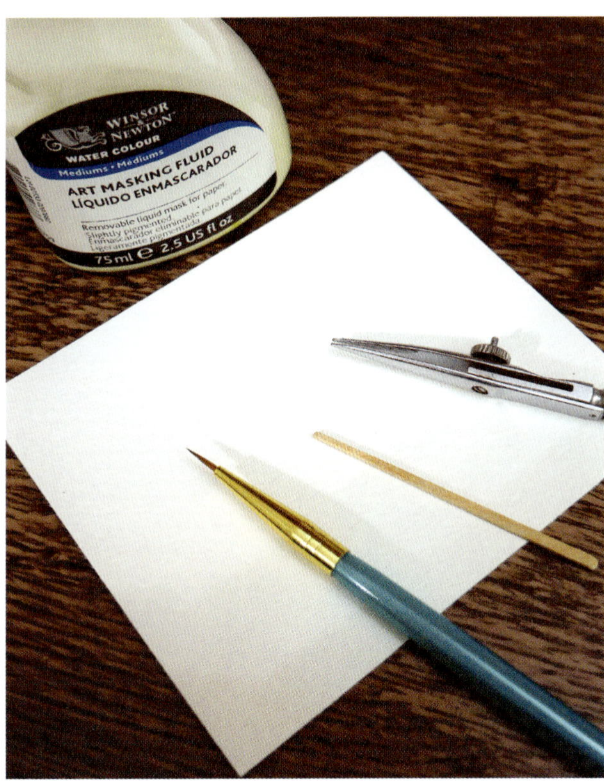

Various tools that can be used to apply masking fluid.

It's important to remove the masking fluid as soon as possible after your painting dries. The longer the masking fluid is left, the harder it'll be to remove and the higher chance there will be of the masking fluid taking your paper with it. We'll be using masking fluid in a couple of projects within this book for lightning (page 73) and a full moon (page 143).

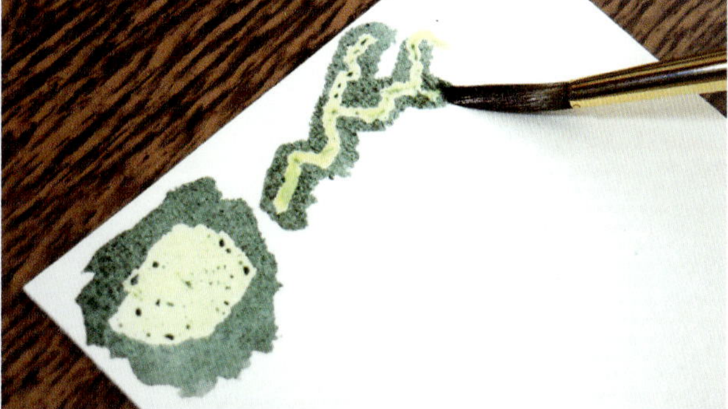

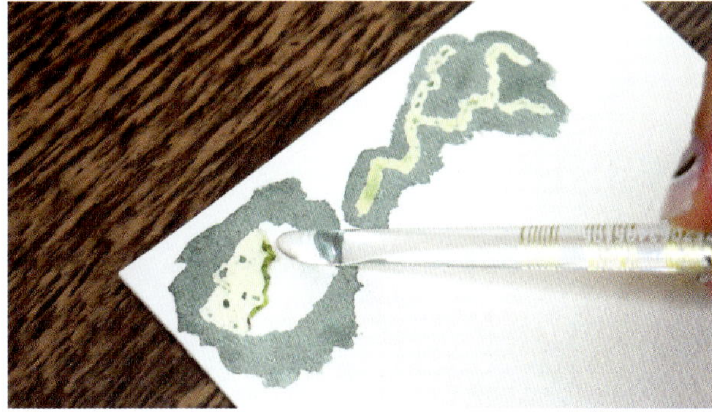

Top: apply the masking fluid to the paper. Middle: once the masking fluid is dry, paint over it. Bottom: once the paint is dry, you can remove the masking fluid with a dull-sided tool.

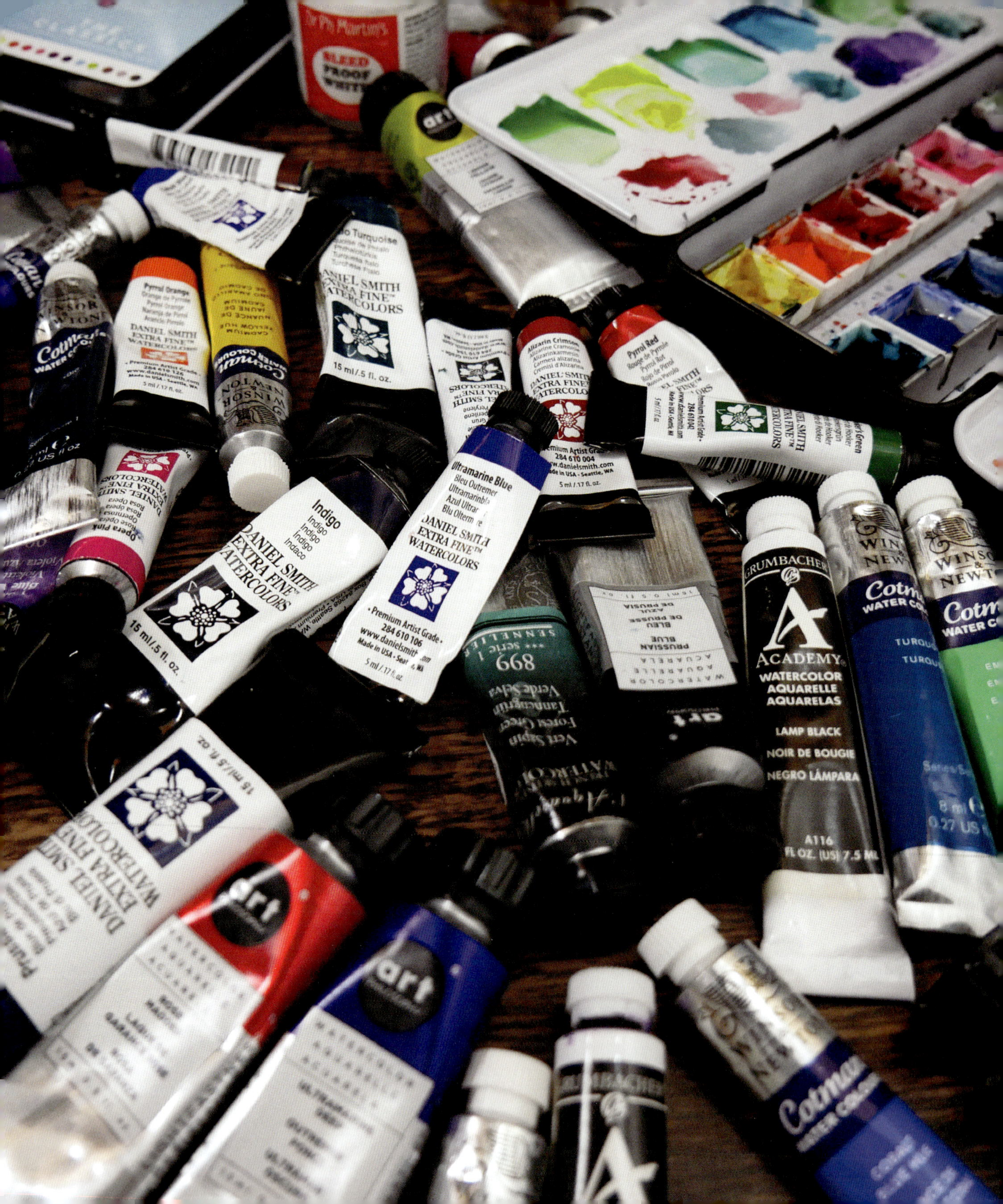

Ultramarine Blue
Bleu Outremer
Ultramarinblau
DANIEL SMITH EXTRA FINE™ WATERCOLORS
Premium Artist Grade
284 610 106
www.danielsmith.com
Indigo
DANIEL SMITH EXTRA FINE™ WATERCOLORS
15 ml/.5 fl. oz.
Pyrrol Orange
Pyrrol Red
Alizarin Crimson
GRUMBACHER
ACADEMY
WATERCOLOR
AQUARELLE
AQUARELAS
LAMP BLACK
NOIR DE BOUGIE
NEGRO LÁMPARA
A116
PRUSSIAN BLUE
BLEU DE PRUSSE
AZUL DE PRUSIA
Cotman
WATER COLOURS

WORKING WITH COLOR

Color Theory

There are books upon books with all of their pages dedicated to the discussion of color theory, but for the purposes of *this* book, we'll only be touching upon important basics. Some of these points may seem obvious, but these fundamentals will guide us in the color decision process, color mixing and more.

A helpful tool for color mixing is creating a color wheel. I always like to make one when I buy a new set of paints. Different brands of paints, though they may carry the same name, have unique formulas. Meaning, lemon yellow made by Daniel Smith may be slightly different than lemon yellow made by Mijello Mission Gold. Experimenting and playing with your paint set before you begin is a great way to become more familiar with the colors and how they may behave on the paper.

Using a color wheel, we can also see all three of our primary colors, as well as our secondary and tertiary colors, all together. A color wheel provides us with a "map" of sorts. From here, you can plan the colors you wish to use for a painting.

One of the questions people ask me the most is how to avoid "muddy colors." Muddy colors typically occur when complementary colors (opposite colors on the color wheel) end up mixing. Thus, if you wish your colors to be simple and bright in a painting, you'll need to avoid mixing complementary colors. Using analogous colors (those that are next to one another on the color wheel) would be one way to avoid creating "mud" in your paintings. Analogous colors have similar color temperatures, referred to as either being warm (reds, oranges, yellows) or cool (greens, blues, purples). Colors that are analogous mix well together due to the close relationships of the hues and, thus, can create vivid, satisfying gradients.

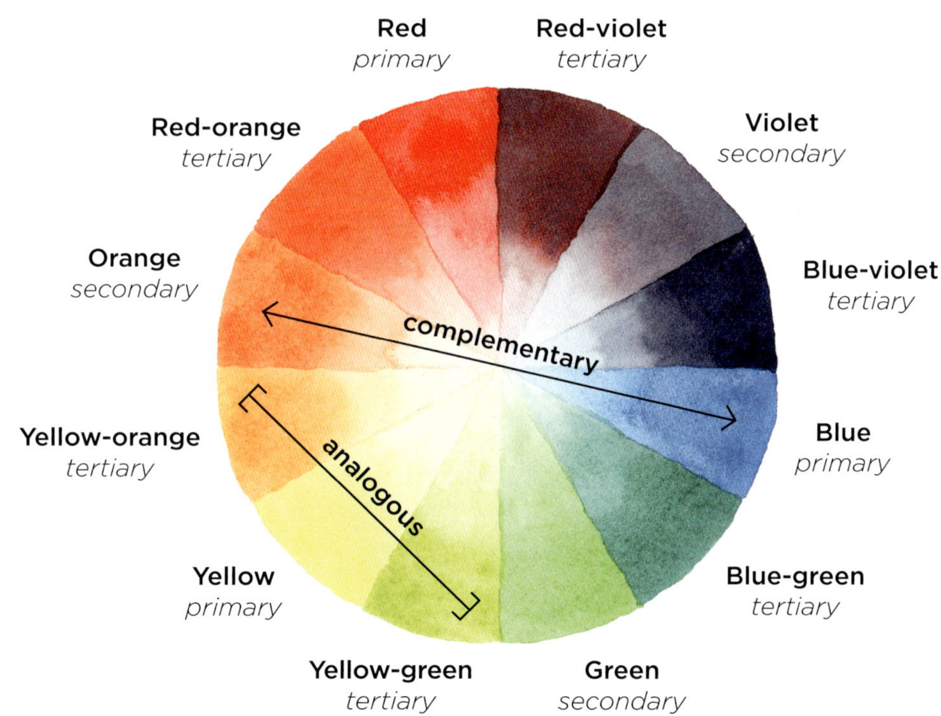

That said, you can create smooth gradients between complementary colors, but it must be done with more care and attention. You should not let the colors touch, otherwise they'll mix and muddy up your piece. This is achieved by careful use of clean water in between the colors and cleaning off your brush many times in between applying paint.

Nonetheless, complementary colors are what they sound like: They complement each other. Complementary colors create the greatest contrast and produce powerful compositions (orange clouds against a blue sky or red flowers scattered across a green field).

And while complementary colors can "muddy" up your paintings, they can also be a powerful mixing tool. For example, you can neutralize a strong red with just a touch of green. This can be useful in a number of ways. Say you're aiming to create a moodier piece and need to dull your intense colors. Adding just a touch of a complementary color may be exactly what you need.

Gradients between analogous colors (lemon yellow and cobalt blue) and complementary colors (pyrrol red and hooker's green). Note how the yellow and blue created a vibrant green, whilst the red and green created a "muddier" brown.

Whether you want to avoid the dull colors mixing complementary colors can produce or embrace the wild world of color neutralization, it's still important to understand what's happening to your colors, both on the palette and on your paper. What's in this section is only a chip off the iceberg of what color theory is, but I hope it helps on your watercolor journey.

To summarize:

- You can still achieve many color hues, even with a small color palette.
- Avoid mixing complementary colors if you want to avoid muddy browns/blacks in your paintings.
- Using analogous colors is a great way to produce simple, yet vivid, gradients. They tend to mix well together and produce pleasing color effects.
- To neutralize, or dull, a color, add in a small amount of its complementary color.

Color Value, Gradients & Flat Washes

Color value is the relative lightness or darkness of a color in its current hue, meaning you won't mix any other colors into it to change its value. In watercolor, a paint's value is determined by its water-to-pigment ratio. You will hear me reference three main values of color in this book, loosely defined below:

- Light-value, a watery, nearly transparent color, more water than pigment
- Medium-value, a less watery, even mix of pigment and water
- Dark-value, a very saturated color, far more pigment than water

Three color values of Prussian blue, from light to dark.

There may be cases where we mix up a color value in between these three, but I always like to have this color scale in my mind. It helps as a reference and a guide. The best way to test color value is to have a scrap sheet of watercolor paper handy at all times! That way you can test each color for its value before putting it in your piece. My art studio is always littered with scrap sheets, full of various color swatches and brush marks.

A watercolor gradient is simply defined as moving from one color value to another within a defined space. For example, moving from a dark-value blue to a light-value blue. You can create gradients using one color (a monochrome gradient) or with multiple colors.

There are multiple ways to create gradients in watercolor, but my favorite way is to apply a dark value of my paint to my paper and, while it's still wet, apply a clean, wet brush and drag that pigment out. You'll need to clean your brush in between each stroke, dragging that pigment out farther and farther across the paper until it's nearly transparent. Creating gradients like this is a fantastic way to see the range of a particular color. It's amazing how many hues there are in what looks like "one" color.

A bichrome gradient with pyrrol red and cobalt blue.

Creating a gradient between two colors is a little like creating a monochrome gradient, in which you apply clean water in multiple brushstrokes to drag out the pigment; however, once you reach complete transparency with the first color, you repeat the process with the second color, moving toward the first. This is depicted in the picture.

A flat wash, however, is exactly as it sounds: one even wash of color, typically of somewhat light value, applied over a large area to help create backgrounds. Washes can be performed with both the wet-on-wet technique and the wet-on-dry technique (page 20). It's often a matter of personal preference for the artist. So, I suggest trying out both ways. Building up wash after wash is referred to as glazing (page 21).

A monochrome gradient of Prussian blue.

A flat wash of phthalo turquoise.

Rachael's Helpful Mixes

Outlined below are many helpful color mixes when it comes to landscape/skyscape painting. I tend to use these colors often and hope you will too! These mixes are not defined to a certain brand of watercolor, but do note that some brands may differ in their paint formulas and, therefore, the color of your mix may be different than what's on this page.

These are pretty simple formulas, and I highly encourage you to try varying concentrations of each color. Explore all of the color values you can achieve! The more you play with your paints, the more comfortable you'll be with them. I like to compare new paints to meeting a new person: You won't get to know them very well in one day! Spend time with them, tell them a clever joke and you'll be friends in no time.

Pastel Orange: This orange is perfect for soft, pastel sunsets/sunrises.

Equal parts yellow ochre and opera pink

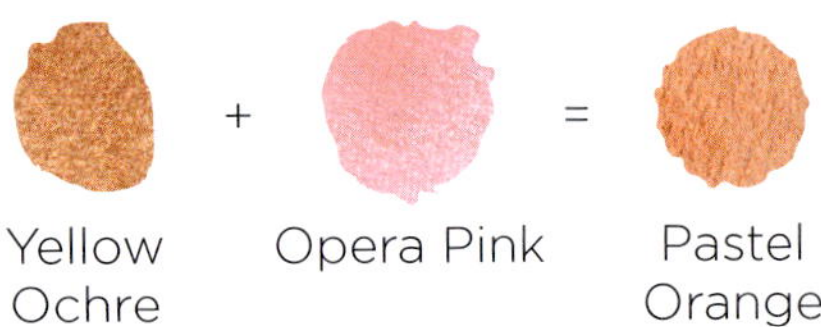

Barn Wood: This is a mixture of burnt umber and Payne's gray, resembling a dark brown akin to old, weathered wood used on farms. It can be used in a variety of applications!

A 3:1 ratio of burnt umber to Payne's gray

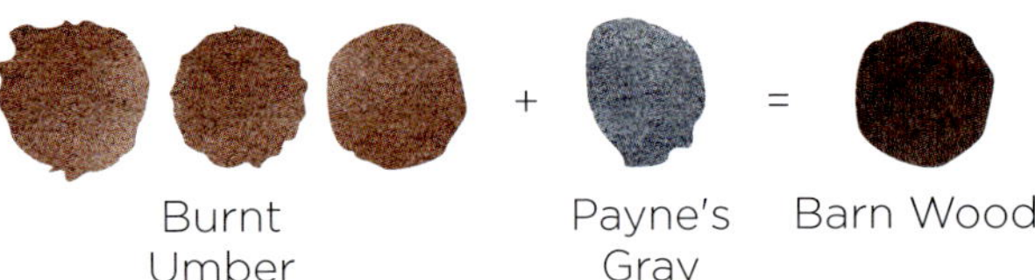

Neutral Gray: Darkening the color value of this will create a near-black color, while lighter color values tend to look gray. This is one of my favorite colors for storm clouds!

Equal parts burnt umber and indigo

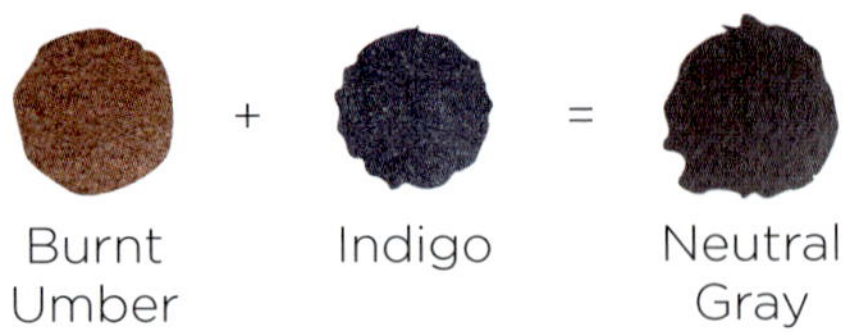

Light Teal: This is perfect for green hills in the distance that have that blue tint to them.

Equal parts cobalt blue and hooker's green

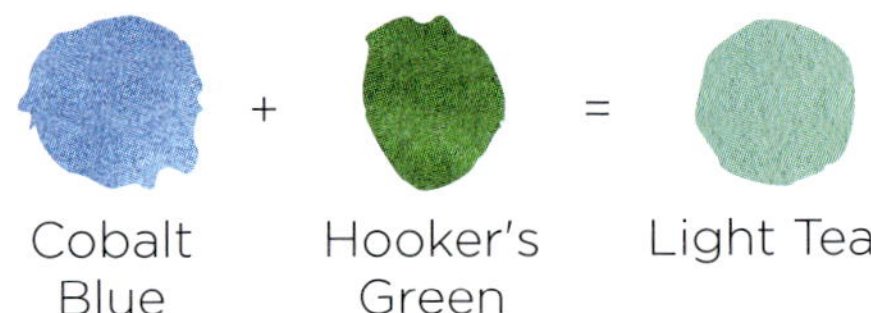

Sea Sage: I discovered this color combination on a whim, playing with my paints while I was painting a misty landscape. Turns out it's perfect to use in that scenario, and I love painting misty pine trees with it.

Equal parts perylene green and Payne's gray

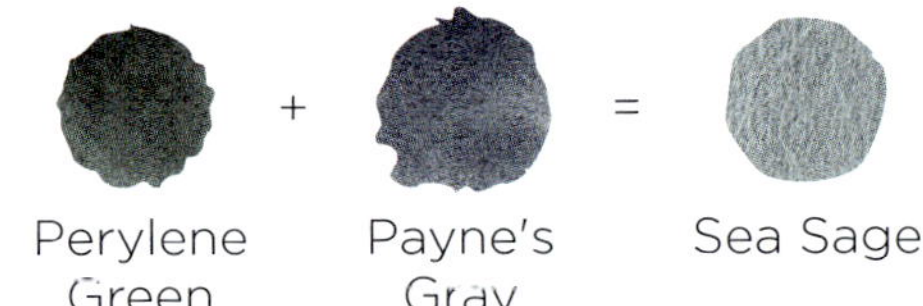

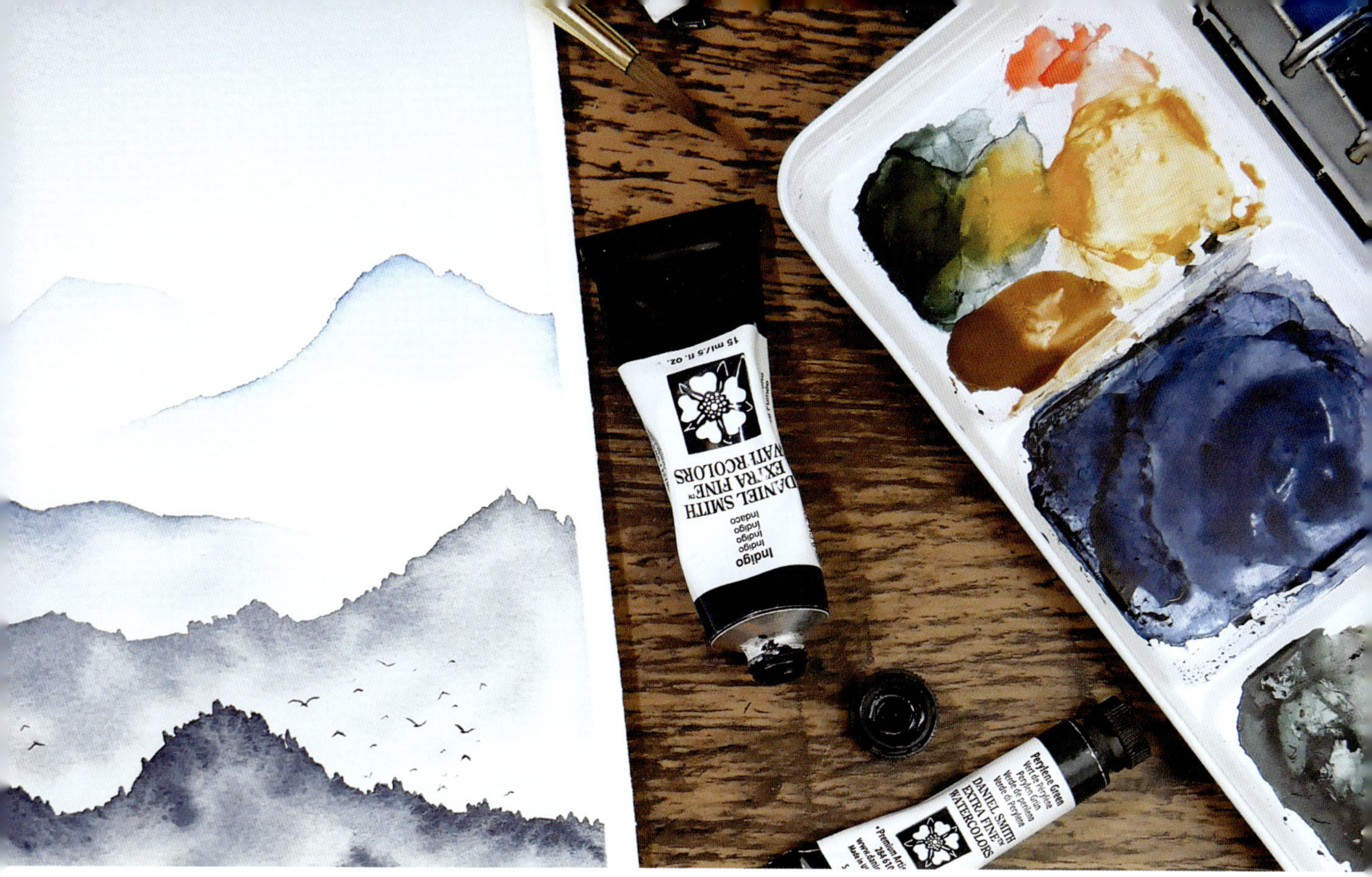

Pewter: This is perfect for those evergreens that need a duller color to capture their moodiness. Similar to my Sea Sage but with the addition of burnt umber to neutralize the blue tint.

Equal parts perylene green, Payne's gray and burnt umber

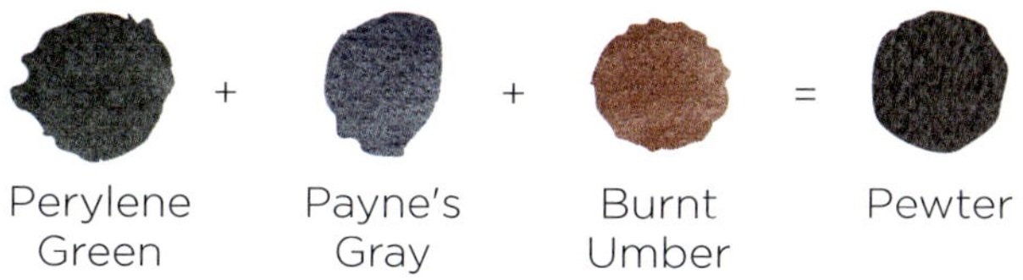

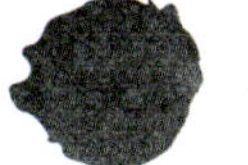 + 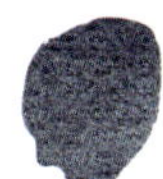 + 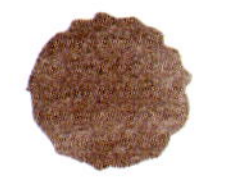 = 

Perylene Green	Payne's Gray	Burnt Umber	Pewter

Nighttime Grass: You'll often hear watercolor artists say they mix their own greens rather than use green right out of the tube. For landscapes, the greens right out of the tube can often be too bright, or perhaps their pigments clash with the paints you've already put down. That's where this green can come in handy. It's bright without being too garish or unnatural. Great for nighttime scenes!

Equal parts lemon yellow, phthalo turquoise and indigo

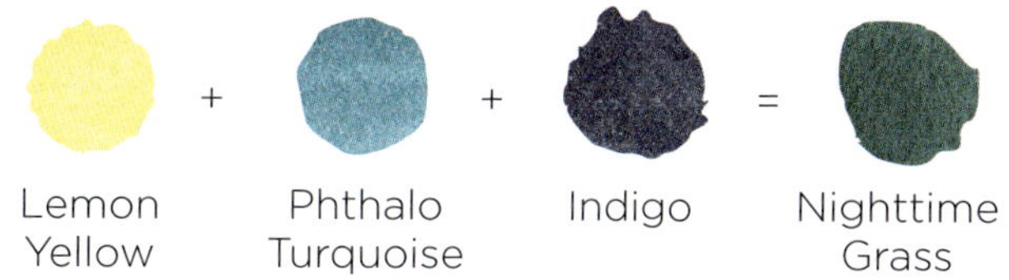

 +  + 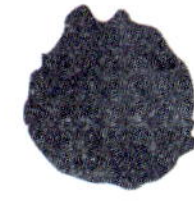 = 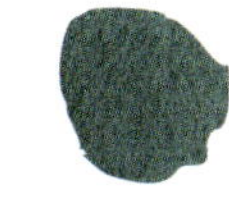

Lemon Yellow	Phthalo Turquoise	Indigo	Nighttime Grass

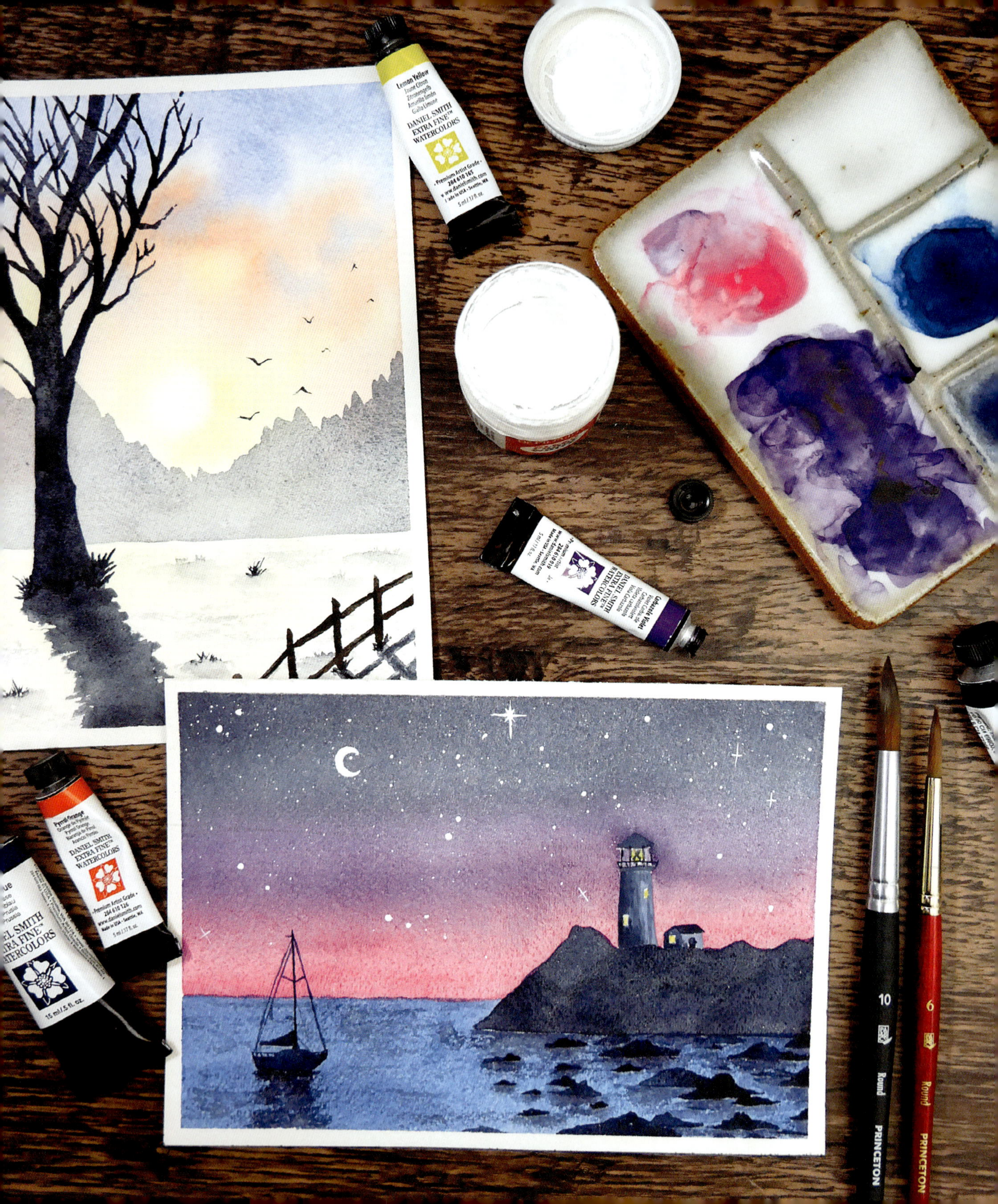
Lemon Yellow
DANIEL SMITH EXTRA FINE™ WATERCOLORS
10
Round
PRINCETON
6
Round
PRINCETON

Soothing SUNSETS & SUNRISES

When I think of vibrant skies, my mind immediately jumps to all the glorious sunsets I've witnessed. Spectacular reds, glowing yellows and oranges, and the deep blue of night encroaching on the day. Sunsets are a beautiful reminder that even the worst of days can end beautifully. In this chapter, we'll create stunning sunsets and sunrises using a combination of essential watercolor techniques. You'll never look at dusk and dawn the same way again.

The sun says goodbye
Light peaks over horizon
Beautiful day done

PEACEFUL MOUNTAIN SUNRISE

The sun has just begun to bring warmth to the morning, red lighting the sky against the contrast of the purple mountains. Let's begin our watercolor sky journey with tackling two important concepts: gradients and glazing.

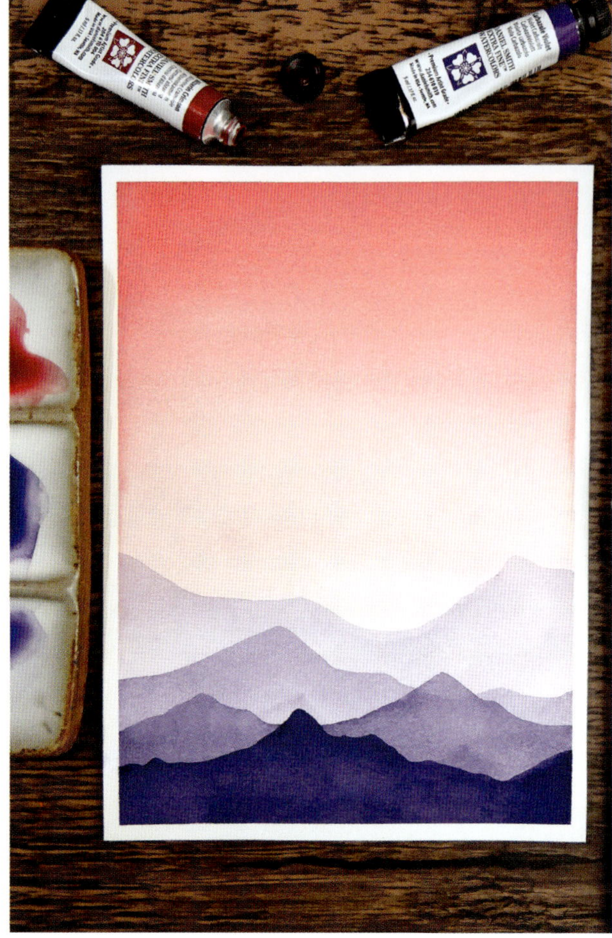

MATERIALS

Paints: alizarin crimson and carbazole violet

Brush: size 12 round

Paper: 5 x 7–inch (13 x 18–cm) cold-pressed watercolor paper

Painter's tape (or washi tape)

Paper towels (or a rag)

SWATCHES

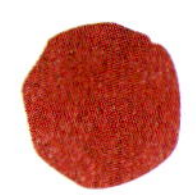

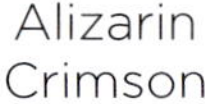

Alizarin Crimson

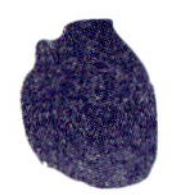

Carbazole Violet

MIX ENOUGH PAINT

Before you begin painting, I recommend mixing up your paints. When working with the wet-on-wet technique (page 20), you have a limited amount of time before your painting begins to dry. Mix up multiple values of the paint colors you'll be using. If you have to mix paint in the middle of your wash, your painting may begin to dry and, when you go back in with freshly mixed paint, you risk creating unintentional blooms due to the substantial difference in moisture. Additionally, always mix up a little more paint than you think you'll need. It's better to have a little leftover paint after a wash rather than having to spend time in the middle to make more.

Be sure to test these colors out on a scrap sheet of watercolor paper; that way you can decide whether you like them or not before you start your painting.

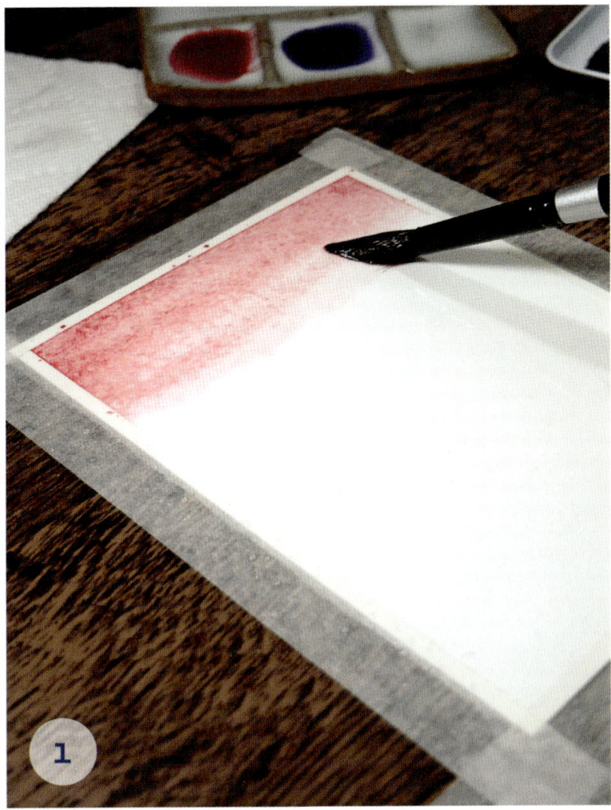

STEP 1: THE MONOCHROME GRADIENT (LAYER 1)

To create that magical glowing sunrise, we're going to use a simple monochrome gradient. A monochrome gradient is a great way to establish depth without creating complexity.

Using a size 12 round brush, begin by wetting the entirety of your paper with clean water. We don't want puddles of water on our paper but enough water that the entire paper has a shiny gloss. Don't rush this process. Watercolor paper, by nature, has a tendency to absorb some water, so make sure you double-check the wetness of your paper before you begin laying down color. You may need to rewet areas again with clean water as it gets soaked up.

Once your paper is nice and glossy, use your brush to apply a light value of alizarin crimson starting at the top of the paper. Gently press the belly of your brush into the paper, working it from one edge to the other in slow, horizontal strokes moving all the way down the paper. As you move down the paper, you'll be dragging the pigment along, naturally creating a gradient as less and less paint is left behind. Be sure to lift your brush up at one of the sides of your paper. If you lift your brush mid-stroke, it'll leave behind pigment that will bloom out, creating a texture that you may not want.

Once you've reached the bottom of your paper, take stock of your gradient. If the gradient isn't as smooth as you'd like, rewet your brush in your light-value alizarin crimson mix, and repeat the process, moving slow with edge-to-edge strokes from the top of the page to the bottom. Moving slow, edge to edge, is key here. If your strokes are too fast, you'll risk creating lines in your sky and, if you lift your brush in the middle of the page, your paint will naturally bloom out.

Let this layer dry, and add more alizarin crimson pigment to your light mix. We're going to intensify the saturation of the sky in the next step.

STEP 2: THE MONOCHROME GRADIENT (LAYER 2)

Building up saturation in watercolor comes from layering. Layering is what allows you to gauge your colors. Since watercolor is a transparent medium, you cannot fix a dark color by simply painting over it. This transparent nature allows it to be used to create paintings that seem to glow from within. The white of the paper in watercolors acts as a light source, illuminating the transparent pigments from underneath (for more information on glazing, see page 21).

We're going to repeat the process from Step 1 but, this time, with a medium-value mix of alizarin crimson. Using clean water, gently wet the entire paper once again. Watercolors can sometimes be activated by reapplying water, so if you're worried about your gradient, apply clean water in the same slow, edge-to-edge, horizontal strokes. Clean your brush off on your paper towels/rags often while applying clean water (this will help prevent you from activating your gradient further).

When your paper is glossy once more, gently apply medium-value alizarin crimson at the top of your page. Gently work your brush back and forth, edge to edge, dragging that pigment down as you go. The goal here is to intensify the crimson color we've already established while keeping the bottom portion of our page fairly bright and white. Our horizon needs to be lighter than the top of our sky to create that glowing effect behind our soon-to-be mountains.

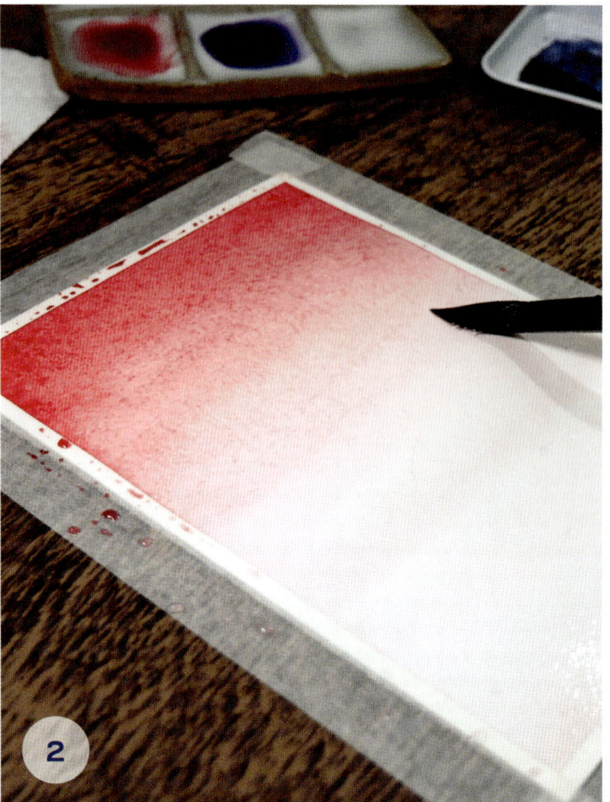

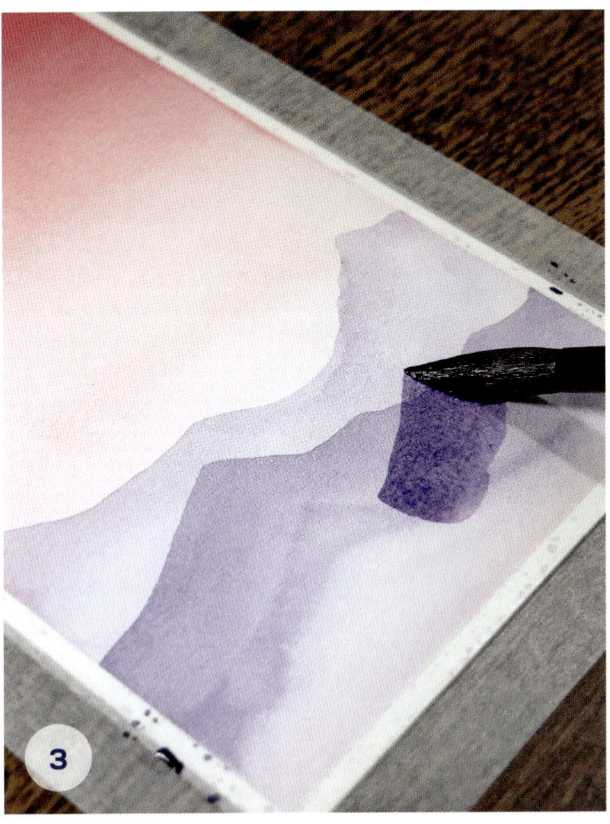

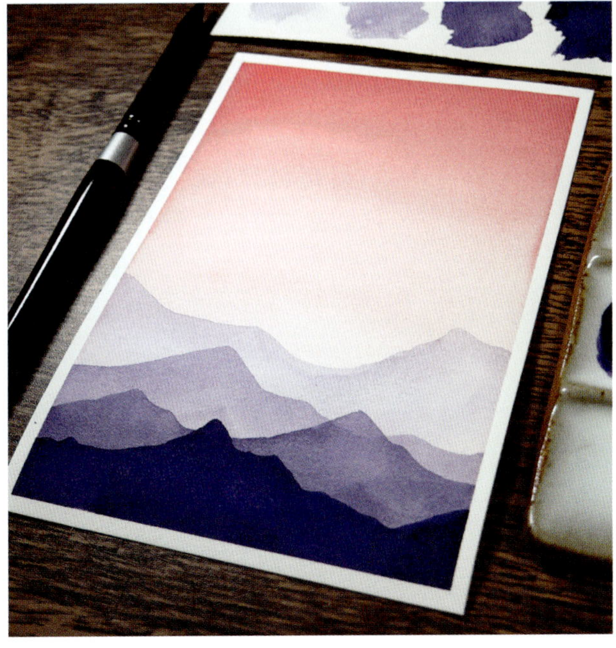

STEP 3: PAINTING THE MOUNTAINS

Now that our sky gradient is complete and dry, let's move on to our mountain range!

To create our mountain range, we're going to use the glazing technique.

About halfway up your paper, apply light-value carbazole violet, dragging your brush from one edge of the paper to the other while creating dips and peaks. Mountains aren't perfect or symmetrical, so keep your brushstroke nice and loose! Once you've applied carbazole violet all the way across, quickly clean off your brush, and gather some clean water. Gently apply the edge of your wet brush along the pigment you just put down, moving from one edge of the paper to the other. By applying clean water to the wet paint, you'll see the violet pigment naturally drag down into that clean water. This creates a soft edge and a "misty" effect for the mountains farther away.

Repeat this step with a darker color value and a different mountain shape. Let dry and then repeat this step until you have four mountain layers in total. Your various mountain layers can overlap if you wish. I like to do this to create some variety and because I believe it looks realistic. Lighter-value mountains will appear as though they are farther in the distance, while the darker-value mountains will appear closer to the viewer. This strategic glazing technique is the key to creating depth in paintings. Background details will appear lighter in value, and foreground details will appear darker in value (i.e., more saturated).

Though our finished painting is flat, we've given it the illusion of depth with both our gradient and our layered mountains.

SERENE PINE SUNSET

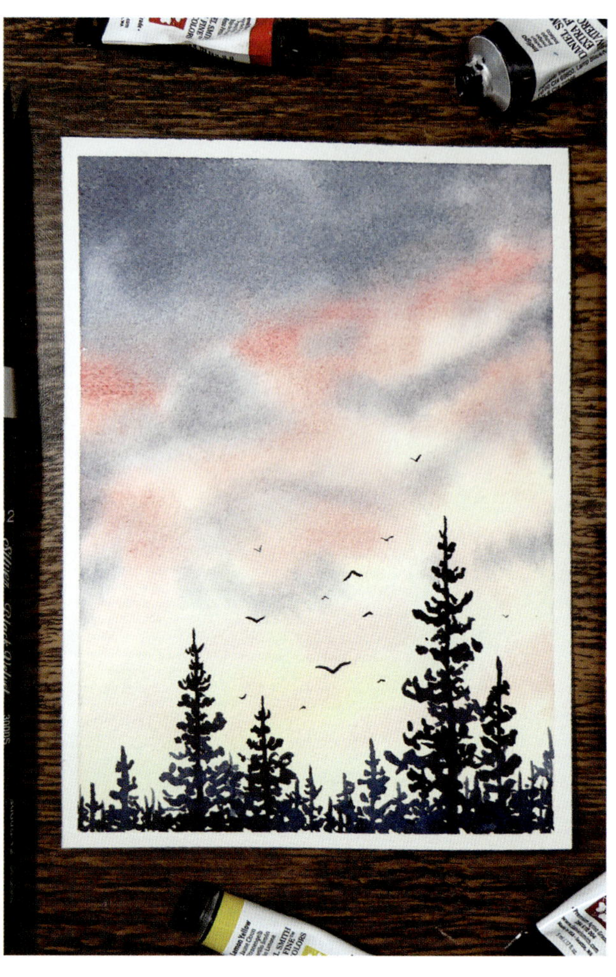

The sun has dipped behind a forest of pines, leaving behind a multitude of colors in the sky, both warm and cool. This piece can be broken down into two parts: the wet-on-wet technique for the sky and the wet-on-dry technique for the trees and details! The wet-on-wet technique will create soft edges and blends between colors for the sky, while the wet-on-dry technique will provide details for the trees and finishing touches.

MATERIALS

Paints: lemon yellow, pyrrol red, alizarin crimson (or rose madder) and indigo

Brushes: sizes 12 and 2 round

Paper: 5 x 7-inch (13 x 18-cm) cold-pressed watercolor paper

Painter's tape (or washi tape)

Paper towels (or a rag)

SWATCHES

Lemon Yellow

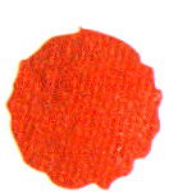

Pyrrol Red

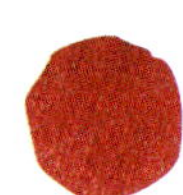

Alizarin Crimson

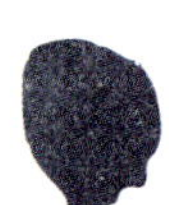

Indigo

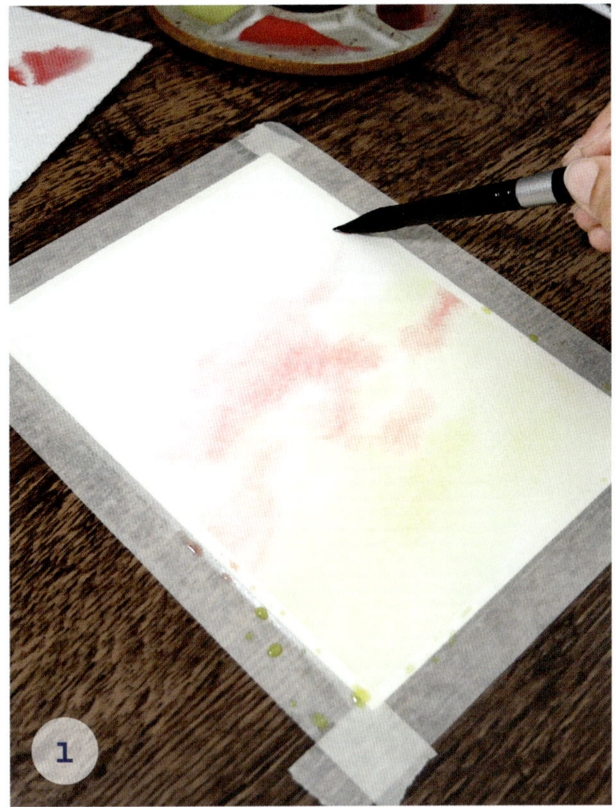

STEP 1: THE SUNSET SKY—LEMON YELLOW & PYRROL RED

Using your size 12 round brush, begin by wetting the entirety of your paper with clean water. Once your paper has a nice shiny gloss of water, use your brush to apply a light value of lemon yellow, starting from the bottom of the paper, stopping about one-third of the way up your paper. Work your brush from one edge of the paper to the other in slow, horizontal strokes moving toward the top of your paper, dragging the pigment along as you go. You'll find that the paint will naturally start to spread on its own.

If you want a more saturated lemon yellow, load your brush with more paint, and reapply it to your paper in the same horizontal strokes. As before, make sure you test your color on a scrap sheet of watercolor paper before applying.

While the paper is still wet, quickly clean off your brush, dab off any excess water on your paper towel/rag and pick up some of your light-value pyrrol red. Apply that pyrrol red above your lemon yellow, making sure your red and yellow sections "touch," and begin the same process, dragging your brush back and forth, edge to edge, working your way up another one-third of the paper. It doesn't need to be perfect, and you can leave some little spots of white here and there.

The goal here is not to have a very smooth gradient but to capture some of the "wispiness" of clouds during a sunset. You can even use some of that pyrrol red and apply a few strokes in the lemon yellow portion of your sunset to create some wispy clouds!

If your paper has begun to dry at this point, do not continue to the next step. Let your paper dry completely before continuing. If you attempt to lay down colors on halfway-dry paper, blooms will begin to appear (for more on blooms, see page 22). Once completely dried, you can reapply clean water to the entirety of the paper and continue from there.

STEP 2: THE SUNSET SKY—ALIZARIN CRIMSON & INDIGO

Making sure your paper is still wet and glossy, we're now going to apply alizarin crimson above the pyrrol red section. With a clean brush, pick up a light value of alizarin crimson, and apply the paint using long, horizontal strokes just like we did with the first two colors. This time, only paint half of your remaining third of the paper (we'll need to leave room for our indigo).

Apply some of that alizarin crimson to the pyrrol red section, again creating some wispy cloud textures with long, smooth strokes. You can even touch the tip of your paintbrush on the page and let the watercolors work their magic to create some smaller clouds. Have fun with this! If you'd like to increase the intensity of the alizarin crimson or pyrrol red section, add some more pigment to your brush, and apply it in those same long, smooth strokes to their respective areas.

While the paper is still wet, we're now going to apply our indigo. If you've noticed your paper has begun to dry again, let it dry completely, and then reapply clean water to your entire paper.

Pick up some medium-value indigo, and apply it to the top of your page, now working down in those long, smooth, horizontal strokes until you meet the alizarin crimson. Apply a few strokes of indigo among the alizarin crimson to create more of that sunset cloud texture. From here, you can go back and forth between applying some darker-value alizarin crimson and indigo clouds in that top one-third of your painting (make sure to clean your brush off in between colors).

Be careful not to overwork this. We don't necessarily want to completely mix these two colors, but instead apply some strokes and then let the water and paint work their magic to create those soft edges and blends.

Once you're satisfied with your clouds and sky, let your painting completely dry before continuing to the next step.

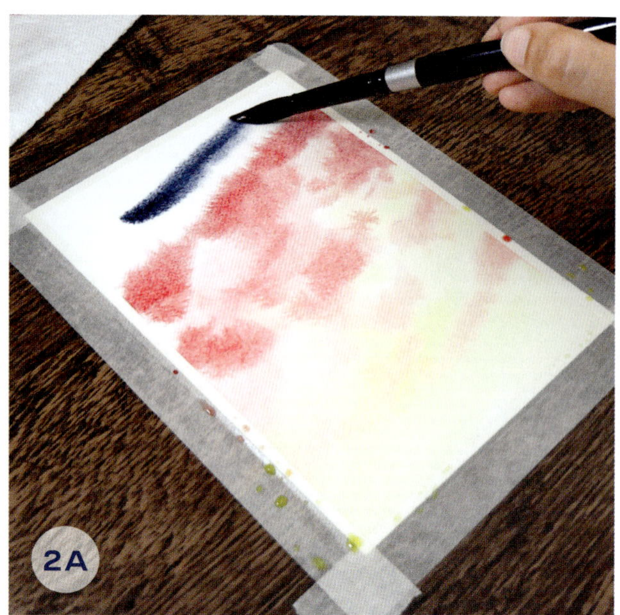

2A

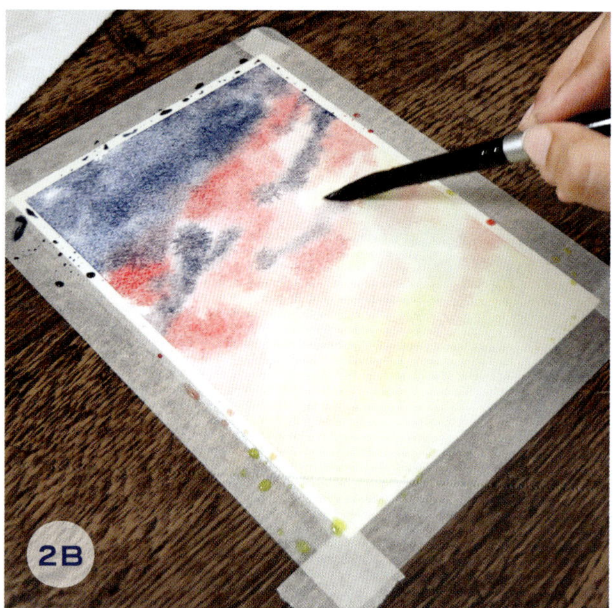

2B

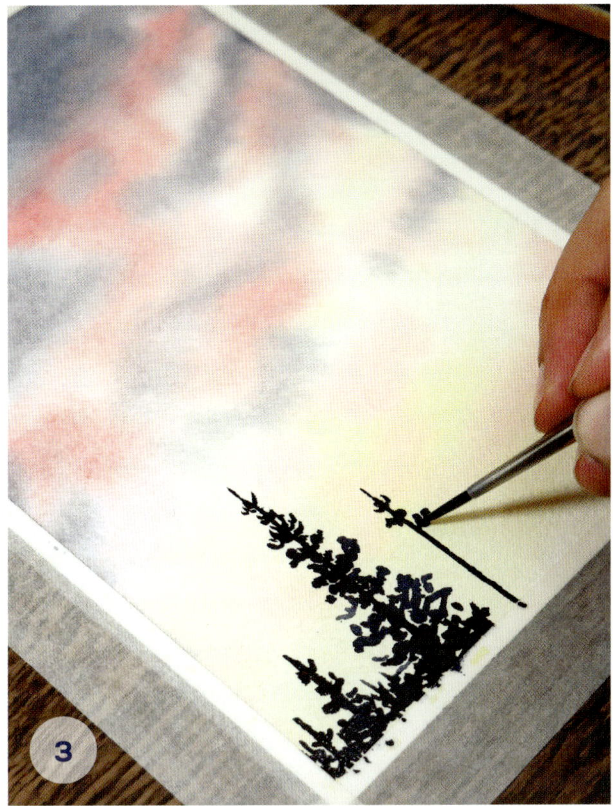

3

STEP 3: THE PINE TREES

Now, our beautiful sunset sky is completely dry! But it's looking like it needs a foreground to anchor the scene in place. That is where our pine forest comes in.

To create pine trees, I like to apply what many artists call the "blobby" technique. It's both a fun name and a fun technique! Switch to your size 2 round brush for this step.

Try practicing a few trees on a scrap sheet of paper before applying them to your painting. Begin by picking up a dark-value indigo with your brush. Create the trunk by painting a small, thin, vertical line. Your brush should be just damp with the paint, not soaking, otherwise you'll have difficulty creating a small, thin line. I always test a few lines on my scrap sheet before I paint my tree trunks.

Then, beginning just below the top, apply pressure to your brush to create a small blob. Continue with these blobs down both sides of the trunk to create a pine tree shape. These blobs are abstract and don't have specific shapes to them. You also don't need to fill in all the spaces, so keep some areas open. After all, pine trees are not perfectly symmetrical by nature. You need to create some "imperfect" parts for the trees to look natural.

When you're ready, paint a line of pine trees along the bottom of your sunset painting. Vary the sizes and shapes to create the effect of a pine forest. Not all trees are going to be the same size or height, so make sure to create variety! I typically place my tallest tree on either the right one-third or the left one-third of the paper, but never the middle. Placing an extremely tall tree in the middle will detract from the beauty of your sunset sky, which is the main attraction of the piece.

Once your pine forest is dry, you're ready to move on to the last step!

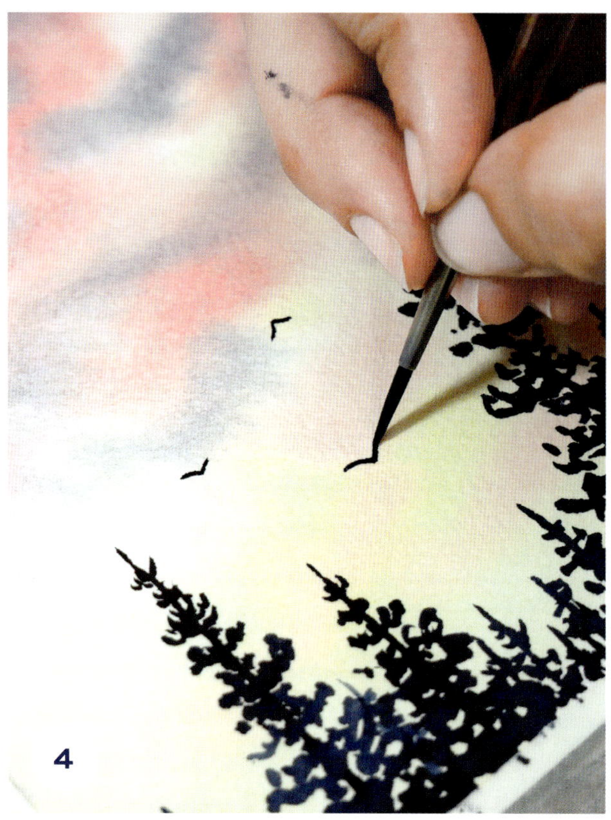

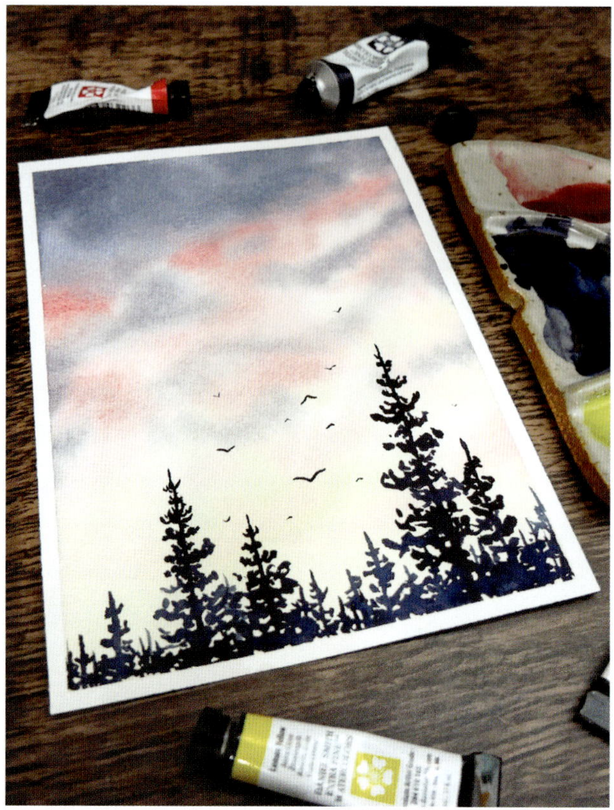

STEP 4: THE FINISHING TOUCHES

We now have a beautiful sky and a sprawling pine forest, so, naturally, the last step is to add some life. Let's paint a few bird silhouettes in our sky.

You'll still be using your size 2 round brush for this and a dark-value indigo (the same value we used for the trees). To paint bird silhouettes, move the tip of your brush in a "V" motion.

For variety, you can stretch out the "V" to mimic the bird stretching its wings as it soars or, alternatively, paint a "V" upside down. Paint between six to twelve birds, some in a cluster and some far away.

Once these details are done, your painting is complete! Carefully peel away your tape (if your piece was taped down), and bask in this peaceful sunset you created.

WINTER MORNING SUNRISE

Snow blanketing the ground, the sun silently rising over the far-off treetops, the first birds taking flight into the chilly air—that's what we're going to depict in this piece! Let's learn how to paint a bare deciduous tree, one that's lost all of its leaves due to winter's chilly air.

MATERIALS

Paints: lemon yellow, pyrrol orange, cobalt blue, Payne's gray and Barn Wood (page 28)

Brushes: sizes 12, 10 and 2 round

Paper: 5 x 7-inch (13 x 18-cm) cold-pressed watercolor paper

Painter's tape (or washi tape)

Paper towels (or a rag)

Ruler

Pencil and kneaded eraser

SWATCHES

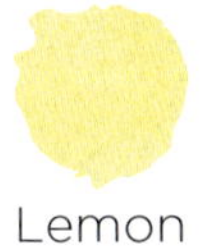
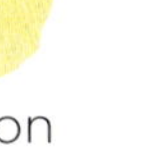

Lemon Yellow

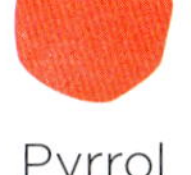

Pyrrol Orange

Cobalt Blue

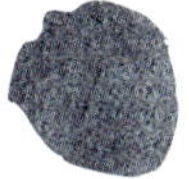

Payne's Gray

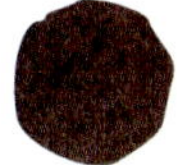

Barn Wood (page 28)

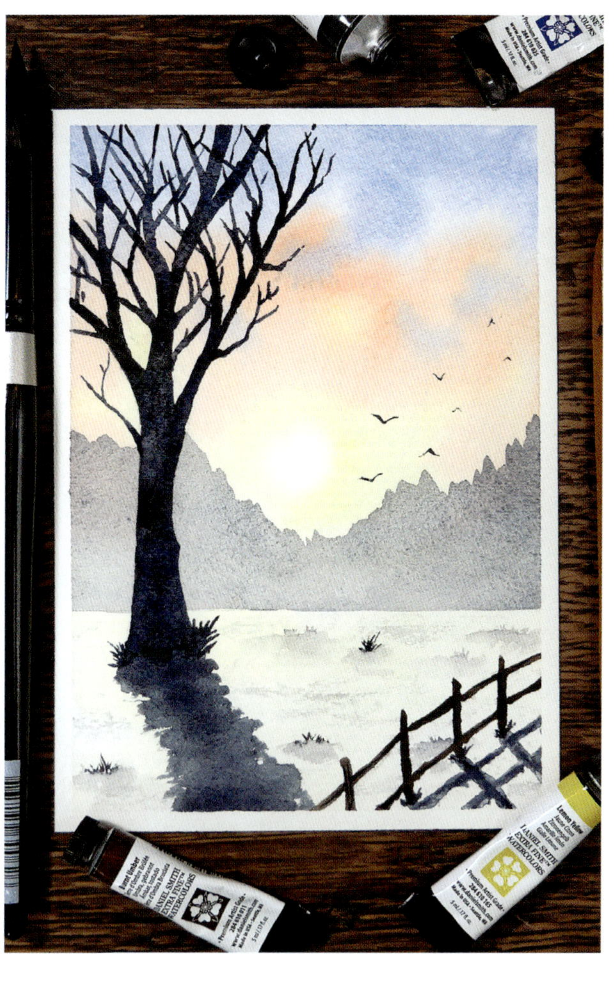

STEP 1: THE SKETCH

For this piece, we'll need to sketch out the foundations of our piece so we have something to follow. Due to watercolor paint's transparent nature, you'll be able to see any dark, thick lines once the painting is complete, so sketch lightly! Or, alternatively, use a kneaded eraser to lighten your sketch marks. You can do this by simply pressing the kneaded eraser repeatedly on the pencil marks. The eraser will pick up the graphite and lighten your sketch.

Place your ruler down horizontally about one-third of the way up the page from the bottom. Take your pencil and lightly drag it across, creating a nice straight line. This will act as our horizon line. Above that horizon line, draw the outline of a distant forest. The sun will be rising in this piece, so the distant forest will only be a silhouette. We won't be able to make out any specific shapes, only the tips of the trees.

Next, let's draw the general outline of our tree. I placed my tree on the left, with the base of the trunk about an inch (2.5 cm) below the horizon line. Lightly begin to draw your bare tree. I extended my branches off the page to give the tree some realism and to make it seem like the tree exists within the painting rather than on top of it.

I actually find it difficult to sketch deciduous trees, but it's far easier to paint them, so don't feel discouraged if you don't like your sketch! Remember, this is just a guide, not something you need to precisely trace when we begin to paint.

Finally, we're going to add in a wooden fence. I lightly sketched in a few fence rails that appear in the bottom right of the painting.

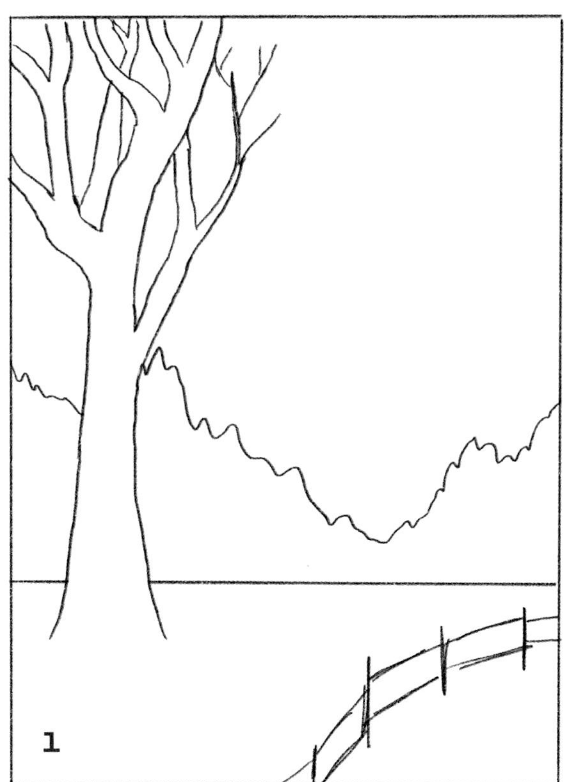

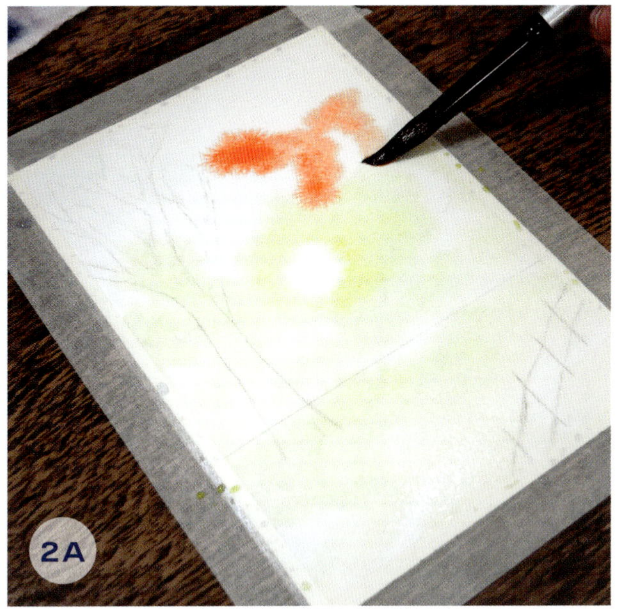

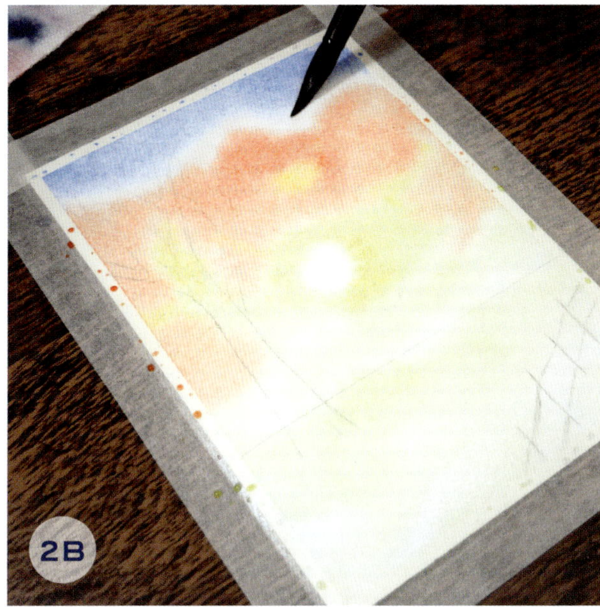

STEP 2: THE SKY

Using your size 12 round brush, wet the entire paper with clean water. Once your paper is glossy, take medium-value lemon yellow, and begin painting loose strokes just above the horizon line. Feel free to also just touch your brush to the page, dropping in paint so that it naturally spreads out on its own. We aren't aiming to create a perfect gradient but, rather, some wispy morning clouds. Then, take the belly of your brush, and gently press it into the paper, painting a circle in the center. Leave the center white, as this will be our sun.

With the same yellow, gently brush a few strokes down in the snow/ground portion of our painting. Snow is very reflective, so it will reflect the yellow color of our early morning sun!

Next, clean off your brush, and take up some medium-value pyrrol orange. We're going to use the same loose strokes above the yellow portion of our sky, leaving the remaining one-third of our sky for our next color. Feel free to drop a bit of pyrrol orange within the yellow portion.

Try not to paint in the pyrrol orange with paint strokes, but, rather, drop the orange in with the tip of your brush, letting the paint naturally bloom out. Dropping in colors with the tip of your brush on a wet page, rather than painting in strokes, will prevent the two colors from mixing too much and will allow them to keep their pure vibrancy.

Finally, clean off your brush again, and pick up medium-value cobalt blue. Carefully apply that color along the top portion of your paper. Be careful to not let the orange and blue mix as your brushstrokes cross the paper. To do this, leave a white barrier between the two colors. The paint will naturally spread out on the wet paper, so there's no need to worry about closing the boundaries between these two complementary colors.

Just like with the pyrrol orange and lemon yellow, use the tip of your brush to drop some cobalt blue in the orange layer. Let the paint bloom out naturally to create more of those wispy morning clouds!

Let dry completely before moving on.

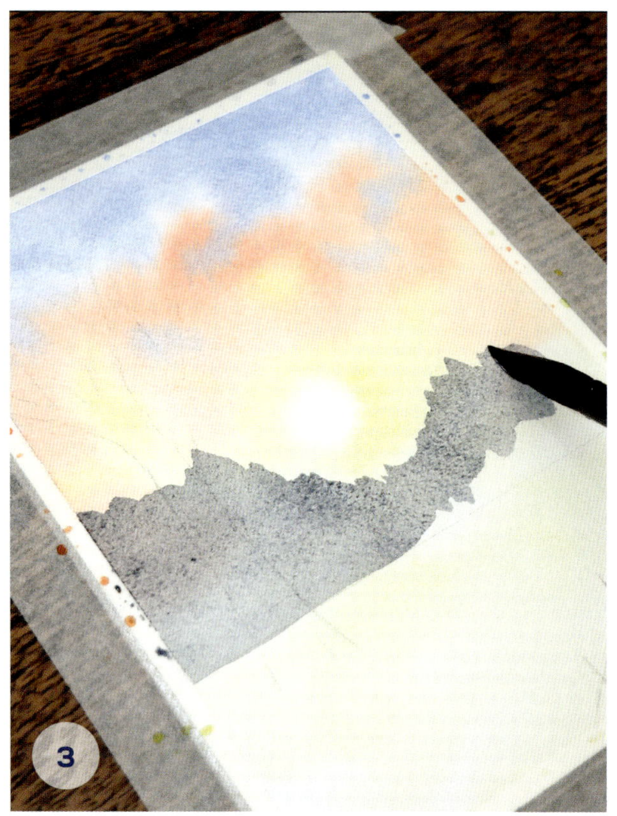

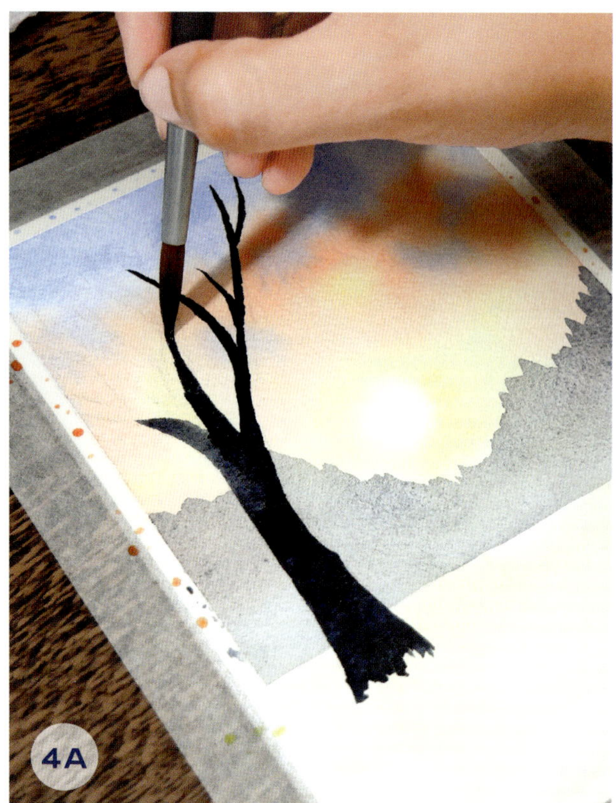

STEP 3: THE FOREST SILHOUETTE

Now that your paper is completely dry, we're going to paint the forest silhouette that's off in the distance. Take up a light-value Payne's gray with your size 12 round brush, and begin filling in your sketch.

Hold your brush so the tip of it is vertical with the page, and use the tip to create the tops and uneven edges of trees in the distant forest. The top of this silhouette will be uneven to represent the tops of trees, but the bottom will be a straight line across the horizon.

The wash doesn't need to be perfectly even. We're simply painting a suggestion of a forest far in the distance. The forest is part of the background and isn't the main draw of the piece, so no worries if it's not perfect.

Let the forest silhouette dry before moving on.

STEP 4: THE BARE DECIDUOUS TREE

Using your size 10 round brush, pick up dark-value Payne's gray. Paint with long, upward strokes to fill in the trunk of your tree sketch. You can leave the bottom of your trunk somewhat uneven, as we'll come back to that portion later.

To paint the branches, we're going to take advantage of your brush's shape. At the base of your branches, closest to the trunk, apply more pressure to your brush, allowing the belly to press into the paper and the bristles to flare slightly. As the branch moves away from the trunk and becomes thinner, begin lifting that pressure off your brush, and you'll see the bristles bounce back into their round shape. The line you're creating will become thinner! When you reach the tips of your branches, you should only apply very light pressure so the tips of your brush bristles are in contact with the paper. This will create an even thinner line!

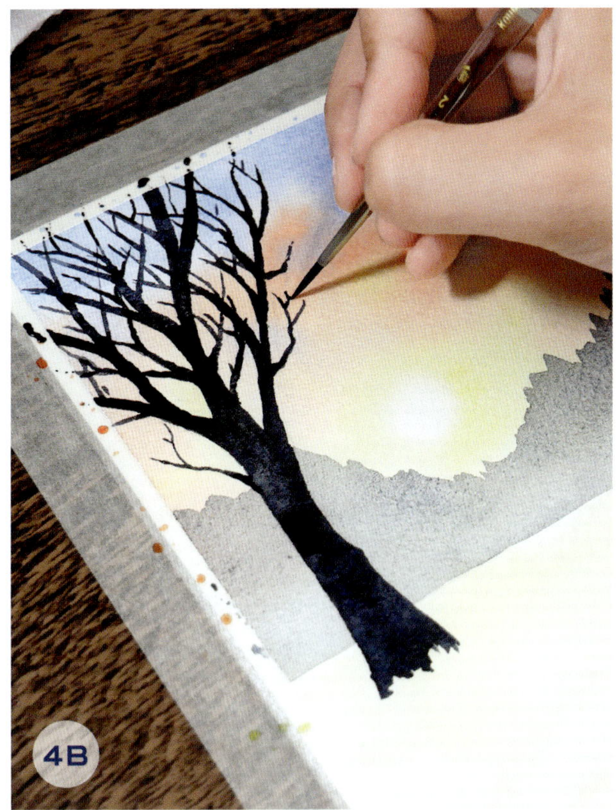

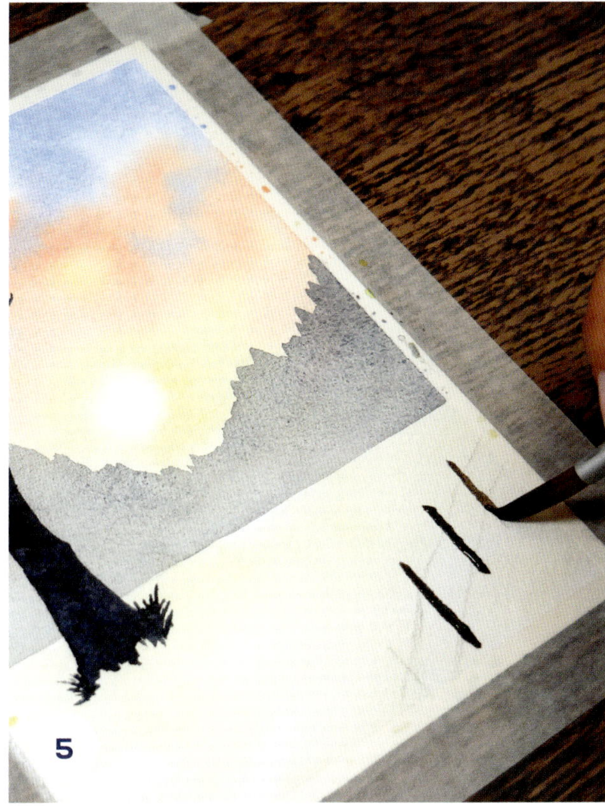

Repeat these steps, painting the branches up and out to create the bare canopy. Let your branches overlap as you go. This will give the silhouette some realism. Trees aren't perfect. They're gangly and tend to grow in all directions, so try not to give too much thought to your brushstrokes. Randomness and chaos in nature is realism. No matter what you paint, there is most likely a tree somewhere on this planet that resembles what you've created. If it helps, look up some images of tree silhouettes on Pinterest. I often do this when painting a new subject to me. Having a reference image is helpful and it's not "cheating." Artists use reference images all the time.

When you've created a few branches, switch to a size 2 round brush. This will allow you to paint the finer details, like the twigs on the ends of the branches. Using that same brush and color, add some grass to the bottom of your tree trunk. This will help to ground your tree in your painting rather than it looking like it's floating on the page. Let dry.

STEP 5: THE WOODEN FENCE

Now, let's add some details! For our wooden fence, use a dark value of Barn Wood. Using your size 10 round brush, paint along your wooden fence sketch. These old wooden fences are usually uneven and warped, so no worries if your paint strokes aren't perfectly straight. Let dry.

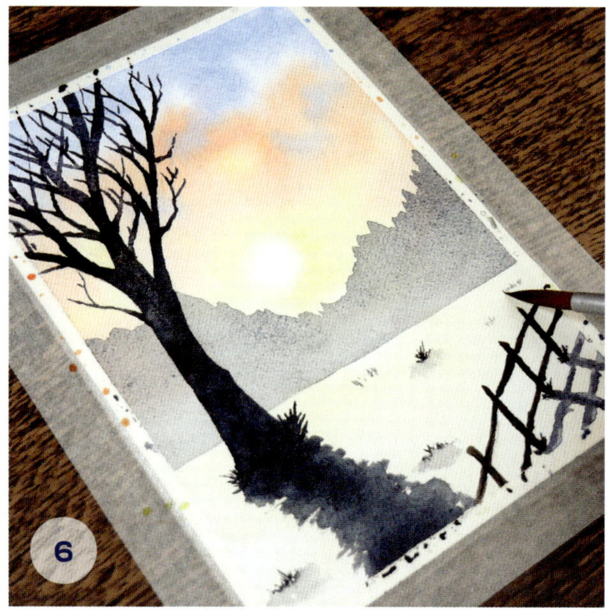

STEP 6: THE FINISHING TOUCHES & DRY BRUSHING

Now, we're going to add in some shadows! Grab your size 10 round brush, and pick up some medium-value Payne's gray. With it being early morning, our shadows will be at a slight angle. Add in your fence's shadow by following the same grid-type structure of the fence.

Using that same medium-value Payne's gray, add in the shadow of your tree! Start at the base, and paint at the same angle as your fence's shadow. Extend the shadow of the trunk off the page, as it is still early morning and your shadows are nice and long!

Also using that same paint color, add in a few sprigs of grass here and there, peeking up through the snow. Then, quickly clean off your brush, dab it on a paper towel until it's damp and gently swipe it along the bottom of your sprigs of grass. This will help drag the color out across your ground to create some natural shadows. I also added some grass popping up along the bottom of each fence post to help ground it in the painting.

For more texture in the snow, we're going to use the dry-brushing technique. Dry brushing is the process of laying down watercolor paint with little to no water. Sounds odd for watercolor painting, right? For this technique, you won't have a completely dry brush but, rather, a brush with a small amount of water/paint. Using this technique can create some interesting and varied textures that are difficult to create otherwise.

I always suggest practicing this on a scrap sheet of paper first before going straight to your piece. Pick up some light-value Payne's gray with your size 10 round brush, and immediately dab your brush on your paper towel until it's nearly dry. Hold your brush with a horizontal grip, meaning the belly of the brush should be nearly parallel to the paper (you shouldn't perform this technique using the tip of your brush). Quickly, and lightly, swipe your brush horizontally across the paper. Your stroke should lightly skim your paper, and you'll notice that the stroke isn't even. In fact, there are white spaces and gaps in between color. This is exactly what we're aiming for!

The speed of your stroke will impact the effects of your dry brushing, so try it at different speeds to practice achieving the effect you desire. Additionally, the type of paper you're using (hot-pressed, cold-pressed or rough) will also impact your dry brushing. Dry brushing is easier on textured paper and, to achieve dry brushing on smooth paper, like hot-pressed, you'll need fast brushstrokes. Dry brushing also works the best on dry paper, meaning that if your paper is wet or damp, you won't achieve the right texture.

In this piece, dry brushing light-value Payne's gray across your snowy section helps to create varied shadows across the ground, mimicking the dips and shadows of snowdrifts across the field.

Lastly, add in a few birds in your morning sky. They are early risers, after all! For more information on painting birds, see page 40.

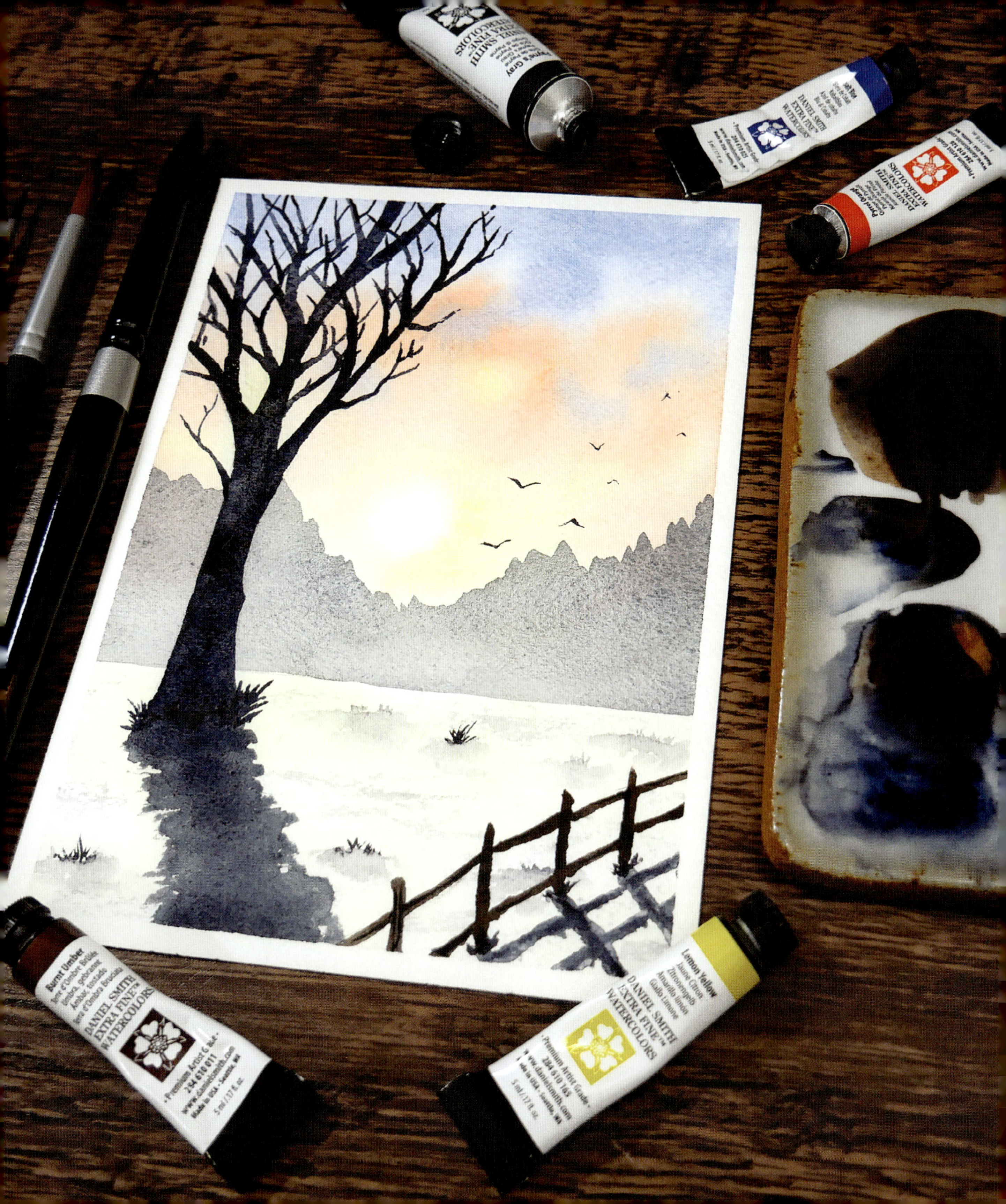
Burnt Umber
DANIEL SMITH
EXTRA FINE™
WATERCOLORS
Lemon Yellow
DANIEL SMITH
EXTRA FINE™
WATERCOLORS

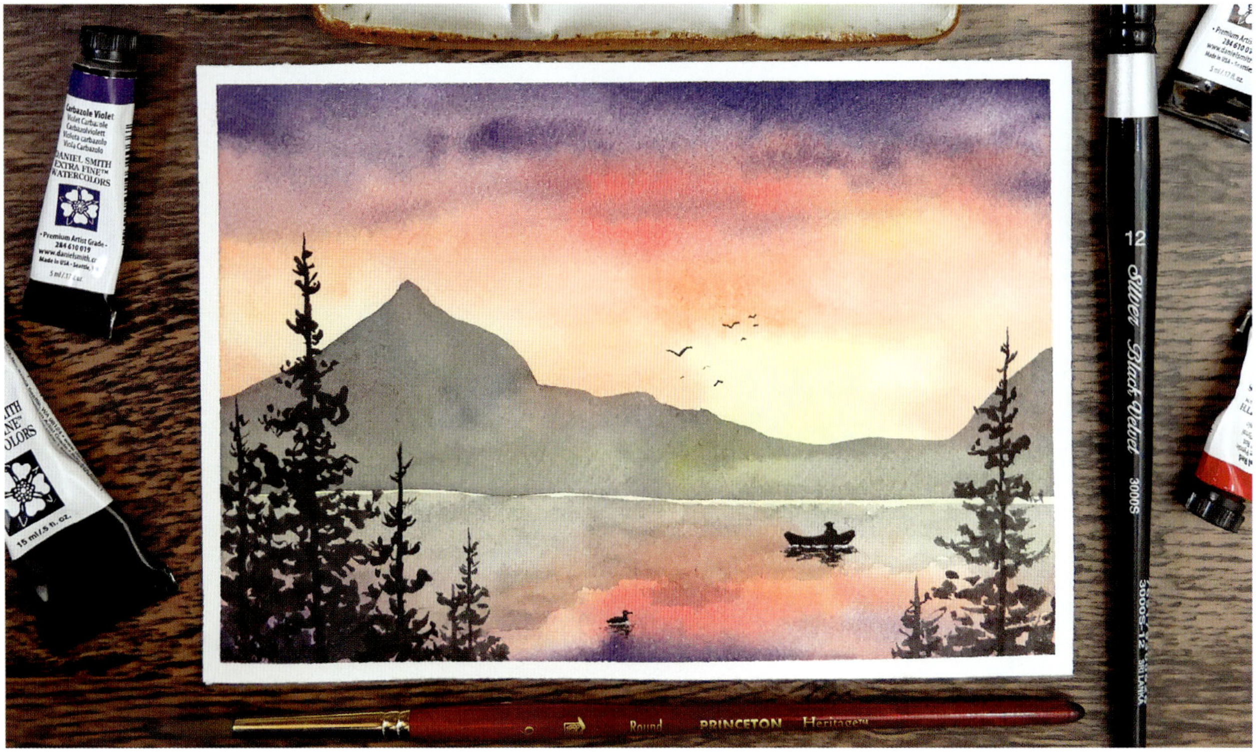

CANOE LAKE SUNSET

The sun has dipped below the mountains, saying goodbye for the last time that day, leaving behind bright warm tones—one last hurrah before the darkness of night takes over. A lone canoe sits out on the lake's nearly still water, but a small loon paddles out from the lake's edge to join the boat in the last few minutes of the sun's brilliant light. In this painting, you will learn how to paint a lake that reflects the sky above.

MATERIALS

Paints: lemon yellow, pyrrol orange, pyrrol red, carbazole violet and Neutral Gray (page 28)

Brushes: sizes 12, 6 and 2 round

Paper: 5 x 7-inch (13 x 18-cm) cold-pressed watercolor paper

Painter's tape (or washi tape)

Paper towels (or a rag)

Ruler

Pencil and kneaded eraser

White gel pen

SWATCHES

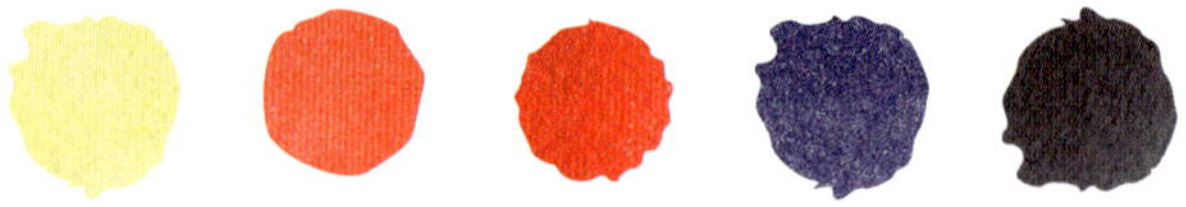

Lemon Yellow

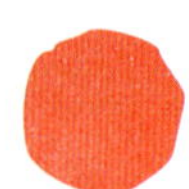

Pyrrol Orange

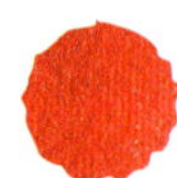

Pyrrol Red

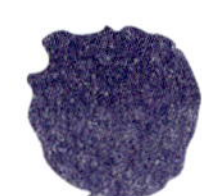

Carbazole Violet

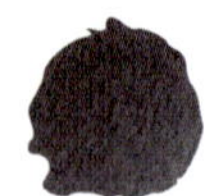

Neutral Gray (page 28)

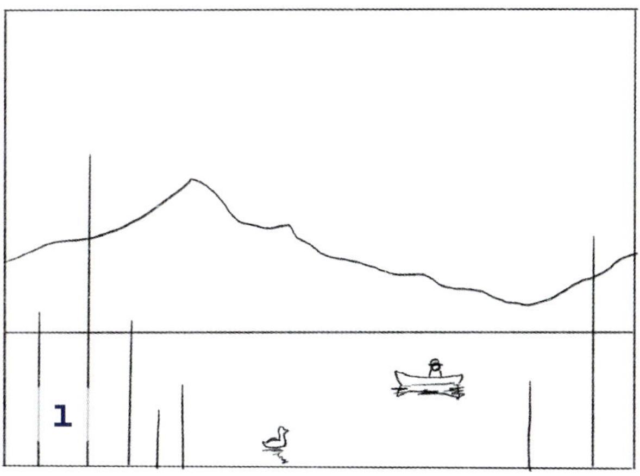

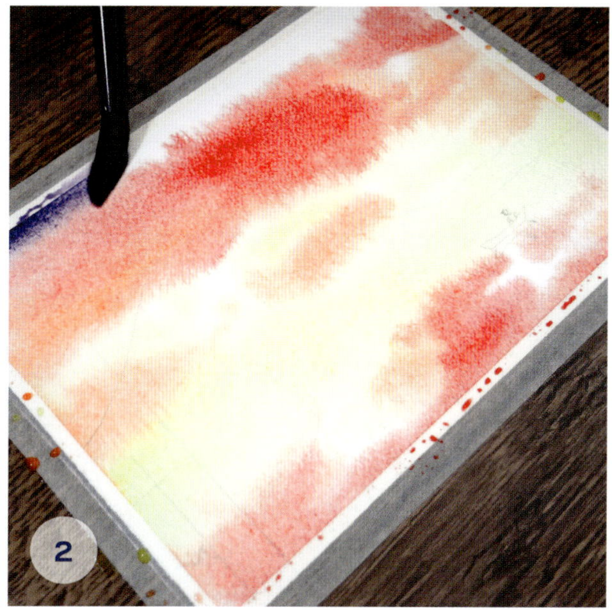

STEP 1: THE SKETCH

Grab your ruler and draw a horizon line one-third of the way up the paper from the bottom. This will be the lake. Next, lightly sketch in your distant mountains, and use a ruler to sketch out where your foreground pine trees will be. I placed some pines in the left- and right-hand corners of the paper. On the right side of the lake, roughly sketch out the shape of a canoe with one man inside. You don't need details here, just the basic shape of the canoe, which is sort of like a banana with a flat bottom. Since the lake will be flat and calm, there will be a reflection of the canoe in the water, so sketch out a few lines directly below the canoe to depict this.

STEP 2: THE SUNSET SKY (LAYER 1)

For this piece, we'll be painting in similar ways to the project Serene Pine Sunset (page 36), with loose strokes of color in a sort of uneven gradient. This time, however, we have the sky's reflection on the lake, so we'll need to replicate those colors there.

So, start out by wetting the entire sheet of paper with clean water using your size 12 round brush. Then, load up your brush with medium-value lemon yellow, and begin applying paint to the paper in long, horizontal strokes. You'll need to paint this lemon yellow color above and below your horizon line, indicating that the color will be both in the sky and on the water. Essentially, we're going to paint a very loose "mirror image" of whatever we paint in the sky.

Next, load up your brush with medium-value pyrrol orange, and paint above and below the lemon yellow, adding some of the orange color within the yellow section to create some wispy, soft clouds. Repeat the same process with medium-value pyrrol red, leaving a small section of white at the top of the paper for our final color. Lastly, clean off your brush, and then load it with dark-value carbazole violet. Paint in the carbazole violet at the top of the paper and then at the bottom of the paper.

Let this layer dry completely, as we'll be painting in a second layer to build up our colors momentarily.

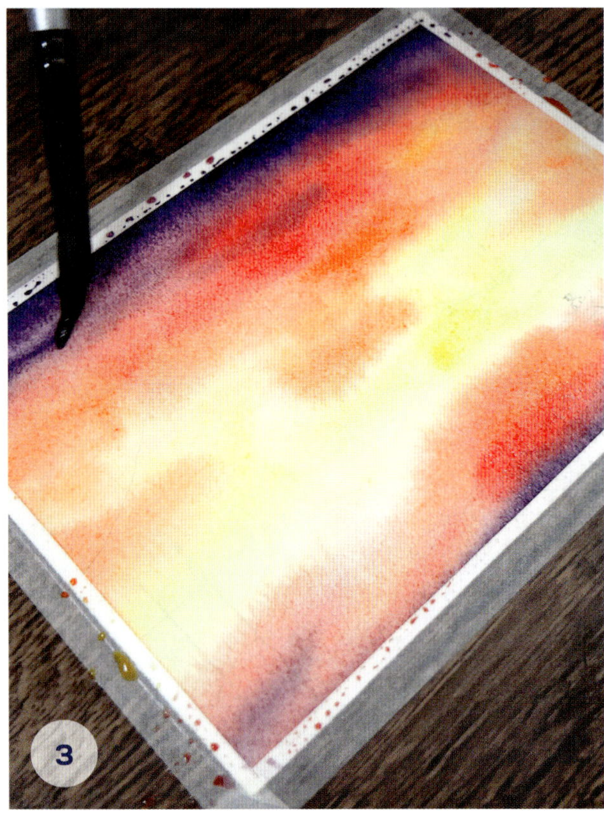

STEP 3: THE SUNSET SKY (LAYER 2)

Once your first layer is dry, go ahead and rewet the entire paper again with clean water, starting from the lemon yellow section and working outward. If you added clean water from the top to the bottom of the paper, for example, the purple pigment may travel downward and end up mixing with the lemon yellow, muddying the bright, vibrant colors we're looking to achieve.

After you've rewet your paper, repeat the same process: adding in darker values of lemon yellow, pyrrol orange, pyrrol red and, finally, carbazole violet. Paint in these colors with loose strokes, letting the analogous colors naturally mix and blend on the wet page. When you're satisfied, let your paints dry completely, reevaluate the saturation of your colors and, if necessary, repeat the same steps again to build up your painting to your desired vibrancy.

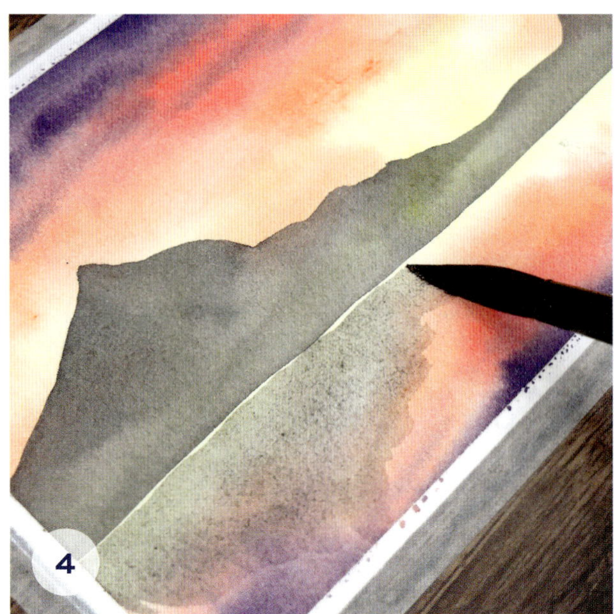

STEP 4: THE MOUNTAIN & REFLECTION

Very similar to our first project, Peaceful Mountain Sunrise (page 32), the mountain in this painting will also be a simple silhouette. Since the sun has dipped below the horizon, there is no light to shine on the details in the distance, hence why we're painting a silhouette.

So, load up your size 12 round brush with medium-value Neutral Gray, and fill in the pencil sketch of the distant mountain range. Let dry and then use a light-value Neutral Gray to paint a reflection of the mountains in the lake. This reflection doesn't need to be perfect, but it should roughly mirror the shape and height of the mountains above it. In fact, as you can see in my painting, the tops of the mountains look rather undefined in their reflections. Giving the reflection this rough edge makes it look as though the water has a slight ripple, warping the reflection of the mountains.

Additionally, for reflections on water, leave a small line unpainted in between your mountains and their reflection. This slight separation helps the viewer of your painting identify where your mountains begin and where the reflection begins.

Let dry.

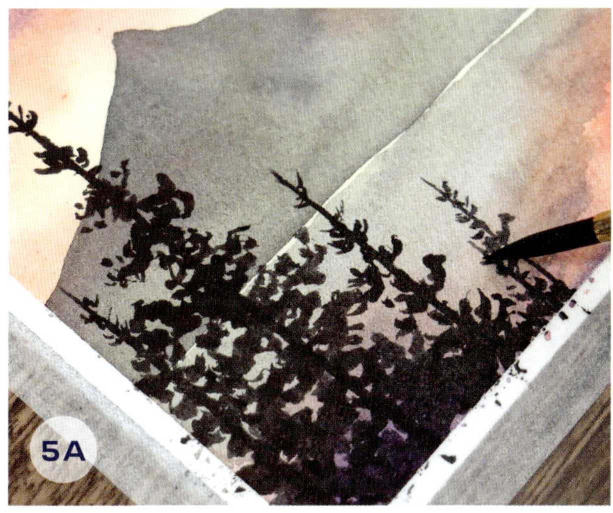

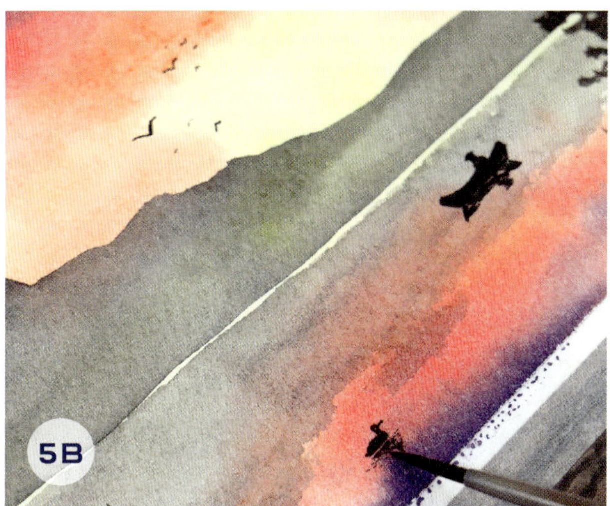

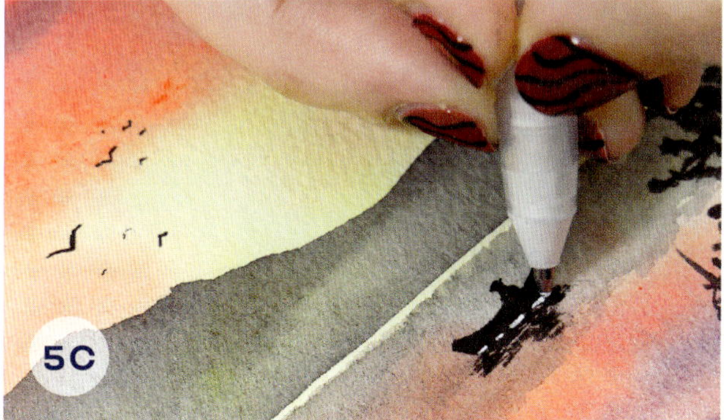

STEP 5: THE PINE TREES, CANOE, FLYING BIRDS & LOON

Time to add in foreground elements to bring magic to our painting!

Using the blobby technique (see page 39) and a size 6 round brush, paint in pine trees with dark-value Neutral Gray. The pines should be of various shapes and sizes in the bottom left- and right-hand corners of your painting. Painting pines on both sides of the paper helps to frame your main subjects, the lone canoe and loon.

Switch to your size 2 round brush, and load it up with dark-value Neutral Gray. In order to paint small details like this one, make sure your brush is well loaded but not dripping with paint. If your paintbrush is loaded with too much moisture, it will be difficult to paint precise lines. Following your sketch beneath, paint in the canoe and its lone passenger, as well as a rough reflection directly beneath. In the canoe's reflection, you don't have to fill it in entirely with paint. Leaving some small unpainted spaces adds to the illusion of a reflection, making it look as though the water is rippling.

After your canoe, paint in a flock of birds high in the sky, above the mountain range silhouette. Vary the shapes and sizes of the birds so it looks like some are closer and some are farther away.

Lastly, let's add in our loon. The best way to describe the shape of the loon is this: a silhouette of an apple pie, with a head and beak attached. As always, if you're unsure of how to approach painting something, try it out on a scrap sheet first before adding it to your painting. I do this all the time, and it takes away the stress of having to "get it right" the first time. Once you've painted your loon, use the dry-brushing technique (page 46) to add in some rippling reflections beneath the loon. I also went back and added some dry brushing to the reflection of the canoe as well.

For some final touches, pick up your white gel pen, and add a few broken lines/dots where the bottom of the canoe and the loon would touch the lake. This helps to break up the subject and reflection.

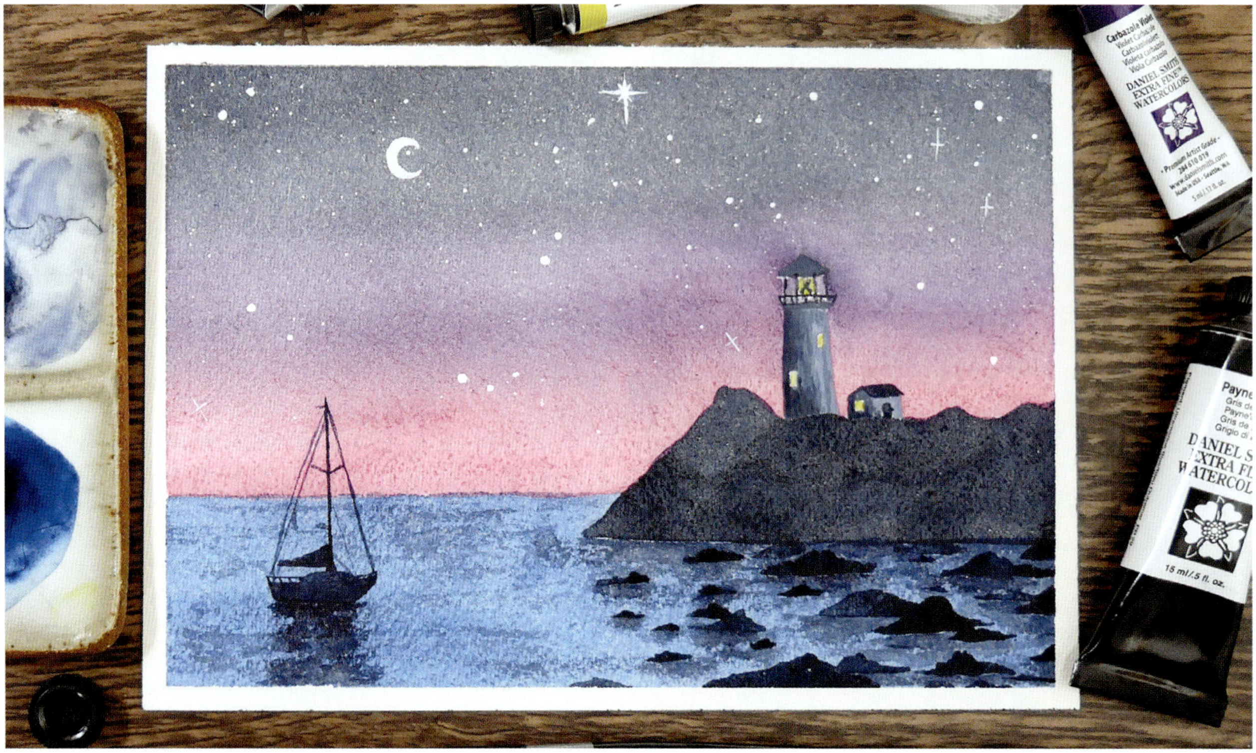

SUNSET SHIFT AT THE LIGHTHOUSE

Nearly all the boats have returned to their docks, as night approaches and shifts the light of day to darkness; there is, however, lingering light on the horizon, silhouetting the last sailboat and the lighthouse bringing it in to shore. In this painting, we'll practice smooth gradients and dry brushing and learn about the spatter technique.

MATERIALS

Paints: opera pink, carbazole violet, indigo, Prussian blue, Payne's gray and lemon yellow

Dr. Ph. Martin's Bleedproof White paint (or white gouache paint)

Brushes: sizes 12, 6 and 2 round

Optional: size 1 or 2 liner

Paper: 5 x 7-inch (13 x 18-cm) cold-pressed watercolor paper

Painter's tape (or washi tape)

Paper towels (or a rag)

Ruler

Pencil and kneaded eraser

White gel pen

SWATCHES

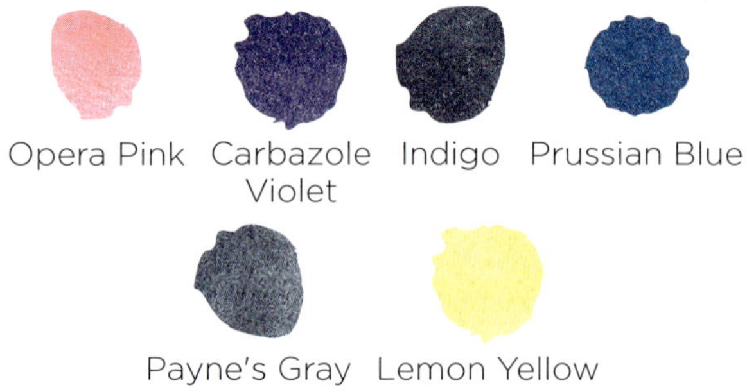

Opera Pink

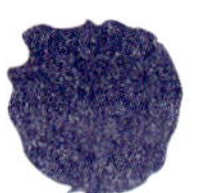

Carbazole Violet

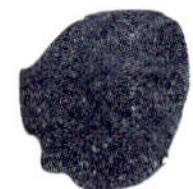

Indigo

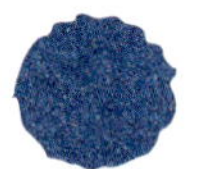

Prussian Blue

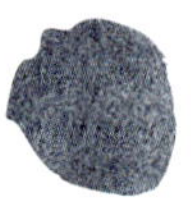

Payne's Gray

Lemon Yellow

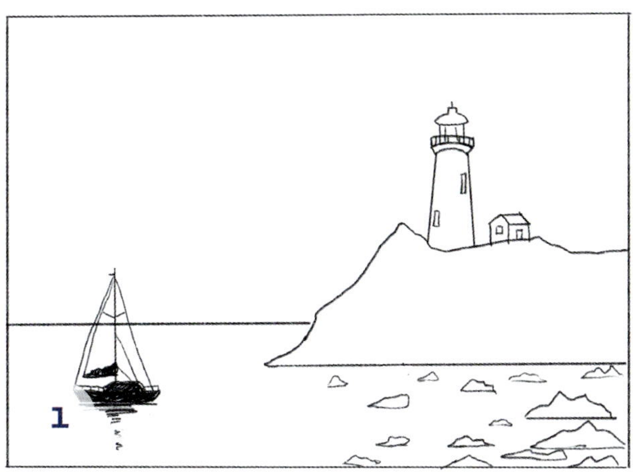

STEP 1: THE SKETCH

Grab your ruler and sketch a horizontal horizon line one-third of the way up the paper from the bottom. About halfway through your horizon line on the right-hand side, sketch in a cliff with a cylinder lighthouse and a small building next to it. Below the stone cliff, sketch a few rocks in the ocean.

In the bottom left-hand corner of the paper, lightly sketch the silhouette of a sailboat, using the ruler to help sketch the straight mast in the middle of the boat. Use the above image as a reference, or look up sailboats online to get an idea of what the shape looks like.

STEP 2: THE GRADIENT IN THE SKY

Using your size 12 round brush, begin by wetting the entire sky portion with clean water. The key here is to avoid painting water over the cliff, lighthouse and small building. Remember: Watercolor paint will only go where water is. Since we'll be painting our gradient using the wet-on-wet technique, if we wish for a portion of our paper to remain white, it must stay dry.

Once you've applied your water and the sky portion is glossy, let's begin our gradient. Still using a size 12 round brush, pick up medium-value opera pink, and begin applying it right along the horizon. Paint the opera pink around the cliff, lighthouse and small building using your sketch as your guide. Clean off your brush, and then pick up carbazole violet, applying it directly above opera pink, moving your strokes horizontally across the paper. Again, be sure to avoid painting over your lighthouse. The pink and purple should begin to bleed into each other on their own, but to further blend the colors together, clean off your brush and dab it on a paper towel so it's damp rather than soaking wet. Lightly run that damp brush along the edge of the colors, where they meet. This will further blend the colors into one another. You may need to do this a few times to blend the gradient smoothly.

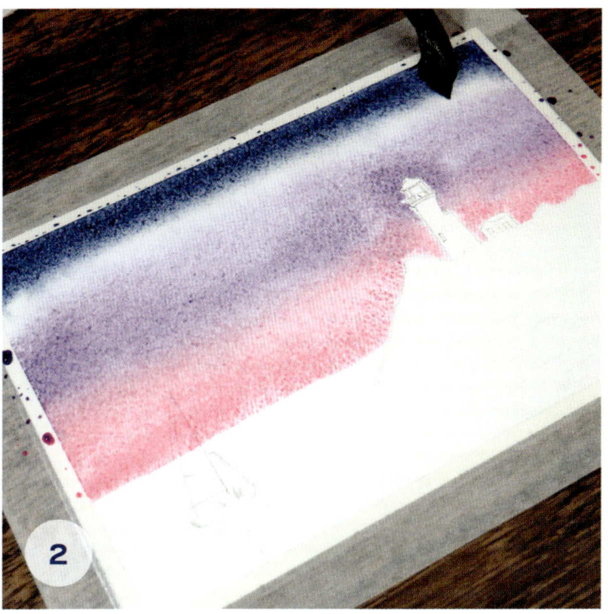

We have one more color to add in this gradient: indigo. This time, pick up some medium-value indigo, and use horizontal brushstrokes, from paper edge to paper edge, to lay down the color. Again, the indigo and violet will naturally begin to bleed into one another, but to smooth out the gradient, use the same technique from the previous paragraph: long, horizontal strokes with a clean, damp brush, where the two colors meet. No worries if the gradient isn't perfect—Mother Nature sure isn't!

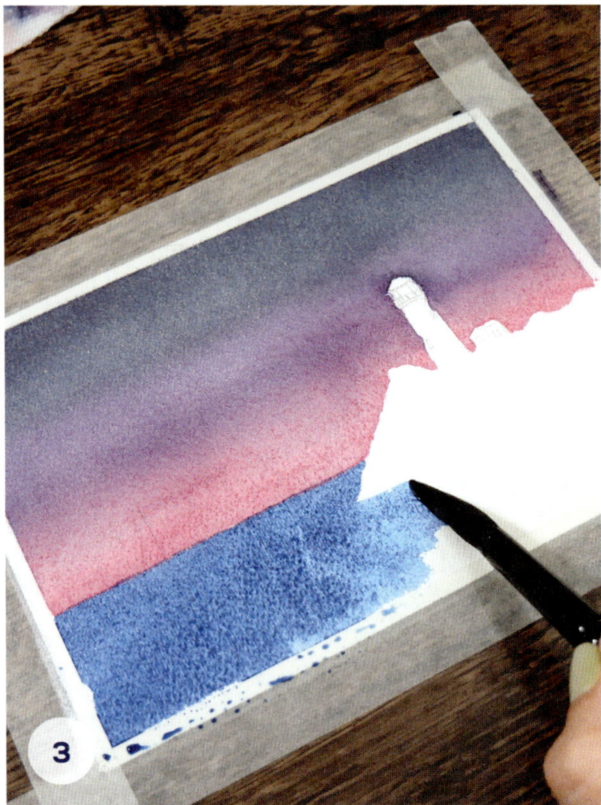

Let this layer dry completely. Then, wet the entire sky portion again with clean water, applying from the pink upward to the indigo. When applying clean water on a gradient like this, it's best practice to start from the lightest color and move to the darkest, as the watercolors will reactivate. Blending from indigo to pink will cause the darker color to muddy the rest, resulting in a less vibrant pink.

Additionally, you may have seen in photo 2, on the previous page, that I accidentally got a little paint within my lighthouse sketch even though I tried to avoid that area. That's okay! In Step 6, we'll be using white gouache, which is opaque and will cover this up. I do my best to avoid painting these areas because it's easier to work with the white of the paper rather than a base of watercolor. After all, the watercolor will react with water and has the chance to blend into the gouache. A small mistake like this is easier to fix rather than a larger painted area.

Once your sky is rewetted, apply the same three colors again, intensifying their values.

When you believe your colors are sufficiently intensified, stop and let the piece dry completely. Watercolors will always appear darker when wet, so wait for the colors to dry, and then you can determine if you want to intensify them in another layer. This is referred to as "color shift."

Color Shift: The "color shift" effect is caused by the way light behaves with water. When the paints are wet, light is absorbed by the water/wet paint, making them appear more saturated. When the paints are dry, they become matte like the paper, and the light then bounces off the paint, making it appear lighter. Additionally, some pigments in the paints behave differently than others and, therefore, will result in varying color shifts.

Waiting for a layer to dry and then reevaluating colors is an important part of watercolor painting. A rule of thumb is that watercolor will always dry a bit lighter, so keep this in mind if you want to create a painting with fewer layers!

STEP 3: THE OCEAN

To create the base of our ocean, use your size 12 round brush to pick up medium-value Prussian blue, and create a flat wash within the outline of your sketch. Like before, make sure to not paint within the cliff, but instead paint around it. You can, however, paint right over your sketches of the rocks in the water. It would take far too long to paint every nook and cranny in between and, most likely, you would not end up with a flat wash of color. Instead, we'll rely on the translucency of our watercolor and look for the pencil sketch below the paint when it's dry. If you can no longer see your sketch, no worries! You can instead reference the final picture of this piece on page 59.

Let the Prussian blue wash dry completely before moving on.

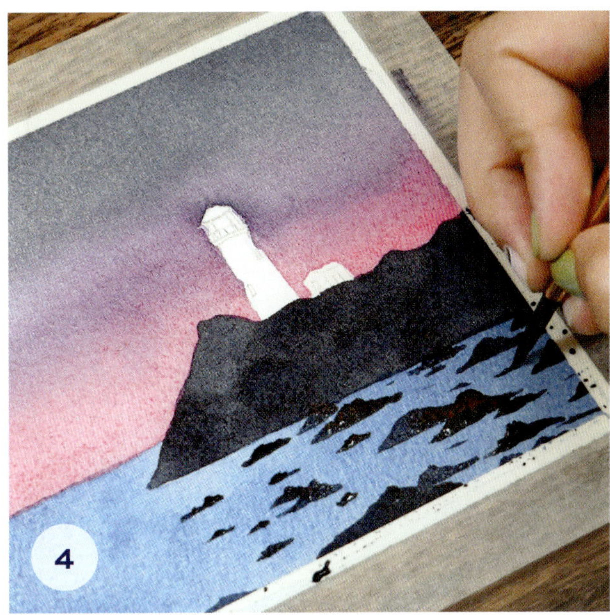

STEP 4: THE CLIFF & ROCKS

Next, let's fill in the cliff. Using a size 6 round brush, apply dark-value Payne's gray to the entire space. This wash doesn't need to be perfectly even. If the paint is a little uneven, it will hint at a bit of texture in the cliff face. Again, let this wash dry before continuing on.

Now, let's add in the rocks in the water. Using that same size 6 round brush and dark-value Payne's gray, paint in various shapes and sizes of rocks. For these rocks, it's important that the bottom of each is flat, as the water is obscuring the bottom portion of the rocks. The tops above the water, however, should vary in shape and size. Make sure to paint some of these rocks as overlapped, as this will help add to the realism of your painting. As I've already mentioned, nature is random, but it can be difficult to paint randomly (we humans like to fall into patterns). It can be difficult to remove yourself from those patterns, so actively bringing this idea up will help you be aware and purposeful with your painting.

Once you've added in plenty of rocks in the ocean, wait for them all to dry before moving on.

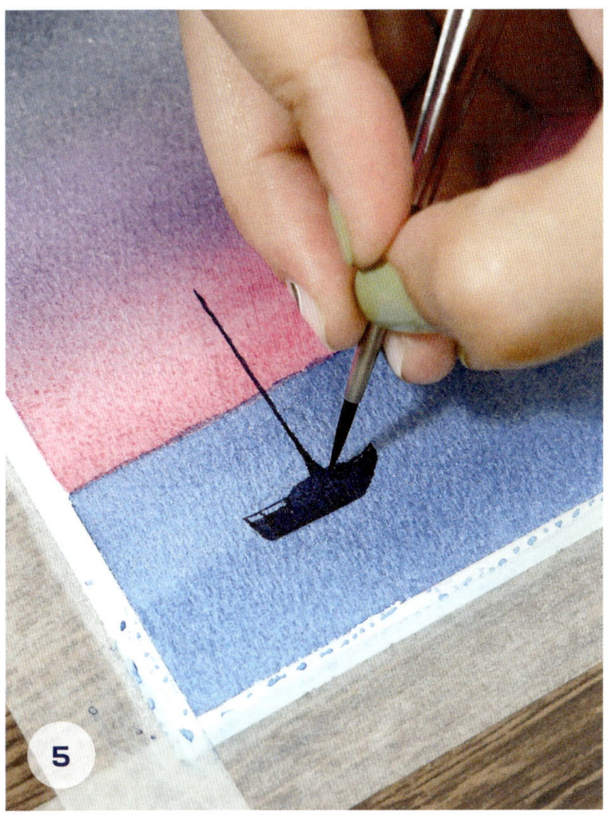

STEP 5: THE SAILBOAT

Pick up some dark-value Payne's gray with your size 2 round brush for this, as we'll be needing the accuracy of a smaller point. My suggestion for this silhouette is to look up pictures of sailboats or sailboat silhouettes online (this is what I always do). It's always easier to paint something with a reference. As with anything, if you aren't feeling confident, practice the silhouette on a scrap sheet of paper. We often have an image in our mind of what we want the outcome to be, but, as with anything, practice makes better—and better is a never-ending journey. Remember, even just putting your paintbrush on the page is a step in the right direction.

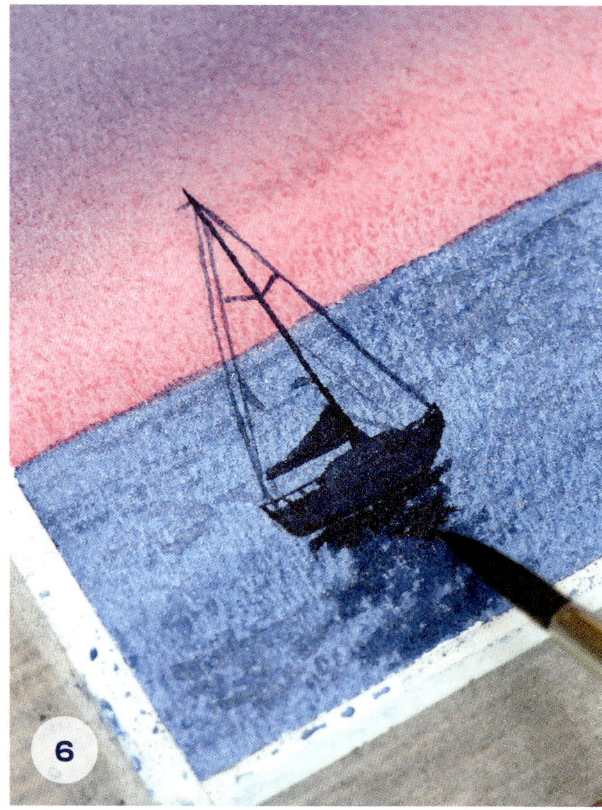

For painting sailboats, I like to break them down into simple shapes. First, I will paint the vertical line of the mast (what the sails attach to). At the bottom of that vertical line, I'll begin painting an almost banana-like shape with a flat bottom (a portion of the boat will be under the water, and the water in this piece is flat and calm). After the basic shape is complete, I'll start adding in details: the railing on the back, the folded-up sail and the various ropes and rigging used for hoisting sails. Be sure to use the very point of your round brush for these skinny lines. If you're having difficulty using your round brush for this and keep painting lines that are too thick, I would suggest switching to a different kind of brush, specifically a liner brush.

Liner brushes are designed for just that: creating lines! I prefer using round brushes simply for their versatility—being able to create thin and thick lines—but liner brushes do come in handy for precise details. In photo 5 on the previous page, I'm using a size 2 round brush. Once your sailboat is complete, let it dry completely.

STEP 6: DRY BRUSHING

Using the dry-brushing technique, let's add some texture to our ocean! For more information on this technique, see page 46.

Using your size 6 round brush, pick up some medium-value indigo, and dab off your brush on a paper towel until it's nearly dry. Then, quickly graze your brush horizontally across the surface of your paper in the ocean section. Use this dry-brushing technique across the entire ocean section, but focus more heavily on the rocky section. Beneath each of these rocks, you can move your brush back and forth, creating almost individual shadows for each. Additionally, add this dry-brush shadow beneath the large cliff. These shadows will help to "ground" each of the rocks and the cliff, making each look like it belongs within the painting. Once you've used medium-value indigo, switch to a darker value, and repeat the process in some areas, adding some color variety to your shadows.

Additionally, we'll need to add some shadows beneath our sailboat. Pick up some dark-value indigo, and dry brush back and forth beneath the boat, letting those shadows extend right to the bottom of the paper.

Let these strokes dry before moving on.

STEP 7: THE LIGHTHOUSE & BUILDING

Let's return to creating our lighthouse! For this, we'll be mixing our watercolors with some white gouache. I used Dr. Ph. Martin's Bleedproof White for this, which is a water-soluble acrylic ink.

Mix a bit of Bleedproof White into your watercolors so that they're opaque. Using Payne's gray, mix up a light-value, medium-value and dark-value opaque gray. The consistency of this mix will be a bit creamier than the watercolors we've been working with so far. There is no set rule for ratios of Bleedproof White to watercolor paint, so use a scrap sheet of paper for testing colors and consistencies as you go. Once you have these three values, let's begin filling in our lighthouse.

Use your size 2 round brush, and load it up with some light-value opaque gray, filling in the bottom two-thirds of the lighthouse (below where the lightbulb is). Make sure to leave one or two rectangular spaces for windows. While this dries, use the light-valued paint to paint the front-facing wall of the small building. Let this dry as well. Then, use a medium-value opaque gray to paint the deck, railing, walls and roof of the lighthouse. Use this same medium value to paint the other wall of the smaller building. These two color values on the building will help to give it dimension. Let dry and then use a dark-value opaque gray to paint on the roof of the smaller building.

Now, let's add some dimension to our lighthouse as well. Pick up some dark-value opaque gray, and begin adding this color to the left side of our lighthouse. This will be the shadowed side. By adding some strokes of this darker value on one side, we're creating a three-dimensional effect. Continue adding a few strokes of darker value, moving toward a medium and then light value again as you paint left to right. Additionally, these strokes should be vertical in direction. These vertical strokes add to the texture of the lighthouse, making it look as old and ancient as the rocks in the ocean below.

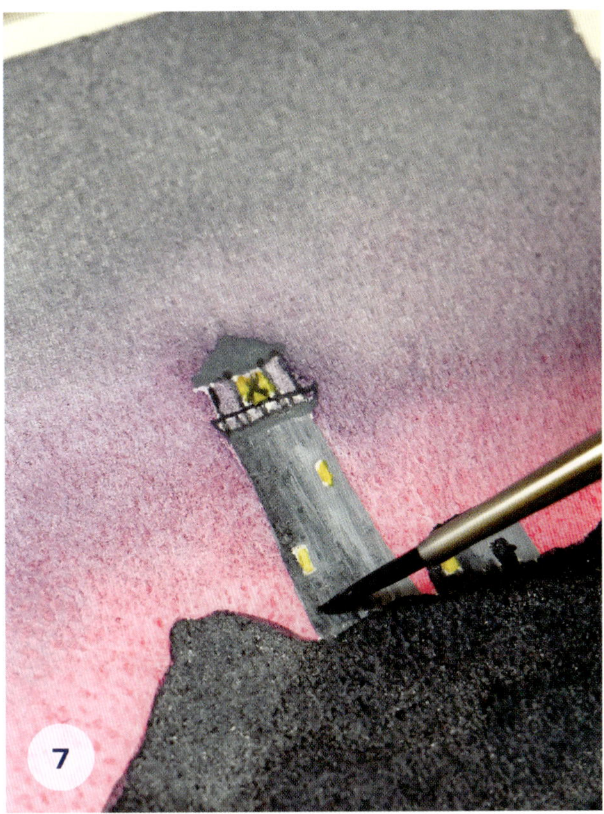

Once you're happy with the gradient on your lighthouse, add in two small lines where the lightbulb is housed in the lighthouse, creating an "X." These represent the inner mechanisms of the lightbulb. Let all of this dry.

Now for the finishing touches. Mix up a light value of lemon yellow and, using your size 2 round brush, fill in the windows of the lighthouse and small building. Also, fill in the middle section of the lighthouse, where the "X" is. Since the top of the lighthouse is built with windows, only paint the middle section yellow. The other two sections next to it should be painted with a medium-value carbazole violet or opera pink, whatever matches the sky adjacent to the lighthouse. Let dry.

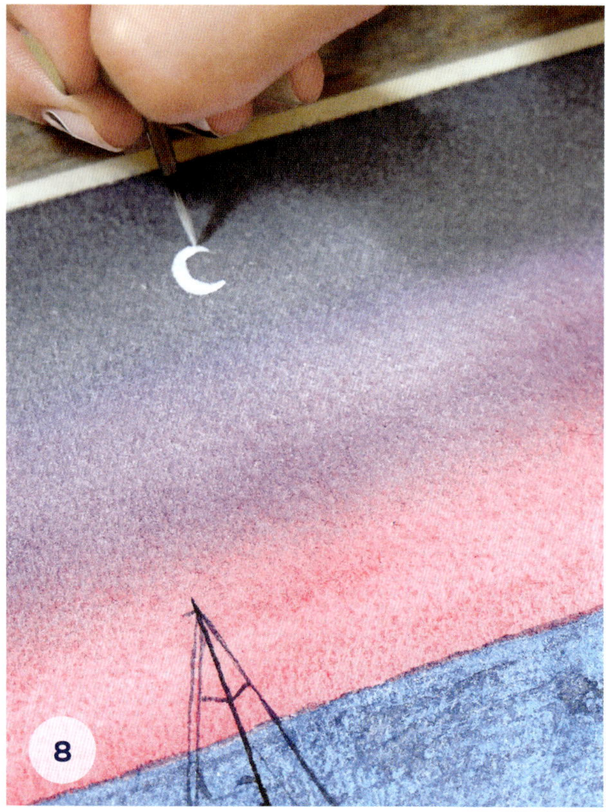

STEP 8: THE MOON & STARS

Time for some final details!

Using your size 2 round brush, pick up some Bleedproof White, and paint a white crescent moon in the sky. We'll use something called the spatter technique to create our starry sky.

To paint stars, load up a small round brush, around size 2 or 3, with Bleedproof White. For the correct consistency of white gouache, add some of it onto your palette (making sure it stays clean), and add in a drop or two of clean water. This will create a smooth, creamy consistency. Next, it's important to cover up any of the areas you don't wish to spatter with stars with some scrap paper or tissues, as this process is a bit uncontrolled. (Yes, you will get white gouache on yourself.) Then, grab a pencil and then begin tapping on your loaded brush. This tapping will send white gouache spattering across your sky, creating stars!

There are many ways to add in random splotches of stars, and you can even forego this step entirely and use a white gel pen if you wish; however, I have found that this process creates a nice variety of randomly sized droplets that would be difficult to achieve with only a white gel pen. Additionally, some artists use a toothbrush loaded with white gouache and flick their finger across the bristles to send stars onto the paper. It's all a matter of personal preference. Experiment with different processes, and find what works best for you.

Wait for the stars to dry completely before adding in further details. The white gouache can smudge pretty easily (I'm speaking from experience). Once dry, let's add in some details with our white gel pen (or you can use a small detailing brush loaded with white gouache).

For twinkling stars, I use a small round brush (size 2 or smaller). Alternatively, you can use a small liner brush if you have one. Twinkling stars are as simple as adding in a few small crosses in the sky, making sure to vary the length of the "arms" of the star. For a larger twinkling star, choose a larger dot (or paint some in if you don't have any). On this larger dot, add eight arms total in various lengths, mimicking the look of a compass that points in all directions.

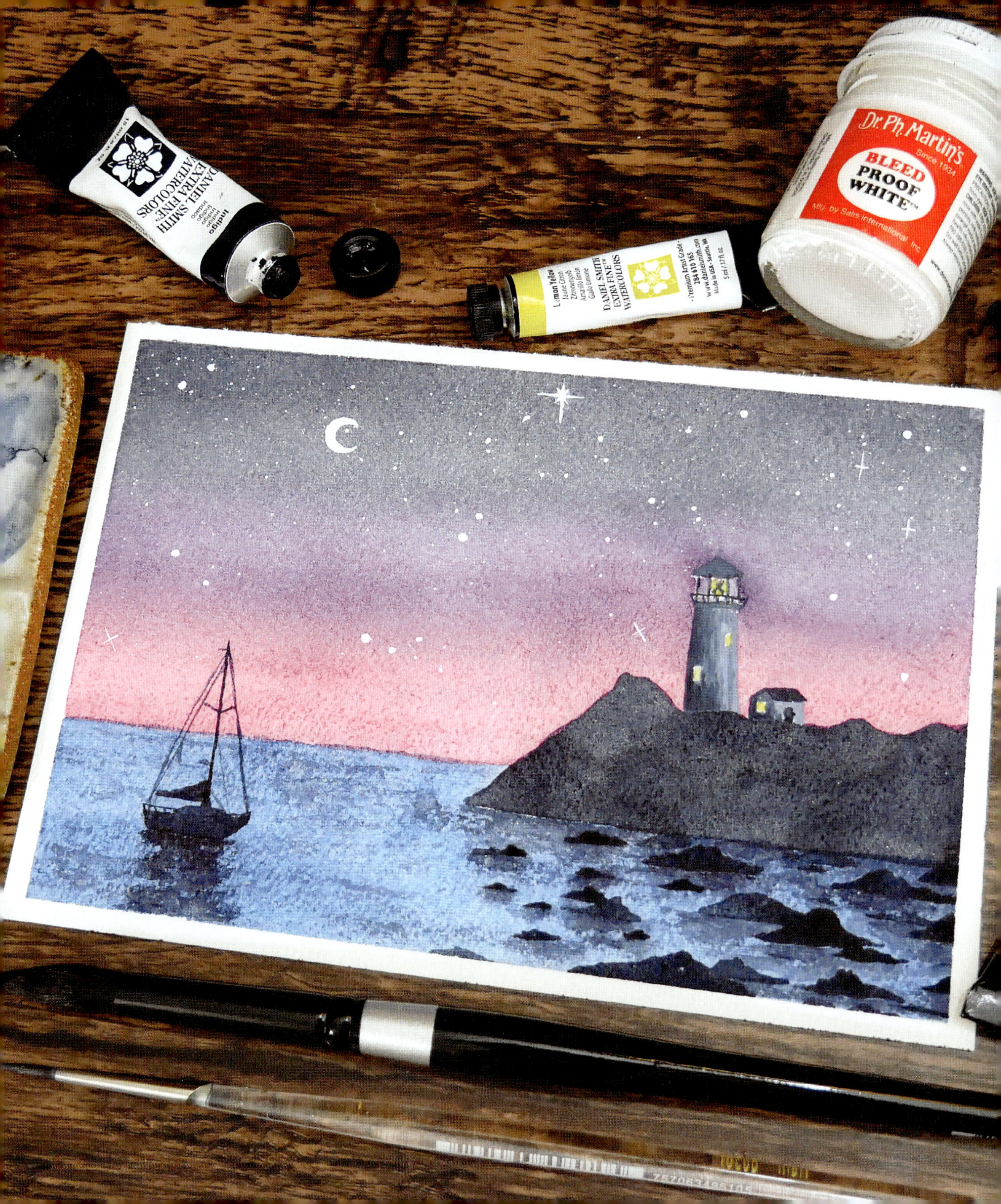

Indigo
DANIEL SMITH
EXTRA FINE
WATERCOLORS
Lemon Yellow
DANIEL SMITH
EXTRA FINE
WATERCOLORS
Dr. Ph. Martin's
Since 1934
BLEED
PROOF
WHITE™

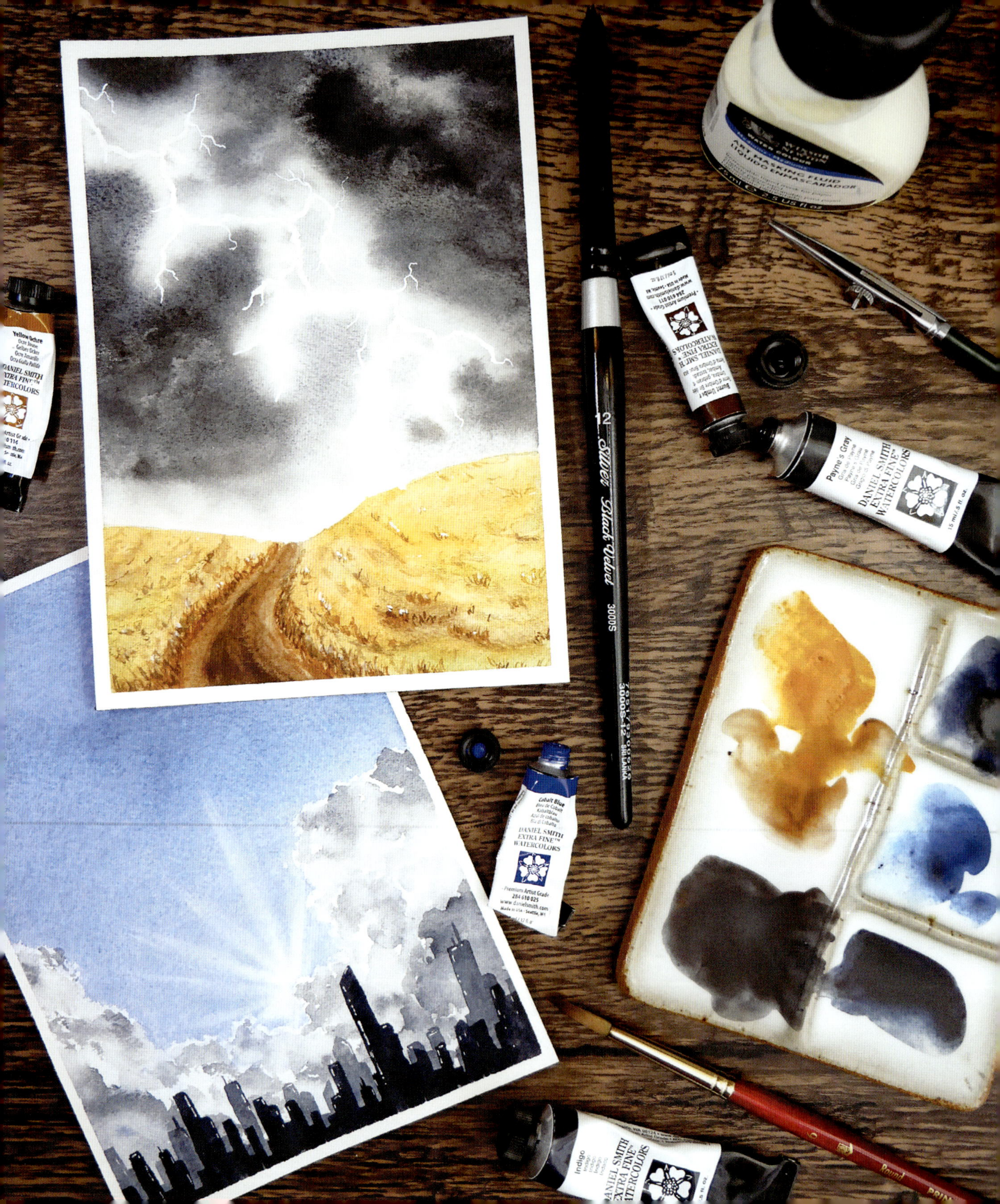
Yellow Ochre
DANIEL SMITH
EXTRA FINE
WATERCOLORS
12
Silver Black Velvet
3000S
Payne's Gray
DANIEL SMITH
EXTRA FINE
WATERCOLORS
Cobalt Blue
DANIEL SMITH
EXTRA FINE
WATERCOLORS
Indigo
DANIEL SMITH
EXTRA FINE
WATERCOLORS
Round

Savage Storms & CALM CLOUDS

Growing up, I used to be afraid of thunderstorms. Loud and jarring, they frightened me, and I used to hide under my blanket until they subsided. As I learned more about them—how air, water and electricity combine to split the sky—my intrigue grew. They're dangerous yet beautiful in their own way. Without the skies in turmoil, how can we ever come to appreciate their stillness and serenity? Giant, soft, fluffy clouds during the summertime provide a peaceful contrast to raging storms. It's incredible how dynamic the sky can be. In this chapter, we'll paint a range of cloudy skies: some foreboding, some raging and some serene.

Deep thunder rumbles
Cotton ball clouds are rolling
The storm has arrived

FLUFFY SUMMER CLOUDS

You've made it! You've made it to the top of that hill you've been climbing. The breeze catches your hair, sending it swirling as you look up to see white, fluffy clouds moving across the sky. The view is stunning, so let's put our paintbrush to paper to recreate this scene. In this piece, we'll use the white of our paper to create these soft clouds.

MATERIALS

Paints: cobalt blue, Prussian blue, Payne's gray, Light Teal (page 28), hooker's green, perylene green and yellow ochre

Brushes: sizes 12, 10 and 6 round

Paper: 5 x 7-inch (13 x 18-cm) cold-pressed watercolor paper

Painter's tape (or washi tape)

Paper towels (or a rag)

Pencil and kneaded eraser

White gel pen or white gouache

SWATCHES

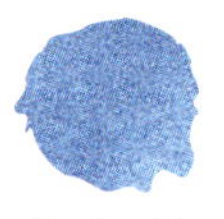
Cobalt Blue

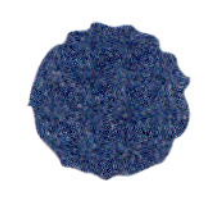
Prussian Blue

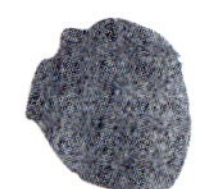
Payne's Gray

Light Teal (page 28)

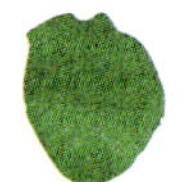
Hooker's Green

Perylene Green

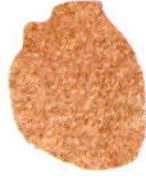
Yellow Ochre

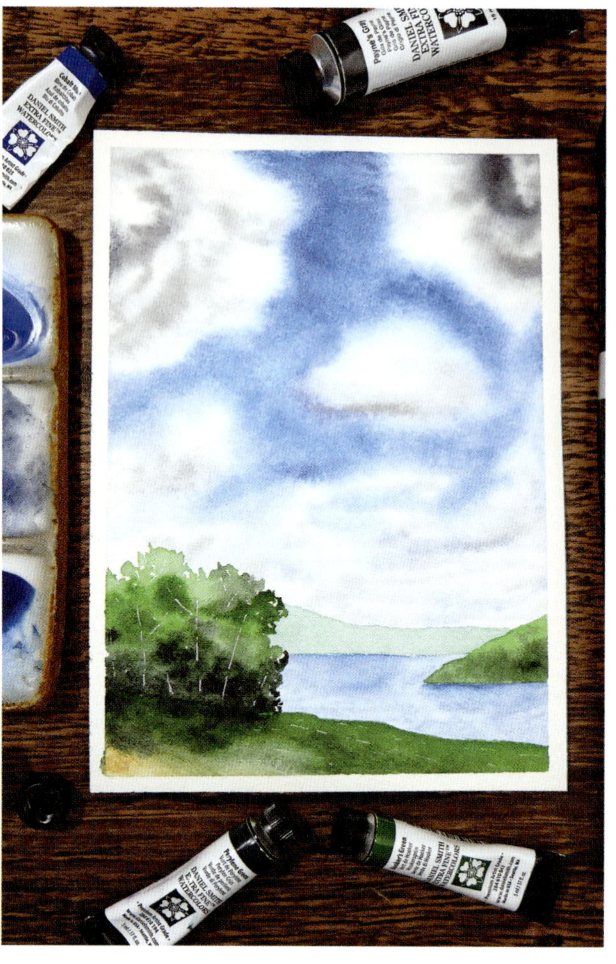

STEP 1: THE SKETCH

Begin by sketching in a gently sloping hill right in the foreground, with a "blobby shape" in the left-hand corner. This "blobby shape" is our bunch of trees. No worries about adding detail here, as we're just blocking out the shape to be filled in later. You can also add a few lines in the tree line, which will later serve as tree trunks.

After the foreground, add a hill in the middle ground and background, both with flat bottoms, as they will be lining a lake.

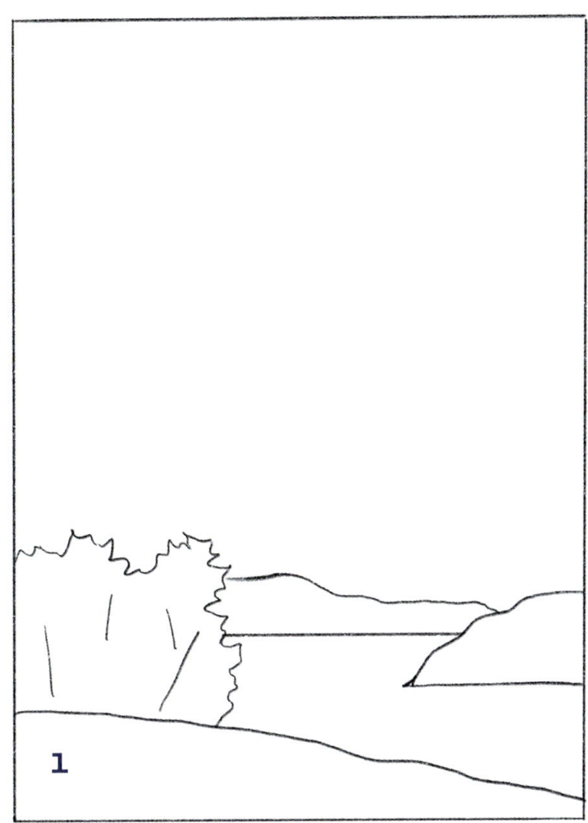

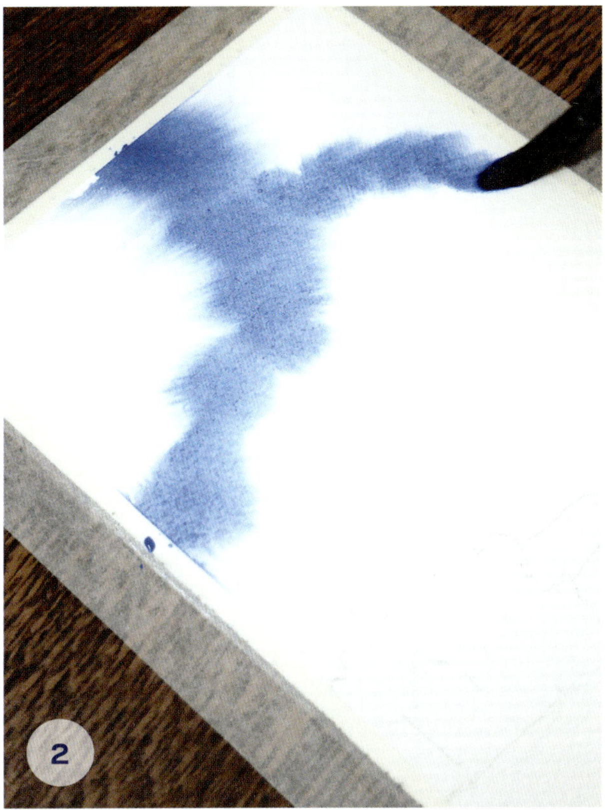

STEP 2: THE CLOUDS

To create our white, fluffy clouds, we'll need to use the white space of the paper. Begin by wetting the sky portion of your painting with clean water. Using your size 12 round brush, pick up some dark-value cobalt blue, and begin applying the paint to the paper, leaving large white spaces for our clouds. Your paint will naturally spread out on the wet paper, so leave larger white spaces than you think you'll need. If you touch the paper with your brush and the paint shoots out across your paper, your paper is too wet. Wait a few moments for the paper to soak up the water and dry just ever so slightly, until the paper is damp rather than glistening.

To give our painting depth, the larger, rounder and fluffier clouds will be on the top of the paper, closer to the viewer. As you move downward toward the horizon line, the clouds will become smaller, skinnier and more horizontal in shape. This will make the clouds appear farther away.

Let's add a bit more color dimension to our sky. Clean off your brush and pick up some medium-value Prussian blue, lightly dropping the color in the sections you've already painted cobalt blue. It's a subtle effect, but doing so in a few sections of already cobalt blue sky will add some variety.

Once you're done creating the white spaces for your clouds, let your paper dry entirely.

STEP 3: THE SHADOWS

It's time to add some shadows to our clouds to give them more dimension. Clean off your brush and apply clean water to the entirety of your paper again. In order to keep your fluffy clouds white, be sure to put down clean water on the white spaces first and then expand outward into the blue sky.

Pick up some light-value Payne's gray, and begin applying shadows to your large, fluffy clouds. In the larger clouds, dab your brush lightly in the white spaces, letting the paint naturally spread out. Then, pick up some medium-value Payne's gray, and apply it to the larger clouds again, moving your brush in small, circular motions to mimic the "fluff" of the cloud.

For the clouds in the middle of the piece, apply that same medium-value Payne's gray to the bottom of the clouds. For this piece, we're assuming the light source is coming from the sun, high in the sky, so the shadows for the clouds will mostly be on the bottom. That being said, clouds are three-dimensional and often have many layers, dips, valleys and swells within them. So, you don't have to only apply Payne's gray on the bottom; you can apply it to the belly of the clouds as well. Just make sure to keep some of the top a lighter value or white!

Once you're satisfied with your sky, let it dry completely before moving on.

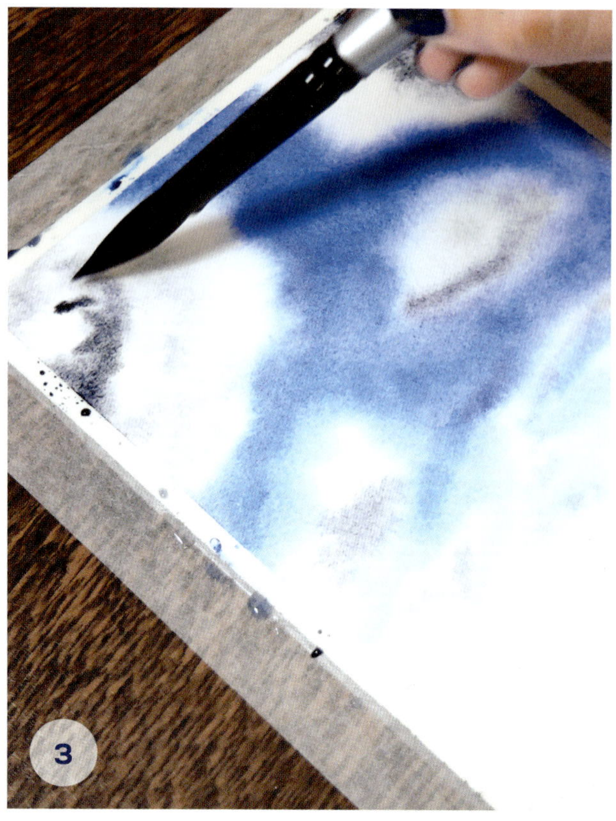

STEP 4: THE HILLS & LAKE

Let's move on to some landscape details and create our middle ground. Using your size 6 round brush, pick up some light-value Light Teal, and apply it with a flat wash to the farthest hill. Let dry.

Next, pick up some medium-value hooker's green, and apply it to the next hill, on the right-hand side of the painting in the middle ground. Without cleaning your brush, pick up some medium-value perylene green, and apply it to the bottom portion of the hill, letting the two greens mix together in the wash. Using these two greens will add some variety and shadows to this hill. Let dry.

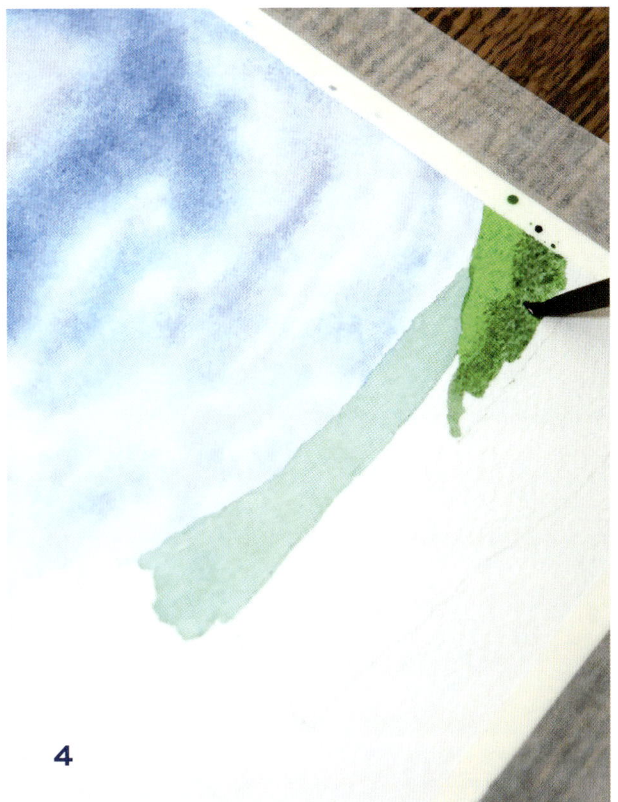

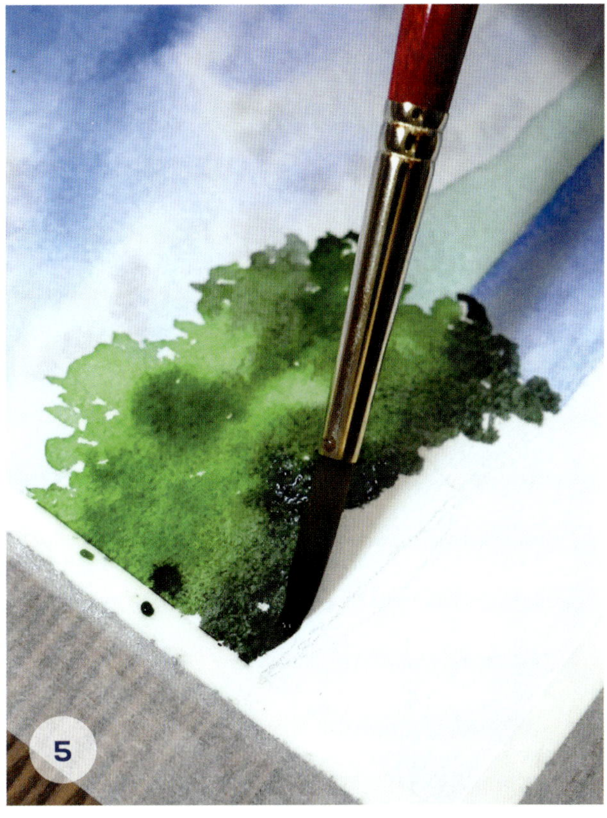

To paint our lake, clean off your brush and pick up some medium-value cobalt blue. Apply a flat wash of this in the lake portion. Don't worry if the wash isn't perfectly even. This is water, after all, and some variety in color saturation and texture will only make it more realistic. While this wash is still damp, pick up some dark-value cobalt blue, and drop color in right below the hill closer to the viewer (on the right-hand side). This will be a slight shadow of that hill on the water, adding some dimension to said hill.

STEP 5: THE TREE LINE

Now, it's time to add our foreground.

Using your size 6 round brush, pick up light-value hooker's green, and begin dabbing your brush in erratic motions to fill in our tree line sketch. Switch back and forth between varying values of both hooker's green and perylene green, letting the wet paints mix as you fill in the outline. The darker values of green will be toward the base of the tree line, whereas the tops of the trees will be lit with sunlight and will, therefore, be of lighter value. Let the trees dry.

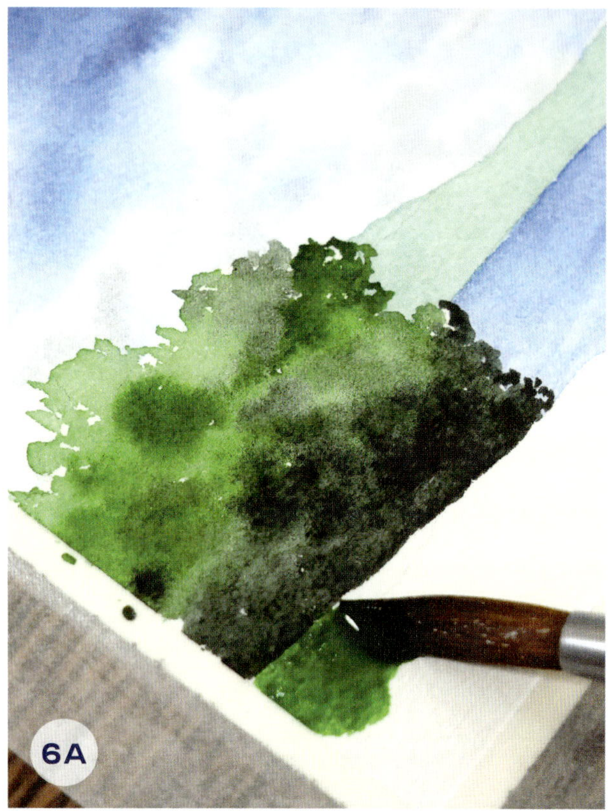

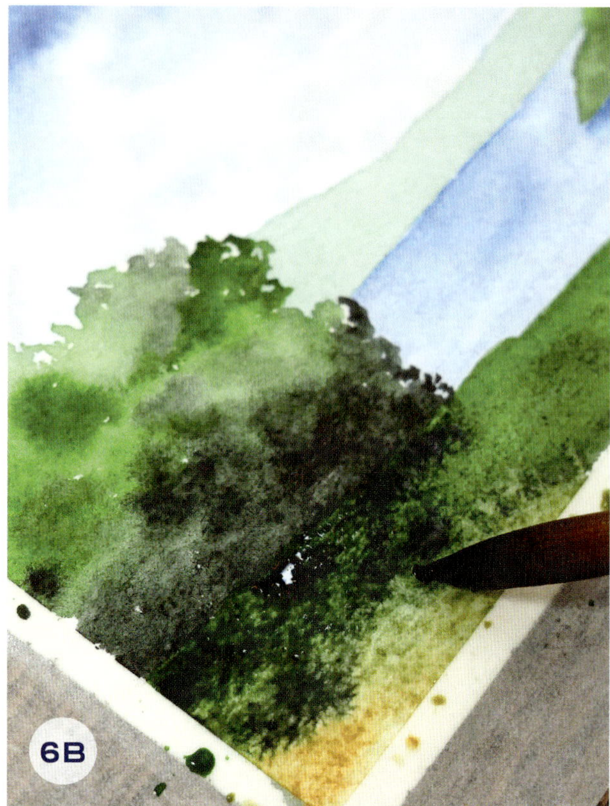

STEP 6: THE GRASSY HILL

Switch to your size 10 round brush, and pick up some medium-value hooker's green. Apply a flat wash of this color along the top of the outline. Then, without cleaning your brush, pick up some medium-value perylene green, and apply it directly below the hooker's green, letting the colors mix and combine in the wash, similar to what we did to the hill in the middle ground.

Clean off your brush and pick up some medium-value yellow ochre. While this portion is still wet, apply the yellow ochre in the bottom left-hand corner, letting it naturally mix with the greens above it in the wash. Adding warmer colors closer to the foreground of paintings is yet another technique used to create depth! Lastly, while the wash is still damp, clean your brush and pick up dark-value perylene green. Dab the perylene green in the field section below the trees, mimicking shadows in the grass. Let this wash dry entirely.

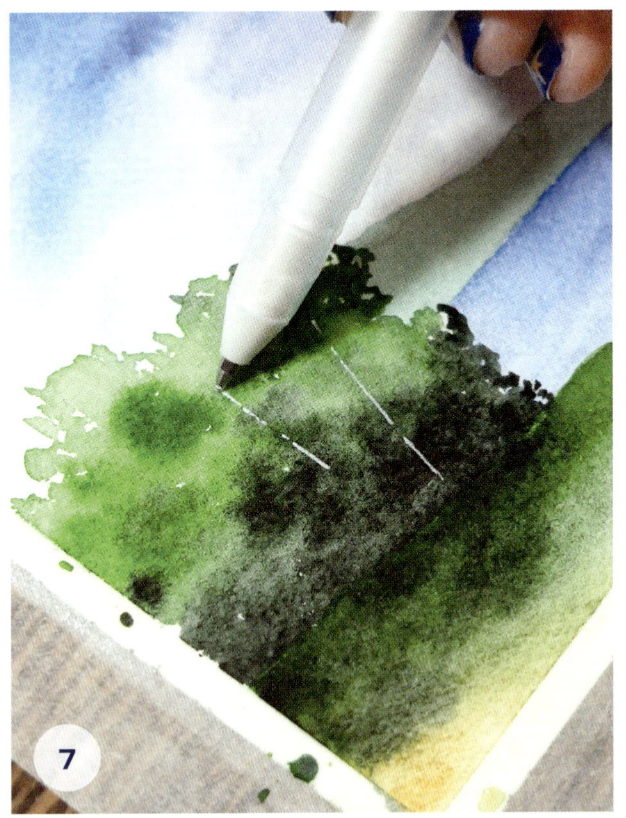

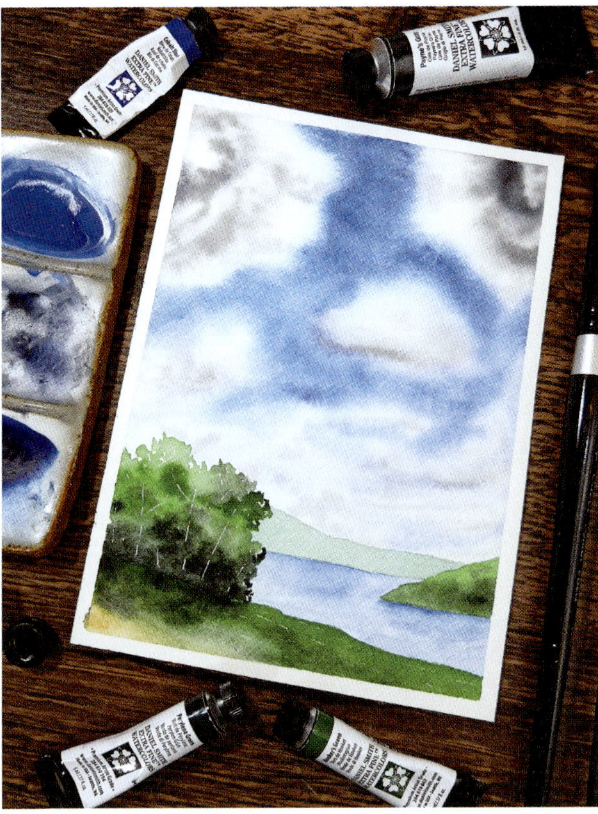

STEP 7: THE FINISHING TOUCHES

Let's add in some final details. Using your white gel pen or white gouache, add in a few tree trunks to your tree line. Leave some spaces/gaps in the trunks and branches, which suggests that leaves are covering up more details. True to life, when you're looking at a forest from a distance, you won't be able to see all of the trunks and branches. Half of being an effective artist is suggesting what's really there and then letting the mind of your viewer fill in the rest.

You can also add a few horizontal lines of white in the grassy field, following the slope of the hill. I like to do this to create highlights and tie things together. Adding in these few white lines gives the illusion of grass gently blowing in the wind.

STORMY BEACH DAY

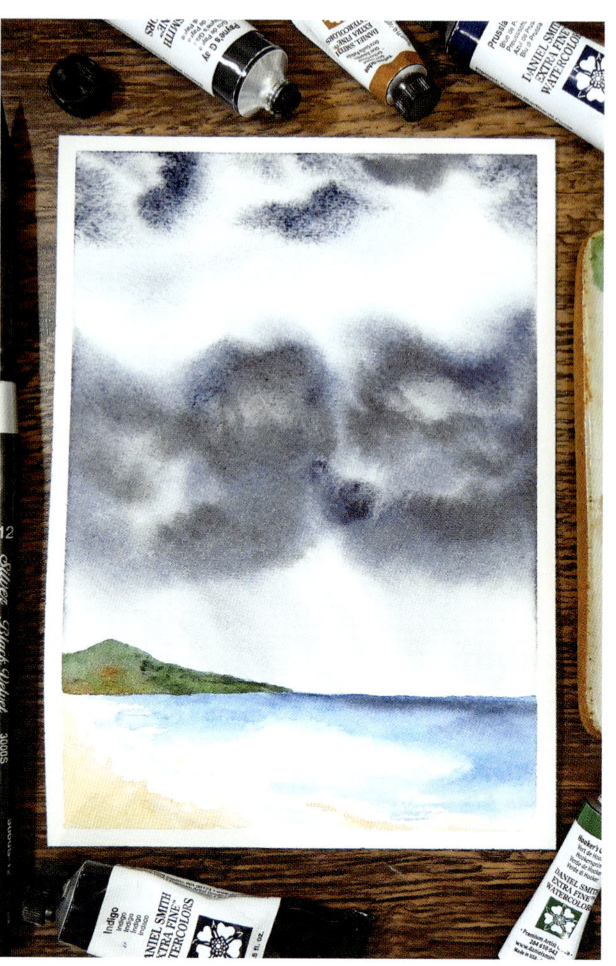

A peaceful day at the ocean is disrupted when the wind begins to blow and rain approaches. The waves begin to stir and froth, seafoam hitting the shore—the brief calm before the deluge. In this piece, we'll practice quick, flicking brushstrokes to create the illusion of rain in the distance.

MATERIALS

Paints: Payne's gray, Neutral Gray (page 28), Prussian blue, indigo, yellow ochre, burnt umber, perylene green and hooker's green

Brushes: sizes 12 and 10 round

Paper: 5 x 7–inch (13 x 18–cm) cold-pressed watercolor paper

Painter's tape (or washi tape)

Paper towels (or a rag)

Pencil and kneaded eraser

SWATCHES

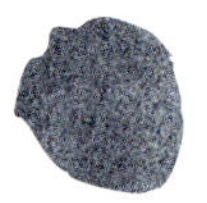
Payne's Gray

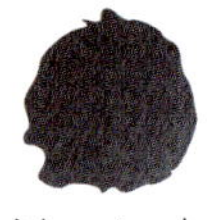
Neutral Gray (page 28)

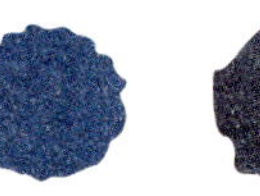
Prussian Blue

Indigo

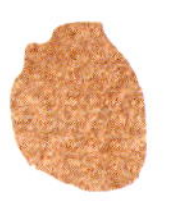
Yellow Ochre

Burnt Umber

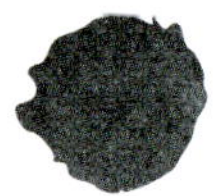
Perylene Green

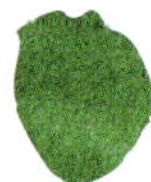
Hooker's Green

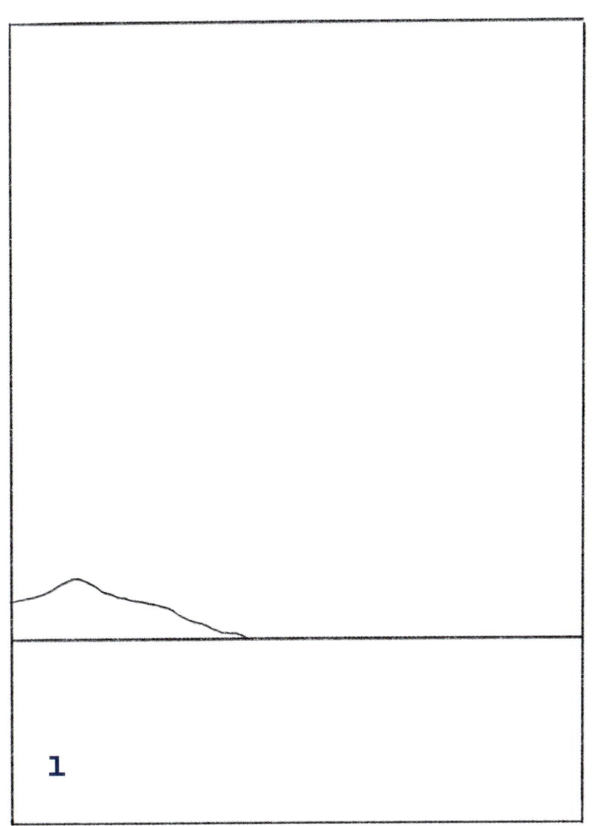

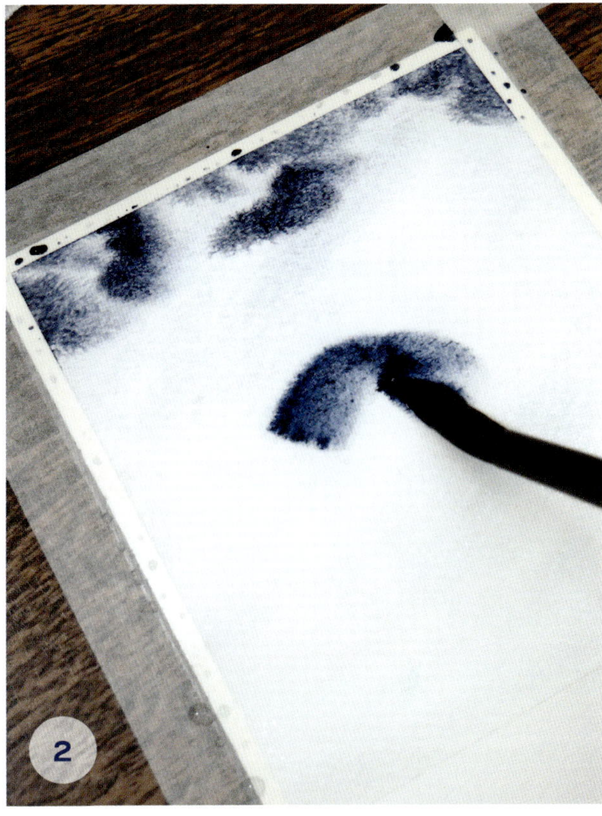

STEP 1: THE SKETCH

Very simple sketch here! On the bottom one-third of your paper, sketch in a straight line, representing our horizon line. Then, on the left side of the horizon line, sketch in a small sloping hill.

STEP 2: THE STORMY SKY (LAYER 1)

Using a size 12 round brush or larger, begin by wetting the sky portion of your painting with clean water. Pick up some light-value Payne's gray, and apply it to the paper in light, wispy brushstrokes, starting from the top and moving down toward the horizon line. This is just adding some color to our background. We'll intensify things next.

While the paper is still damp, pick up some medium- to dark-value Payne's gray, and apply a few strokes right at the top of the page. Leave some white space in between the clouds for highlights. Next, move about halfway down the page, and apply that same Payne's gray in large, circular strokes to mimic round, fluffy storm clouds. This storm cloud will take up the middle portion of our sky, so make sure to leave some room about an inch (2.5 cm) above the horizon.

Move on to the next step quickly, as we need our paper to still be damp! If your paper has begun to dry, stop, let it dry completely and then rewet the paper with clean water before continuing on to the next step.

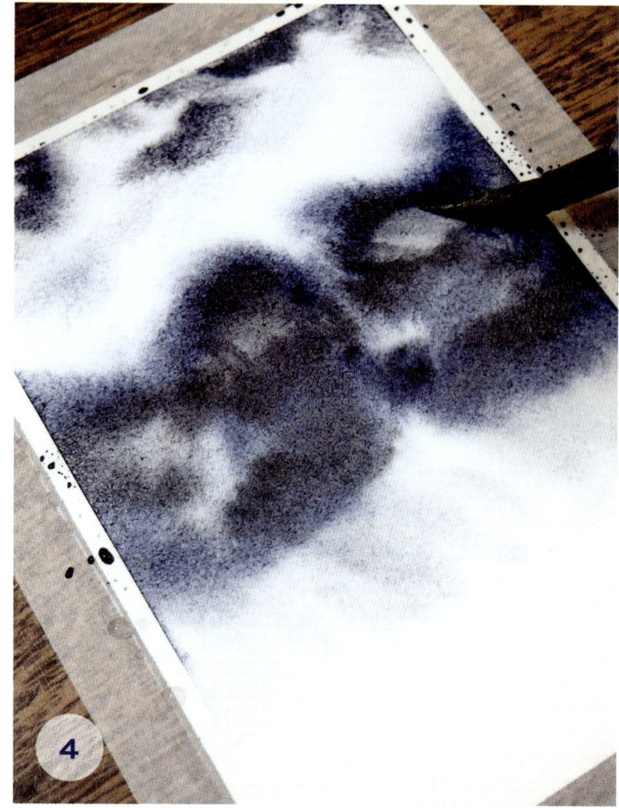

STEP 3: CREATING RAIN

To create our rain, pick up some light-value Payne's gray, and dab your brush on a paper towel. Dabbing your loaded paintbrush on a paper towel will help to reduce the concentration of water in your brush. For this technique, we don't want a fully loaded brush but rather an only slightly damp one. We'll be relying on the dampness of the paper to soften our strokes.

Starting at the bottom of the main storm cloud, gently press your brush into the page, and swipe downward quickly, at a slight angle.

Since the paint on the paper is still wet, we'll end up dragging some of the paint from the cloud downward too. This is exactly what we want. Rain is simply an extension of clouds rather than a separate entity. Perform these quick, angled brushstrokes a few more times, dragging both the paint in the cloud and the paint on the brush downward.

In the photo of this step, my brush is blurry because it's moving so fast. These are short and lightly pressured flicks, very similar to the dry-brushing technique on page 46. You can always practice this technique on a scrap piece of paper as well!

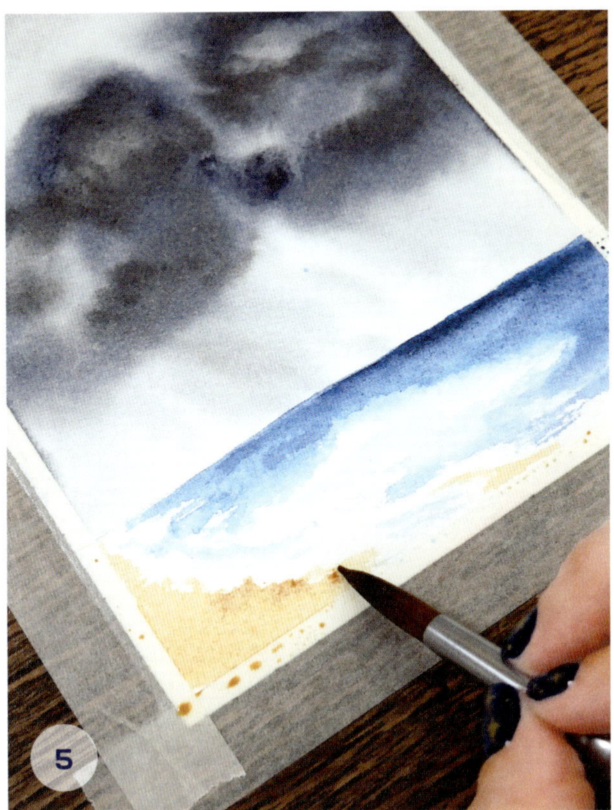

STEP 4: THE STORMY SKY (LAYER 2)

If your paper is still damp from the previous steps, you can start right in on this step. If your paper has begun to dry, stop and wait for it to dry completely, then add fresh, clean water to the sky again.

In this step, we're going to intensify the dark colors of our clouds. Using your size 12 round brush, add some additional dark-value Payne's gray to your main storm cloud. Then, pick up some dark-value Neutral Gray, and add some of that color into your main storm cloud as well. You can drop in color here with your brush or add these dark values with small, swirly strokes.

To add some highlights and texture to your clouds, let's lift some paint off the page. Clean off your brush and dab it on a paper towel, so it's "thirsty," and lift some paint in the clouds to create highlights. For more information on lifting, see page 21.

Let your sky dry entirely before continuing on.

STEP 5: THE OCEAN & BEACH

Let's add in our ocean! Using a size 10 round brush, pick up some medium-value Prussian blue, and begin painting in the ocean. Start at the horizon line, and work your way downward, leaving more white space as you approach the bottom left-hand corner. As you approach the left-hand corner, dab off any excess water/paint on your brush on a paper towel, and then add dry brushstrokes as you approach the corner in Prussian blue. Leaving this white space will create the illusion of white foam and waves breaking on and off the shore. While the Prussian blue is still wet, pick up some medium-value indigo, and apply it to the ocean along the horizon line. Since our storm is in the distance, the ocean in the distance will also appear darker and more "stormy."

Clean off your brush and pick up some light-value yellow ochre. Apply this to the bottom left-hand corner, adding a few strokes in between your white seafoam to imitate the beach peeking through the waves. Clean off your brush and pick up some medium-value burnt umber. Lightly dab on some burnt umber to the top of your yellow ochre section, where the seafoam meets the shore. Applying some of this darker color will create a shadow beneath the wave, helping to give it shape. It also helps mimic the wet sand.

Let dry.

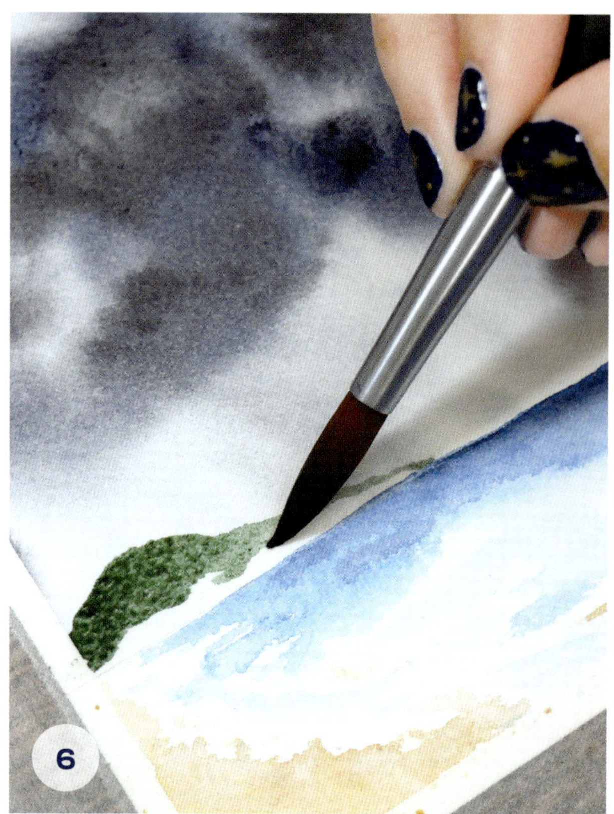

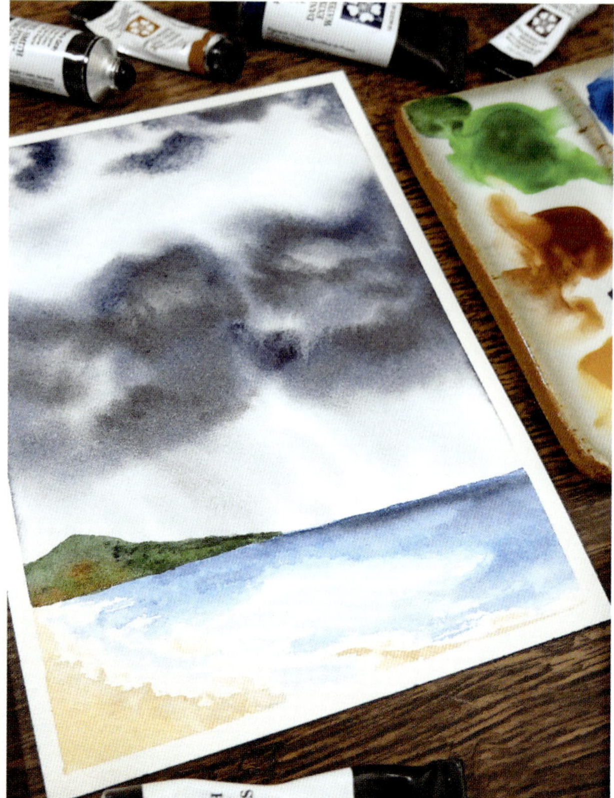

STEP 6: THE DISTANT HILLS

The last step is to create some land in the distance. Using your size 10 round brush, pick up some perylene green, and paint some hills in the distance. Drop in some hooker's green and burnt umber to give some variety and texture to the landmass.

LIGHTNING STRIKES

Thunder rumbles in the distance, the wind picks up and, before you know it, the storm is upon you. Lightning shoots across the sky, and the resulting thunder shakes you to your core. Let's capture this strike on paper using a fantastic tool for watercolor artists: masking fluid!

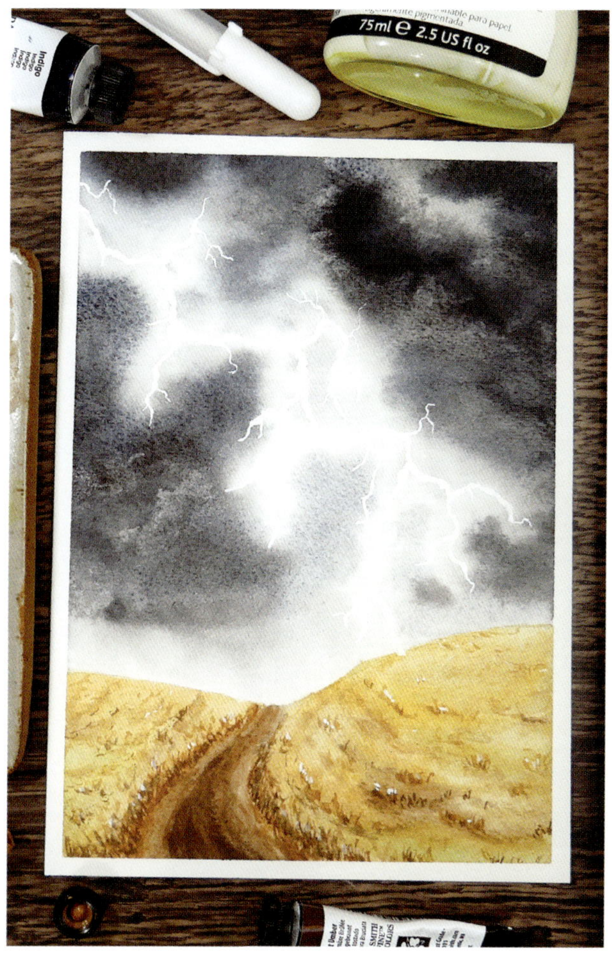

MATERIALS

Paints: indigo, Payne's gray, Neutral Gray (page 28), yellow ochre and burnt umber

Brushes: sizes 12, 6 and 2 round

Paper: 5 x 7-inch (13 x 18-cm) cold-pressed watercolor paper

Painter's tape (or washi tape)

Paper towels (or a rag)

Pencil and kneaded eraser

White gel pen or white gouache

Masking fluid

Ruling pen, toothpick or small brush devoted to masking fluid

SWATCHES

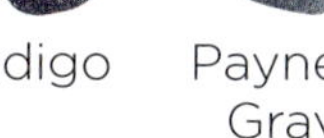
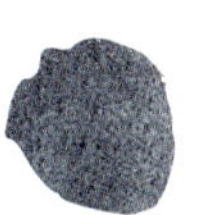
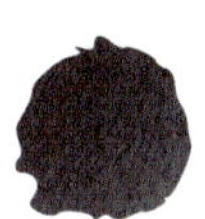
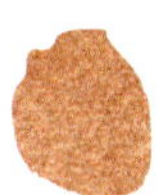
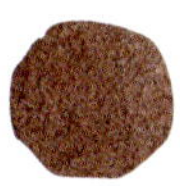

Indigo	Payne's Gray	Neutral Gray (page 28)	Yellow Ochre	Burnt Umber

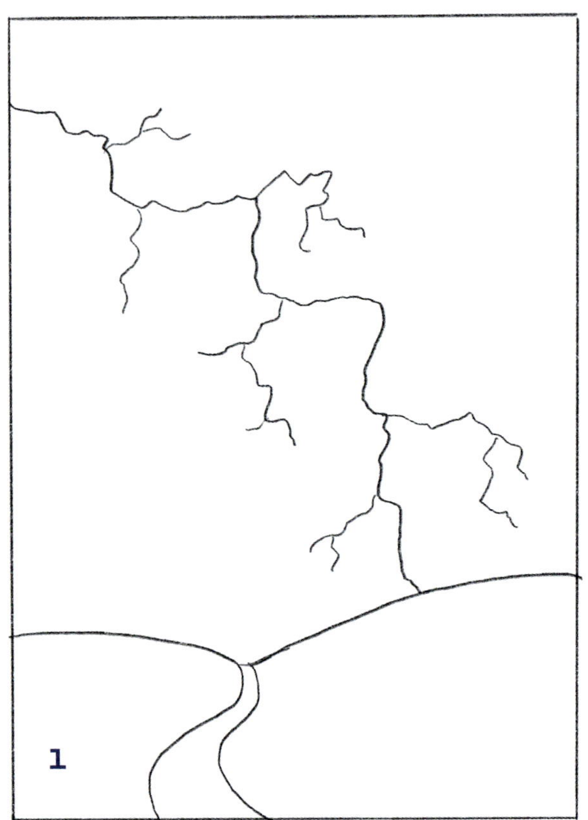

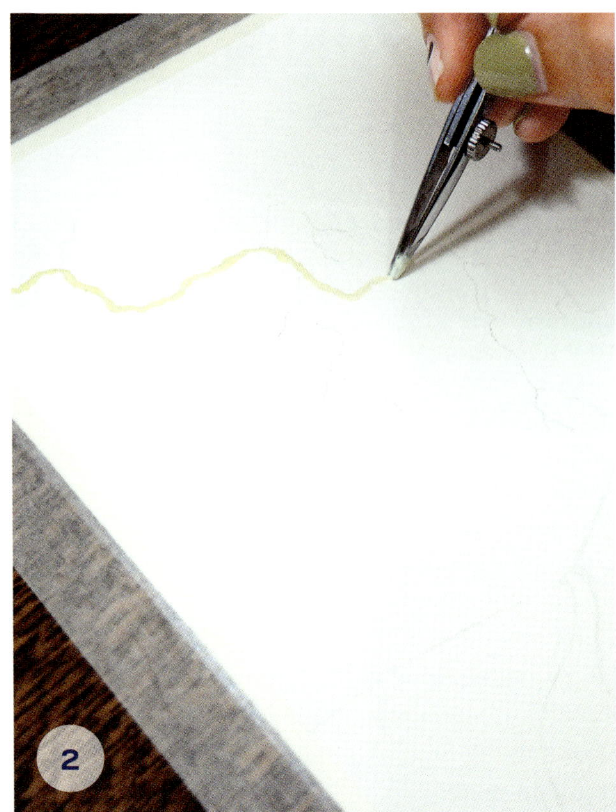

STEP 1: THE SKETCH

Let's begin with our simple sketch. Our lightning is going to take up most of our paper, and we will also sketch in two hills and a path that splits them on the bottom one-third of the paper.

To draw your lightning, hold your pencil loosely. Start at the top left corner of your paper, and begin lightly jiggling your pencil as you work your way down to the hill on the right. This is the main branch of your lightning, the path of least resistance for all that electricity. Add in a few branches here and there, still keeping your grip on the pencil loose and the lines "jiggly." Lightning doesn't move in perfectly straight lines (nearly nothing in nature does)!

Lastly, if needed, lighten up your sketch by using your kneaded eraser (or a regular eraser).

STEP 2: MASKING FLUID

Now, it's time to apply our masking fluid to create our lightning (for more information on masking fluid, see page 22). I use a ruling pen for applying my masking fluid, but feel free to use the tool that works best for you. Once you've applied masking fluid on top of your lightning sketch, wait for it to dry completely before continuing on to the next step.

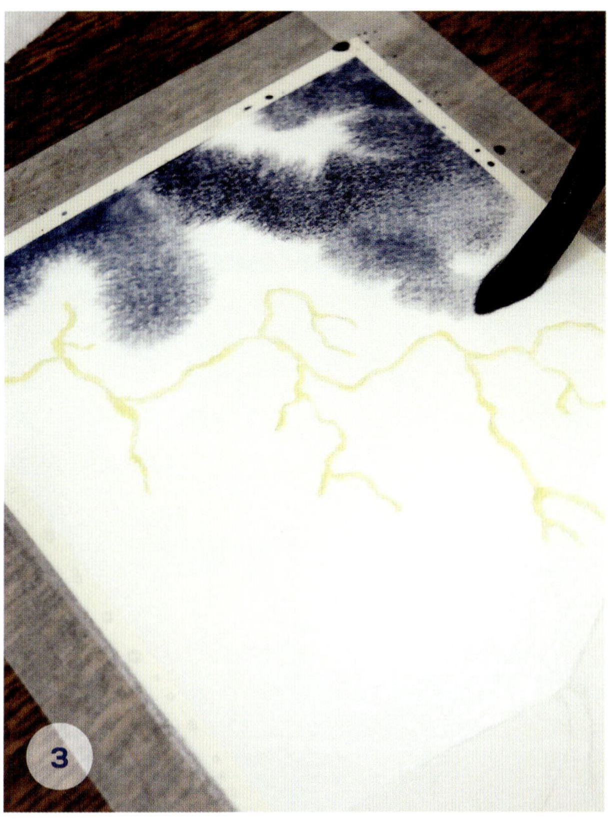

Note: You don't have to use masking fluid for this project. If you have white acrylic paint, white gouache or even a white gel pen, you can still paint this masterpiece! You'll just need to paint over your lightning sketch at the end with white opaque paint. I like to use masking fluid because it provides such a stark white line; then I add in the details with white gouache or a white gel pen.

STEP 3: THE STORMY SKY

Apply clean water to the sky portion of your paper. Using your size 12 round brush, apply medium-value indigo around your lightning strike. You can apply darker-value indigo in some areas versus others. We're not aiming for an even wash here but rather a multitude of colors like those of a storm cloud. Add in various colors of Payne's gray, Neutral Gray and indigo in various values. Leave some white space as well; this helps us give off the illusion of more lightning illuminating the sky high above in the clouds. I suggest leaving about ½ inch (1.3 cm) or less of white space at the bottom of your sky, close to the horizon line. When your paints naturally spread out, it will look as though rain is falling from the dark storm clouds.

We're relying on the white of the paper to demonstrate the luminosity of our lightning; therefore, the key is to not paint directly over the masking fluid. Since we're using the wet-on-wet technique, the paints will naturally spread out and soften around the lightning strike. If your paint spreads out too much, simply use a clean, damp brush to lift the paint off the paper.

We'll be intensifying our clouds in the next step, so let this layer dry completely before moving on.

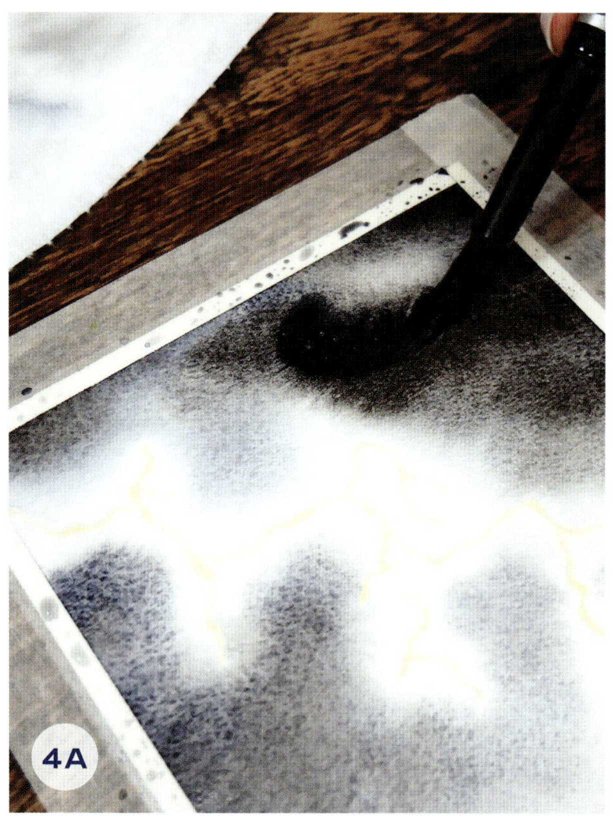

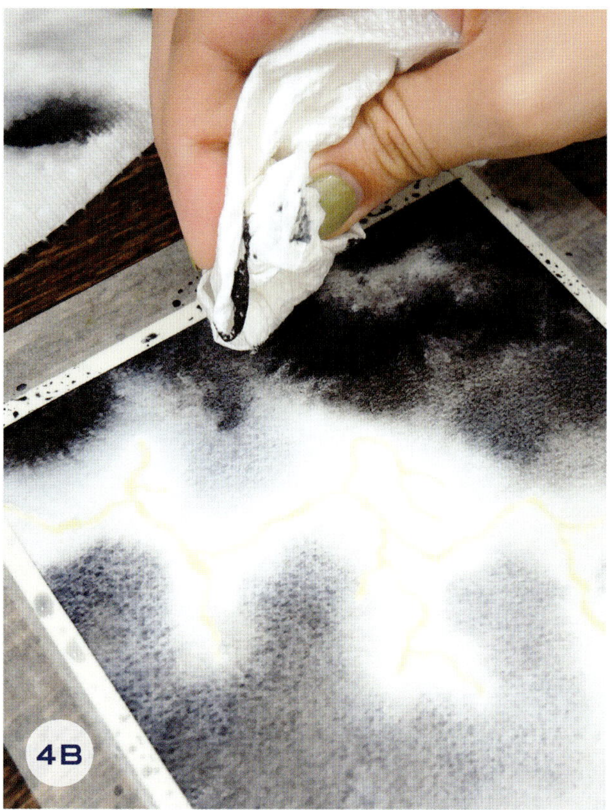

STEP 4: INTENSIFYING THE SKY

Now, we're going to intensify the darkness of our sky. Begin by applying another wash of clean water to the sky portion of the paper. Remember: Apply your clean water from the lightest portion of your painting to the darkest (i.e., the lightning → outward) to discourage the reactivated watercolors from muddying our luminous lightning.

Apply a dark value of Neutral Gray in a few places in the sky. I applied my paint in the top right corner and the bottom left corner of the sky, but feel free to add in darker clouds wherever your heart desires.

Let the paints spread out on their own for a moment and then, using a clean, bunched-up tissue, lightly dab the tissue on the paper to lift some of the paints (for more information on lifting with tissues, see page 21). Using a bunched-up tissue creates random lifts of color, leaving behind a stunning texture that cannot be achieved with our watercolor brushes. These lifts will also create additional highlights so it looks like lightning is flashing among the clouds!

Let dry.

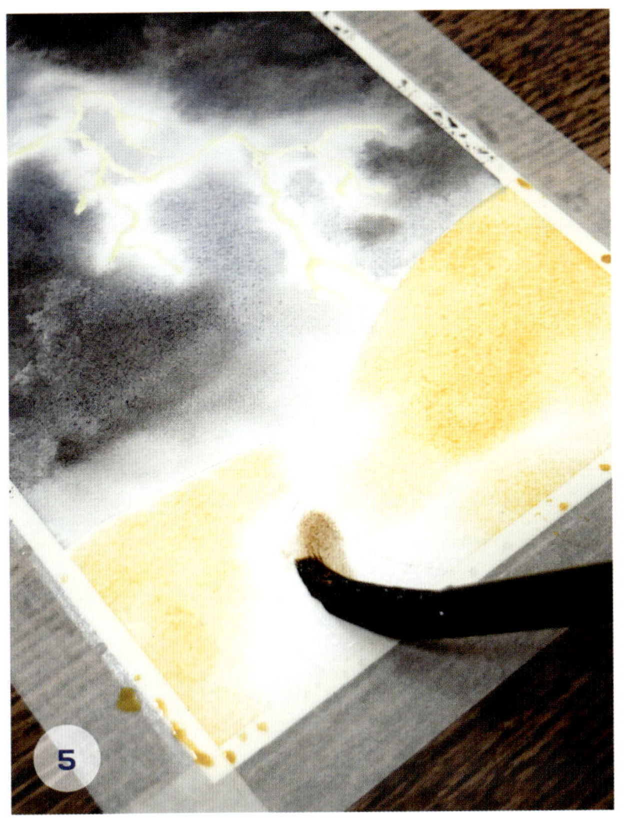

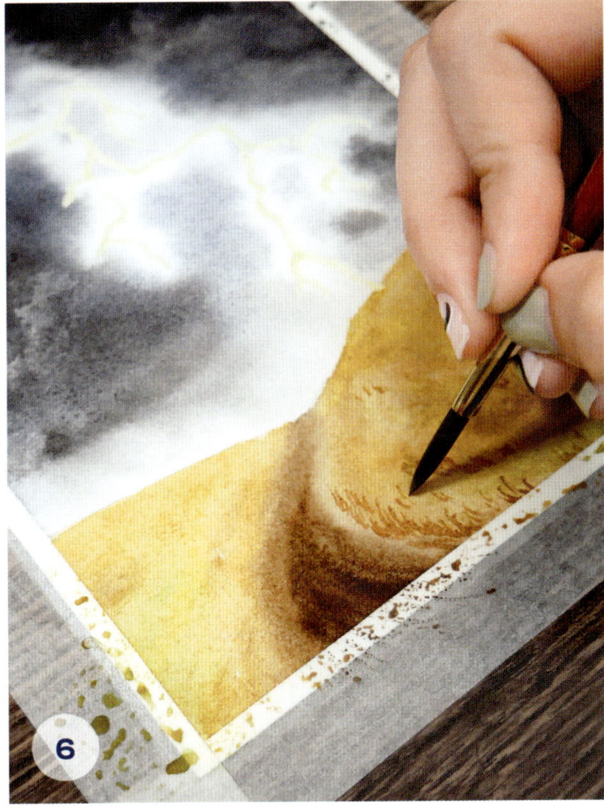

STEP 5: THE FIELD (WASH)

Let's move on to our field. Using your size 12 round brush, apply a wash of light- to medium-value yellow ochre on both sides of your path. This also doesn't need to be a perfectly even wash of color; it's just a baseline to build off of.

Before your paper dries, clean off your brush, and pick up some light-value burnt umber. Paint your path with your round brush, using the tip to paint the path in the distance and then pressing the barrel of your brush into the page as you draw it closer to the bottom of the paper. Dab a few drops of dark-value burnt umber on the path closest to the bottom of the page, and let that layer dry.

STEP 6: THE FIELD (DETAILS)

Once the previous layer is dry, it's time to add some details to our field. Using a size 6 round brush (or smaller like size 4 or 2), pick up some light- to medium-value yellow ochre. Using short flicks of our brush, add in various grass stalks throughout the field. You can also use the dry-brushing technique to add additional textures (see page 46 for more information). Once you've added some yellow ochre, clean your brush off, and pick up some light- to medium-value burnt umber. Add in a few stalks of burnt umber through the field as well. The darkest grassy areas will be surrounding the path, as here we'll be able to view the cross section of the tall grass rather than just the tips of it in the field. Outline the path with those small flicks and brushstrokes. Keep the strokes light and random, just using the tip of whatever round brush you're using.

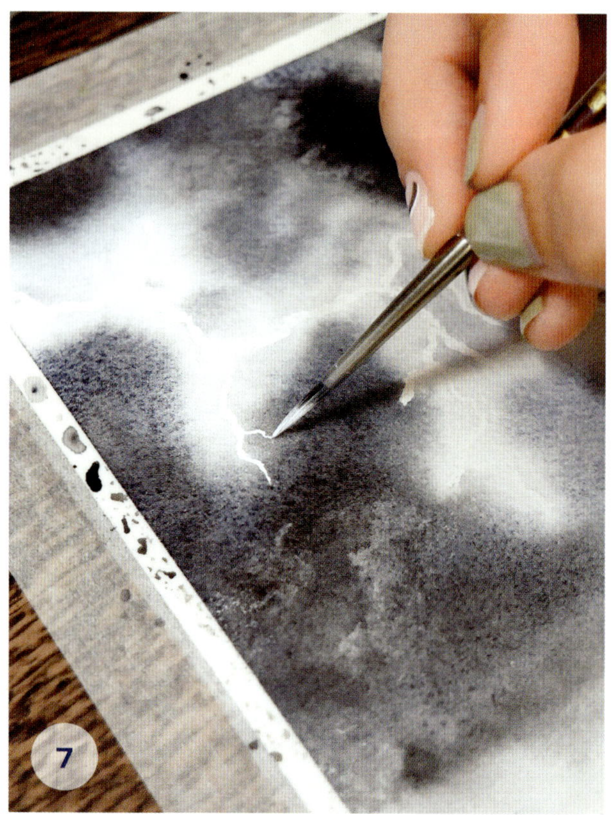

STEP 7: REMOVING THE MASKING FLUID & FINISHING TOUCHES

We're nearing the finish line for this piece! Using a kneaded eraser, the blunt end of a paintbrush or even your fingers, gently remove the masking fluid. For more information on removing masking fluid, see page 23.

Once the masking fluid is removed, use your white gel pen or a small round brush loaded up with white gouache to add in final details. On each branch of the lightning, add a few smaller branches, always ending in a sharp point. Additionally, add a few white highlights to the tips of some grass in the field, replicating the reflection of light that the lightning creates.

It can be easy to nitpick and overdo adding details to the grassy fields, so if you find yourself asking the question "Is it done?" and not having an answer, take a break. Get up, get a drink of water and then return to your workstation to view your masterpiece again. Oftentimes, once you have "reset" your eyes, the answer will come to you rather quickly.

TEMPEST SEA

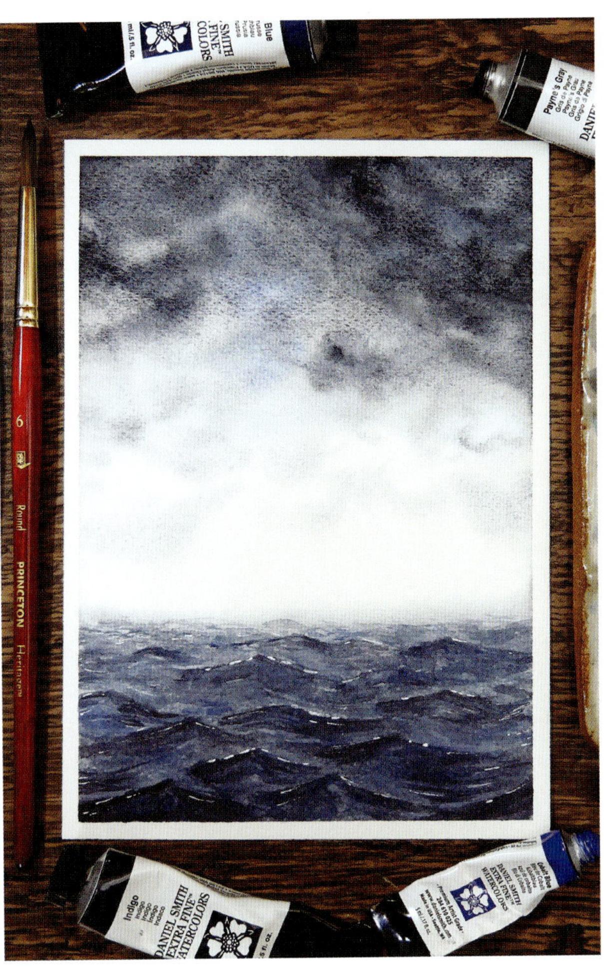

Waves can prove to be a difficult subject. Capturing the illusion of movement on still paper can be a daunting task, yet so many painters are drawn to their beauty (myself included!). Let's break down the creation of realistic-looking waves into simple, repetitive steps in this misty, stormy ocean scene.

MATERIALS

Paints: Payne's gray, indigo and Prussian blue

Brushes: sizes 12 and 6 round

Paper: 5 x 7-inch (13 x 18-cm) cold-pressed watercolor paper

Painter's tape (or washi tape)

Paper towels (or a rag)

White gel pen or white gouache

SWATCHES

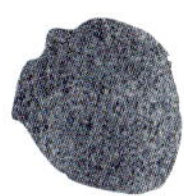
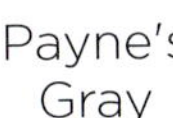

Payne's Gray

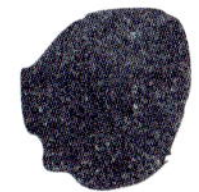

Indigo

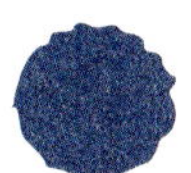

Prussian Blue

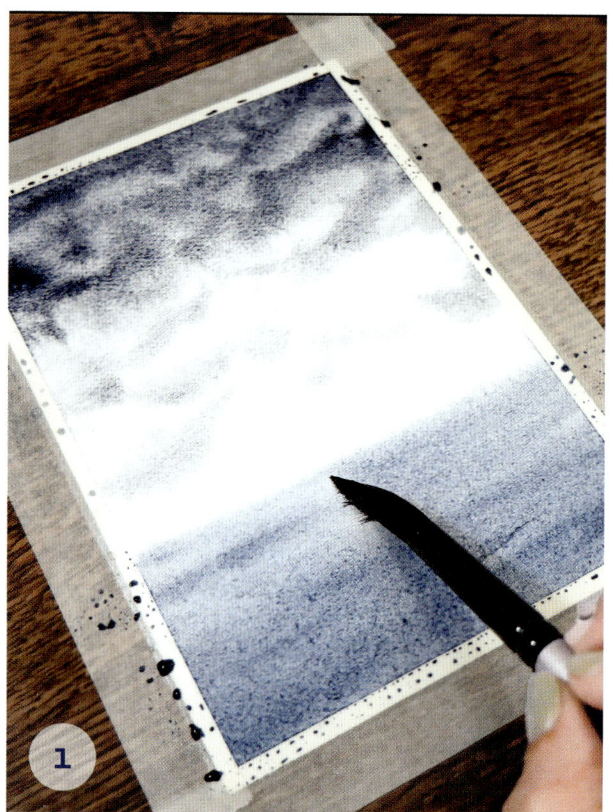

STEP 1: THE BACKGROUND WASHES

Begin by wetting the entire paper with clean water. Using your size 12 round brush, apply some light-value Payne's gray to the top one-third of your paper. Beneath that top one-third, apply that same Payne's gray in light, wispy strokes to paint misty, faraway clouds. You can create those clouds on the way down until you reach a little over half of the page. Next, pick up some medium-value indigo, and on top of your Payne's gray, apply some indigo clouds. Be careful not to mix the paints too much, as we want the clouds to appear misty and soft. Letting the paints naturally mix on your wet paper will create that effect.

Now, before your paper dries, pick up some light-value indigo, and apply that to the bottom one-third of your paper. This doesn't need to be a perfectly flat wash of color, and it's okay to leave some streaks. After all, some streaky textures may actually add to the movement of the water! This is the base color for our waves—it's just something to build off of.

Let your paper fully dry.

STEP 2: INTENSIFYING THE WASHES

Let's intensify some of those colors! Wet your entire paper again with clean water. Apply your clean water from the middle of the page up and again from the middle of the page down. We want our horizon line to stay clean and bright, not too muddied from either the sky or the water. Once your paper is wet again, pick up some medium-value Prussian blue, and tap that color into the sky with your brush. Next, do the same with some dark-value indigo, creating the darkest clouds toward the top corners of your paper. Leave some white space in between a few of your strokes to create natural highlights. We want these clouds to look both misty and soft but also like they're overlapping in the sky.

Next, intensify your ocean by applying another layer of light- to medium-value indigo (depending on the value of your first layer), again stopping about one-third of the way up the page from the bottom. Let that indigo naturally spread upward to create a blurry horizon line (this will give the effect of rain/mist in the distance). If you find your paint is spreading too intensely up the paper, you most likely have too much water on your paper (see page 20 for more information on this).

Let your paper dry before continuing on to the next step.

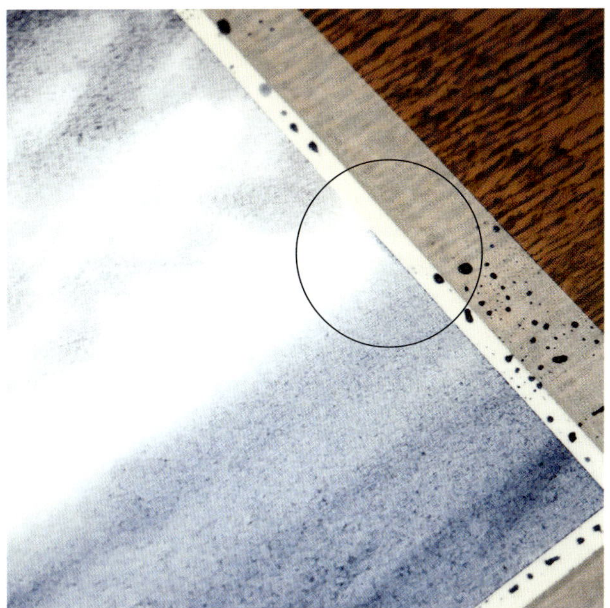

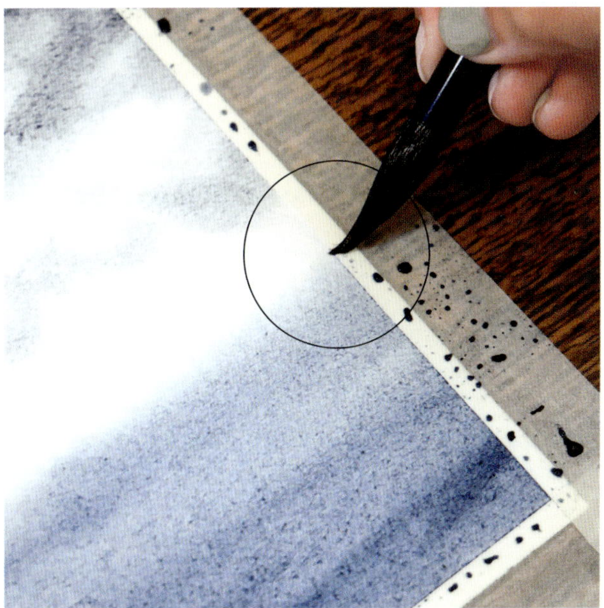

Removing Unwanted Paint: If you find your "ocean" traveling up the edges of the paper, simply clean off your brush, dab it on your paper towel so that the brush is "thirsty" (i.e., only just damp) and press your brush into the wet paint you'd like to remove. Then, dab off your brush on the paper towel to clean it off between each swipe with your brush.

Lifting like this only works while the paint is still wet, so make sure you work quickly before it dries (for more on the lifting technique, see page 21).

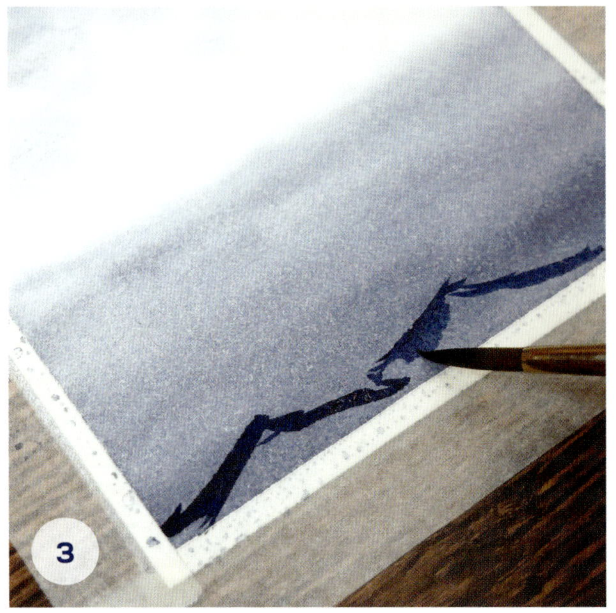

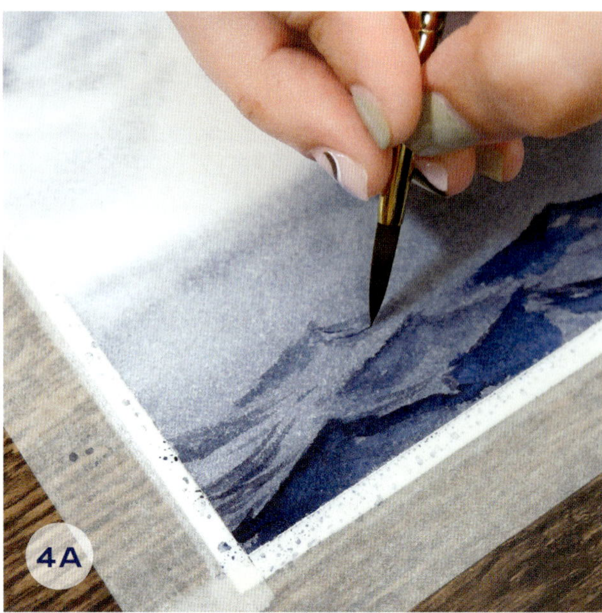

STEP 3: STARTING THE WAVES

Now, it's time to paint our waves! This process takes a long amount of time due to the number of layers it requires but is easily something you can stop, take a break and return to later since it mostly involves using the wet-on-dry technique of painting.

Our waves in the foreground of the painting will be the darkest, as they are closest to the viewer of the painting; therefore, pick up some dark-value indigo with a size 6 round brush, and paint a few mountain-like shapes. The easiest way I have to describe painting waves is painting overlapping "mountains." Some will have a sharper peak (waves about to crest or break), while others will be rounded like hills. The more variety you can add, the more realistic your waves will be.

Once you've created a few waves, clean off your brush and, while they're still wet/damp, apply some clean water to that dark outline you've created. The pigments will naturally travel downward in the clean water to create a wash. Don't despair if the outline of your waves was dry and your wash with clean water didn't reactivate your paint very much. That is plenty okay. In fact, it will begin to create those swooping textures we're aiming for here.

STEP 4: ADDING MORE DETAILS TO THE WAVES

Next, pick up some medium-value Prussian blue, and create a few swooping waves and "mountains" around and behind your first few waves. I dart back and forth between my palette, paper towel and paper often throughout this whole process.

The steps more or less go like this: dark-value indigo or Prussian blue to outline the shape of the wave, some clean water (or light-value indigo/Prussian blue) for a little wash and then rinse and repeat. Make sure to add some swooping strokes in various values of indigo, Prussian blue and even some Payne's gray if you'd like. The ocean is varied in both textures and colors when in motion, so we're attempting to replicate this with repetitive and strategic layering. Keep applying a mix of wet-on-dry strokes, followed by washes, in various values of blues and grays, all while moving toward your horizon line.

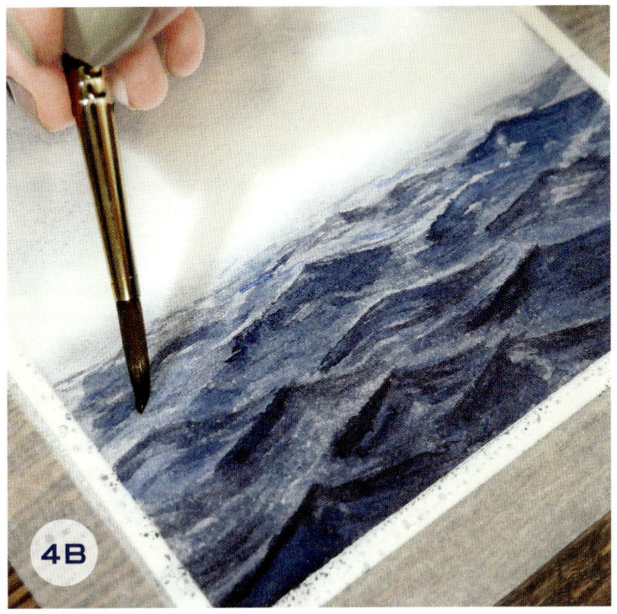

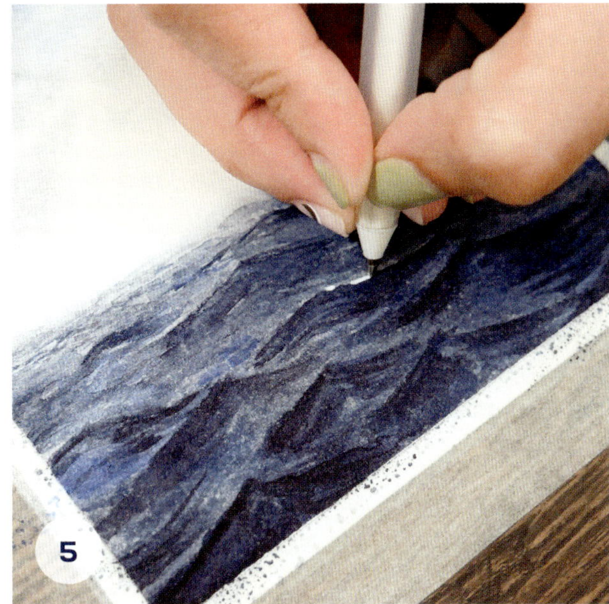

The key here is to create your larger, darker-value waves at the bottom of your paper and your smaller, lighter-value waves nearer the horizon line. Right at the horizon line, I use fewer swooping strokes and more short, quick dry brushstrokes to give just a hint of texture (for more information on dry brushing, see page 46). Less is more as you work your way toward the horizon line. Less detail, less saturation. This will help us create the illusion of depth, as the waves farther away will be harder to make out.

For this process, I take frequent breaks. It can be easy to lose yourself in the painting, adding details here and there, not knowing when to stop. When you find yourself frustrated or even feeling apathetic toward your piece, don't despair! Instead, get up from your workstation and take a break. Your painting will be patiently waiting when you return with fresh eyes. Layering over and over again can be tedious, but this is the slow-building magic of watercolors. With practice—and patience with yourself—you can create a tempest sea. Remember: Keep your strokes varied, actively avoid perfect patterns and create with joy! Once you're satisfied with your waves, let everything dry.

STEP 5: WHITE HIGHLIGHTS

Once you're satisfied with your waves, let's add some finishing highlights. Grab your white gel pen or white gouache, and add some lines/small dots along the tops of some of your waves. I always like to add a bit of sparkle to water, as it reflects even the smallest bit of light around.

I find that it's often adding the finishing touches, such as white highlights or stars, that seem to tie the painting all together. Never underestimate the power of a few finishing details!

SUNBEAM SKYLINE

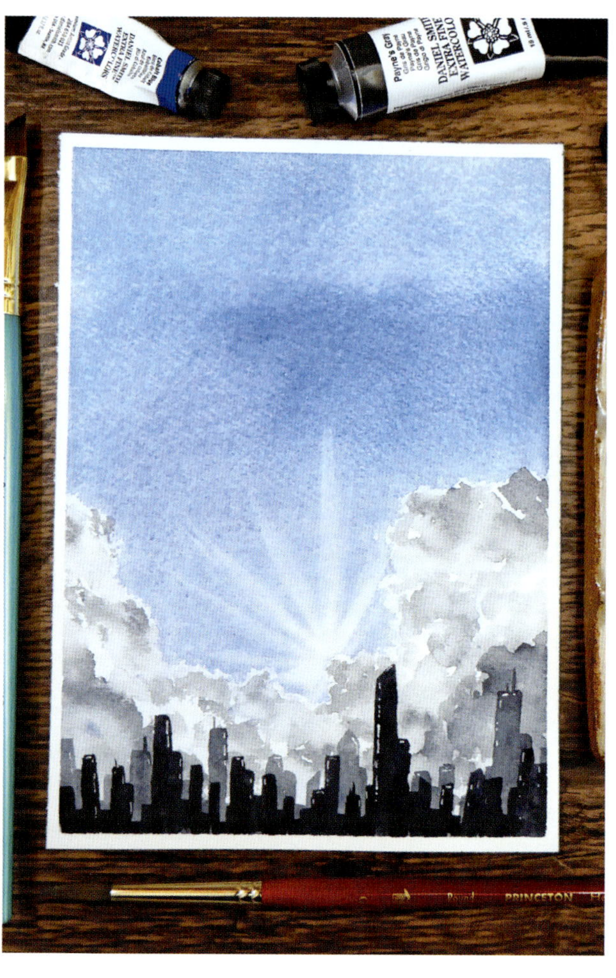

Hiding behind towering, fluffy clouds, the sun brightens the city below, its sunbeams stretching high into the sky. The city, with its tall and mighty skyscrapers, is silhouetted against the bright cloudscape, while the blue sky promises a beautiful, sunny day. In this painting, we'll use tissues to lift and stamp out our towering clouds and an angled or flat brush to paint the city skyline.

MATERIALS

Paints: cobalt blue, Prussian blue and Payne's gray

Brushes: sizes 12, 10 and 6 round and size 3/8 angled (or flat)

Paper: 5 x 7-inch (13 x 18-cm) cold-pressed watercolor paper

Painter's tape (or washi tape)

Paper towels (or a rag)

Pencil and kneaded eraser

White gel pen or white gouache

SWATCHES

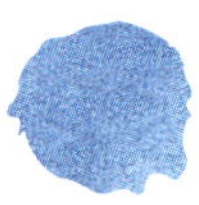

Cobalt Blue

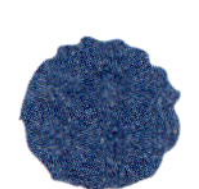

Prussian Blue

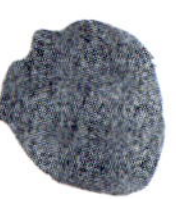

Payne's Gray

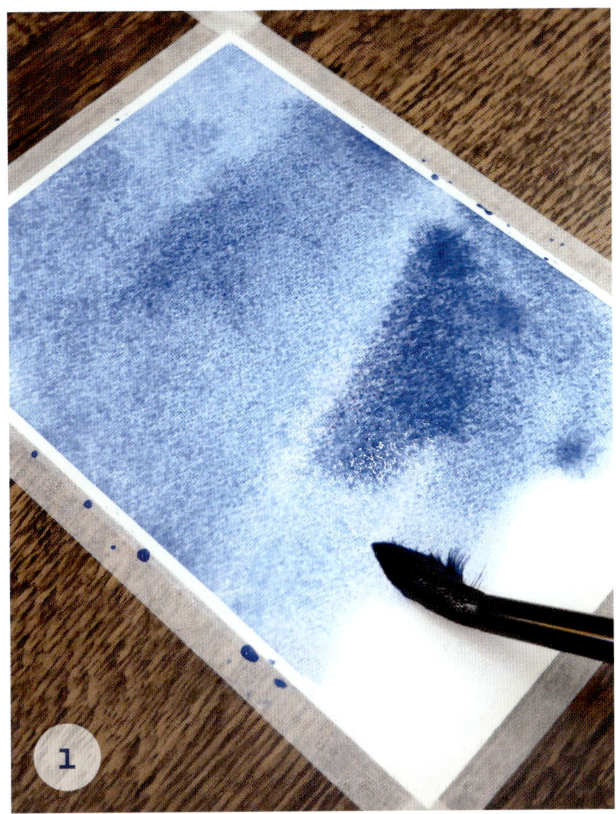

STEP 1: THE BLUE SKY

No sketch is needed for this piece, so let's dive right into painting.

A majority of the sky in this piece is completed in one layer, unlike other projects in the book. This is because we're relying on the white of the paper below to create our clouds. If we tried to stamp out white clouds in the following layer, it would be more difficult to achieve the whiteness of the paper again. On the same degree, we'll need to lift out pigment with our brush for the sunbeams before our blue sky dries. So, you'll need to work a little faster than usual.

Begin by wetting the entire paper with clean water until it's glistening. Then, using your size 12 round brush, paint the entire paper with dark-value cobalt blue, adding in medium-value Prussian blue here and there for a variety of blue in your wash. Quickly, before the wash dries, move on to the next step.

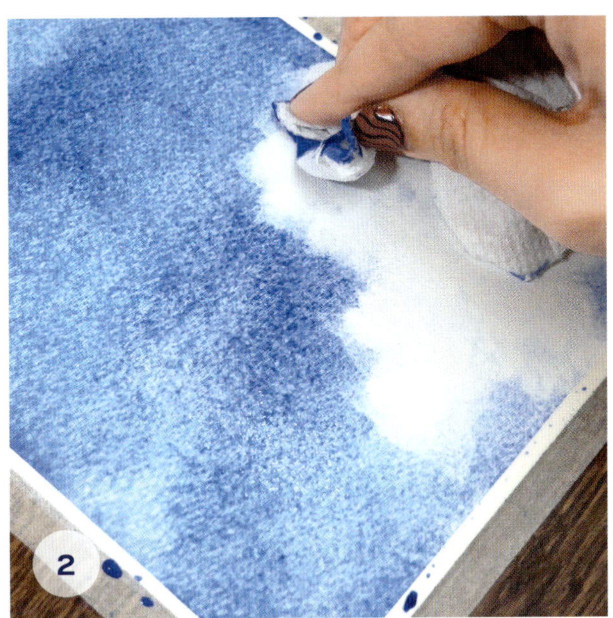

STEP 2: STAMPING OUT CLOUDS

Grab a clean paper towel or rag. Scrunch it up in your hand so the edges are uneven, and then press the paper towel into the bottom of the paper to lift the paint. You'll need to apply decent pressure to stamp out all the pigment, so don't be afraid to really press into the paper. You will also need to scrunch and re-scrunch your paper towel or tissue as it picks up pigment, using a clean portion to lift further, otherwise you'll risk applying the pigment you just absorbed out of the paper.

Continue lifting out the blue pigments with your paper towel, creating the shape of towering clouds that are taller on the sides than in the middle. Another reason I like to use a scrunched-up paper towel versus a folded one is that it creates random, rounded edges rather than predictable shapes. Clouds are wild and unpredictable in shape—no two are ever the same—so we should attempt to replicate that.

Additionally, as you're lifting up the blue pigments, you don't have to get them all. In fact, leaving little hints of blue behind will only add to the textures of your clouds.

Once you've stamped out your cloud shape, move on to the next step before the blue wash above the clouds dries.

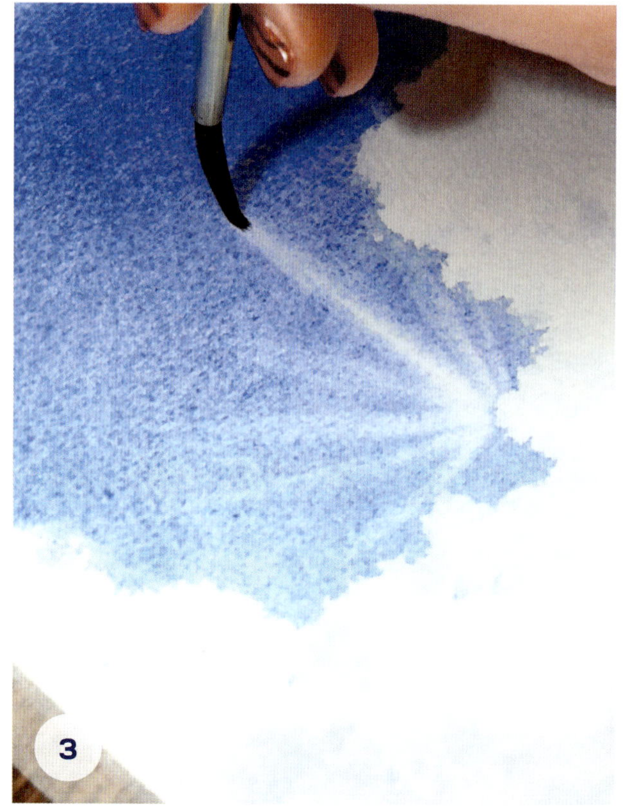

STEP 3: THE SUNBEAMS

We'll create the sunbeams by using a thirsty round brush to absorb pigment off the paper. Grab your size 6 round brush, and make sure the brush is clean and thirsty. Press the tip of your brush into a spot just above the cloud shape you stamped out, somewhere near the middle of the painting. Drag your brush straight up, lifting the pigments as you go, to create a sunbeam. More than likely, you'll need to make multiple passes of your brush for each sunbeam. So, make sure to clean your brush off on a paper towel or rag every single time, removing it of the pigment you just absorbed off the paper. If you don't clean off your brush in between each pass, you won't lift pigment but instead will apply it to the paper.

Lift out sunbeams in multiple directions using your thirsty brush, making sure to vary the lengths of them. If the sunbeams are all the same length, they won't look real. Variety is the key to recreating natural settings!

Once you've lifted out enough paint to make your sunbeams nice and vibrant, let the entire layer dry before moving on.

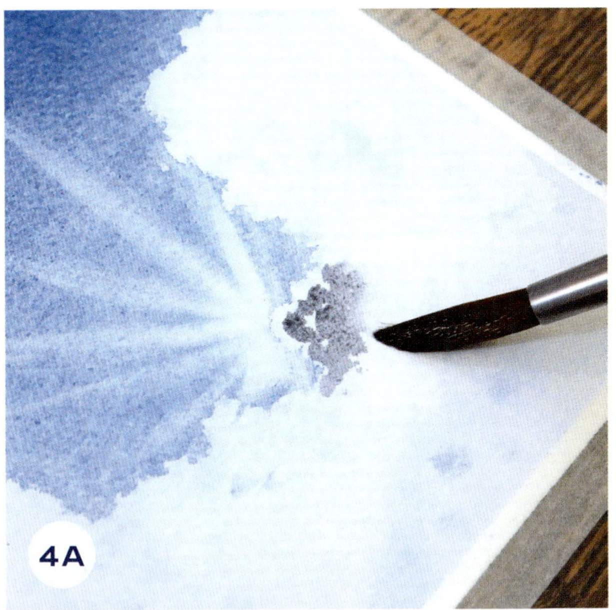

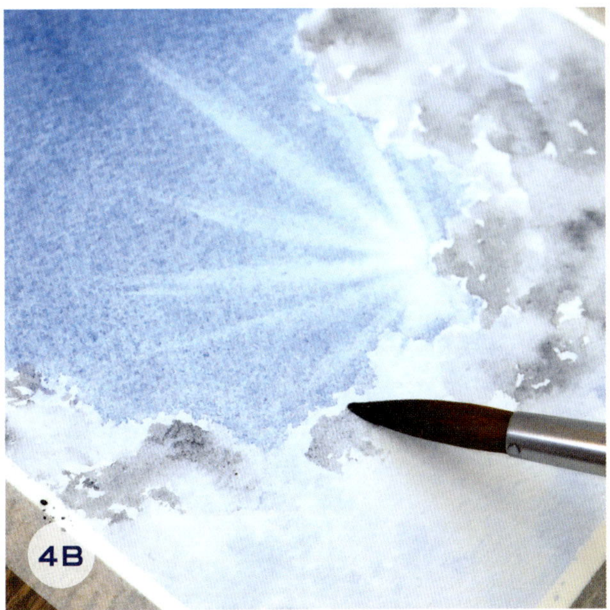

STEP 4: THE CLOUDS' SHADOWS

Now, you can certainly leave your clouds nice and white if that's the way you like them. If so, skip this step and move on to the next one. If, however, you want to add shadows to your clouds, keep following this step. In my opinion, painting in shadows creates more depth and dimension.

So, start by grabbing your size 10 round brush and loading it up with light- to medium-value Payne's gray. Leaving a little white on the edges of the clouds, paint in some Payne's gray, roughly following the edges of the clouds you stamped out. Since the sun is shining brightly behind the clouds, there is bound to be a bright white border reflecting the intense light of the sun. Right behind that bright border, however, will be a shadow.

Before this small wash of Payne's gray dries, clean off your brush and dab it on a paper towel until it's damp. Run this clean, damp brush along the edge of the Payne's gray, softening and blending the edges. Repeat this process throughout your clouds, using various values of Payne's gray. Leave some edges harsh and soften others. It's all about variety! Increase the value of your Payne's gray paint as you approach the fluffy clouds in the bottom corners. This increase in saturation will create the illusion that those portions of the clouds are closer to the viewer, once again adding depth to your painting.

You'll need to work in small sections. If you paint too large of a section of Payne's gray, you risk it drying before you can return to soften some of its edges. Applying paint, cleaning your brush and then returning to soften and blend edges requires quite a bit of manual brushwork, but it's worth it in the end.

Have fun with this part! One of my favorite things to do while watercolor painting is to watch the pigments flow into clean water, eliminating the sharp edges of the previous brushstrokes.

Let dry before continuing on to the city skyline.

STEP 5: THE CITY SKYLINE (LAYERS 1 & 2)

Pick up your size ⅜ angled or flat brush, and load it up with medium-value Payne's gray. Tilt the brush on its side so that you paint with the flat edge of the bristles (photo 5). Similar to how we use the shape of our round brush to our advantage to paint the tips of trees, we'll be using the flat, square-like shape of the angled (or flat) brush to paint our buildings.

Begin on one side of the paper, moving from left to right (if you're right-handed) or right to left (if you're left-handed). That way, as you move, your hand won't smudge what you've already painted. Paint in various sizes and shapes of skyscrapers, some with flat tops, some with angled tops and some with little antennas sticking out. Again, be mindful to add variety. If you paint skyscrapers that are all the same size/height, it won't look realistic and will make your painting appear stiff. Let this first layer of skyline dry before moving on.

Now, load up your angled (or flat) brush again, this time with dark-value Payne's gray. Repeat the same process of painting skyscrapers and various-size buildings all the way across the bottom of your paper. These buildings should be a bit larger than the ones you previously painted, as they are in front of and closer to the viewer than your previous layer. Once done, let dry.

Adding in silhouettes of skyscrapers can be quite fun! I find the repetitive motions of the brush to be relaxing.

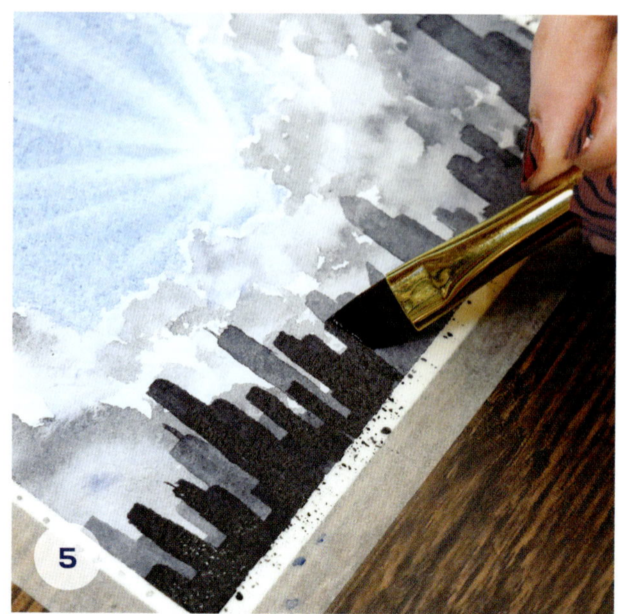

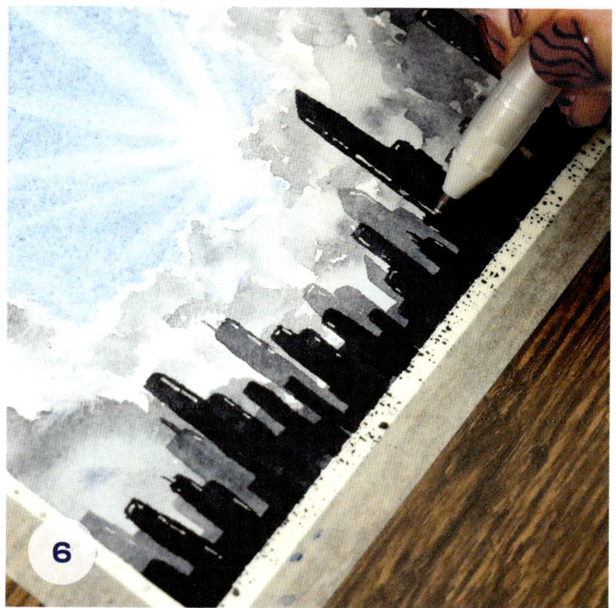

STEP 6: THE FINAL HIGHLIGHTS

For some final highlights, pick up your white gel pen or a small brush with white gouache. Draw/paint in some lines of various lengths along the sides and tops of the skyscrapers, demonstrating the light of the sun reflecting off the buildings' surfaces.

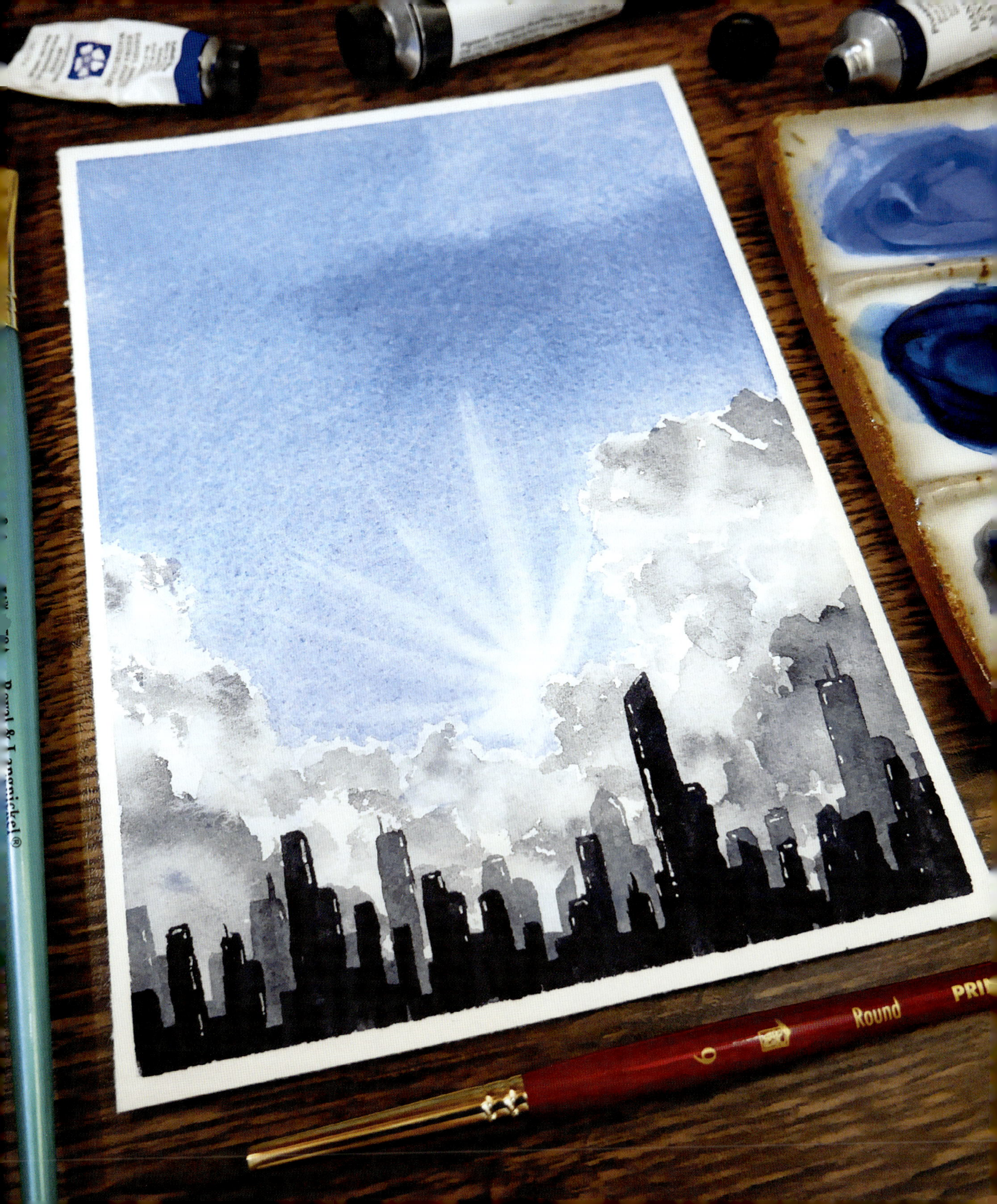
Round

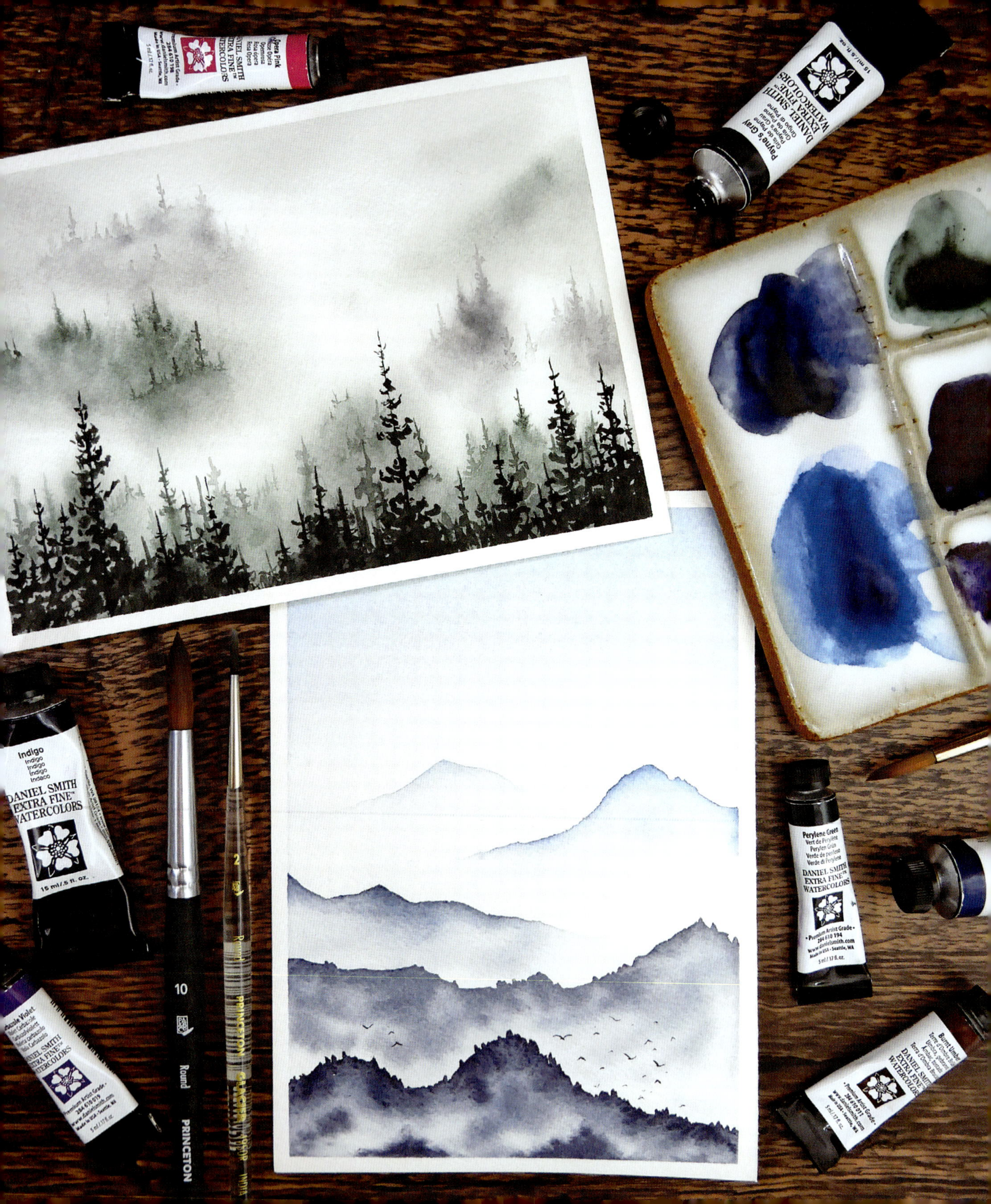
Indigo
DANIEL SMITH
EXTRA FINE
WATERCOLORS
15 ml/.5 fl. oz.
Perylene Green
DANIEL SMITH
EXTRA FINE
WATERCOLORS
Payne's Gray
DANIEL SMITH
EXTRA FINE
WATERCOLORS
10
Round
PRINCETON
2
PRINCETON

Misty MORNINGS & FOGGY FORESTS

What do you think of when fog settles on the earth? Is it eerie? Cold? Do you find morning mists peaceful? Calming? Personally, I feel a combination of all these things. Mists and fogs occur when the clouds in the sky come to visit us down on the earth, blanketing the surrounding landscape in moisture and mystery, wiping away the boundaries between the ground and the sky. In this chapter, we'll use water control and strategic layering to capture misty and foggy landscapes on paper.

Mist shrouds the forest

Clouds touch the ground: a visit

Earth and sky are one

MISTY MOUNTAINS

A flock of birds takes off from the treetops, escaping the fog settled in the deep valleys between mountains. It's quiet, peaceful, serene. In this piece, we'll use color value to create depth and use clean water to soften harsh edges and create magical fog.

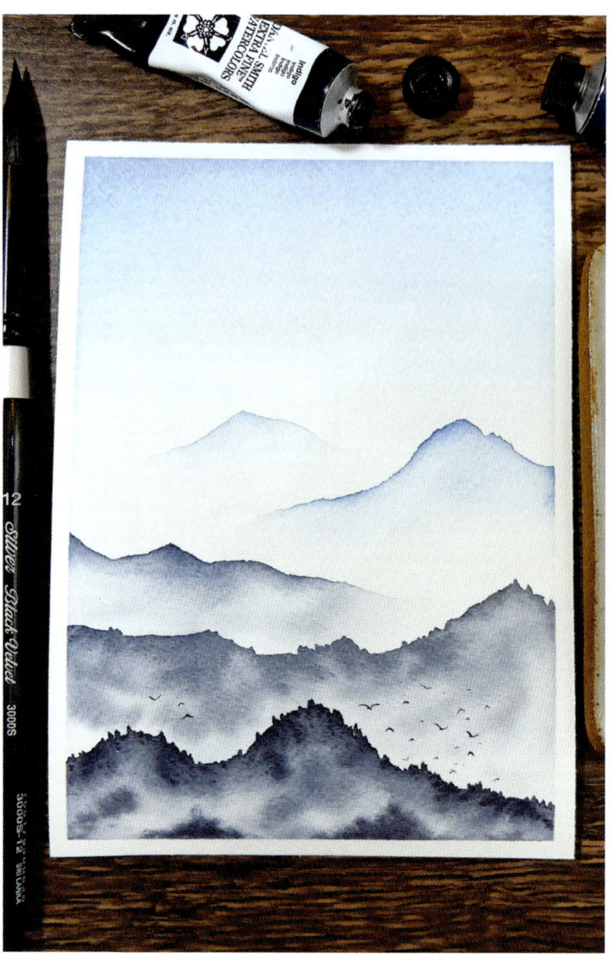

MATERIALS

Paints: Prussian blue and indigo

Brushes: sizes 12, 10, 6 and 2 round (these are the brush sizes I used, but you could get away without using a size 6)

Paper: 5 x 7-inch (13 x 18-cm) cold-pressed watercolor paper

Painter's tape (or washi tape)

Paper towels (or a rag)

Pencil and kneaded eraser

SWATCHES

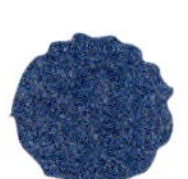

Prussian Blue

Indigo

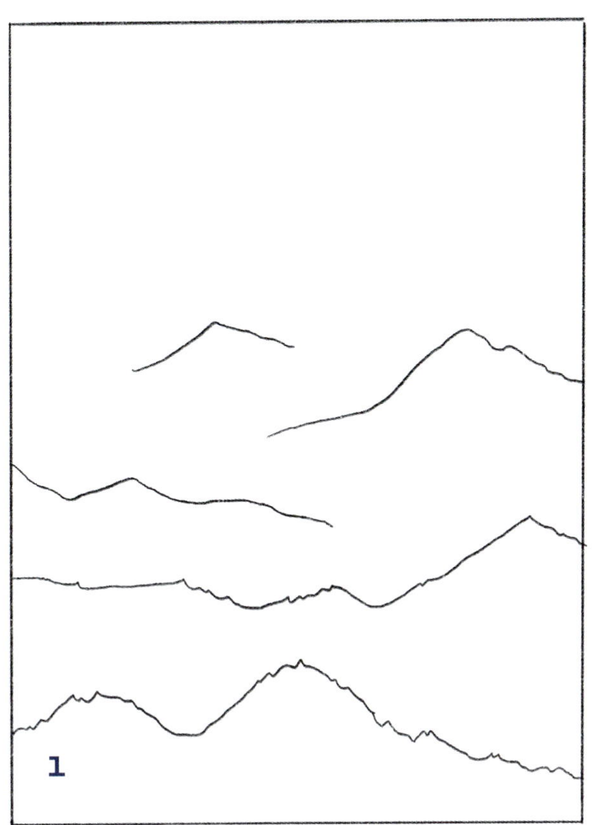

STEP 1: THE SKETCH

This painting has a fairly simple sketch: We simply need to outline where our mountains will go. I've included five peaks in my painting, but feel free to do more or less! It's entirely up to you. Our first three peaks will fade into the fog, so your sketch lines do not need to extend to both edges of the page. The two mountains closer to the viewer extend all the way across the page.

Don't forget to lighten your pencil sketch with a kneaded eraser!

STEP 2: THE GRADIENT

We'll be starting off with a simple gradient of Prussian blue for our sky. Pick up your size 12 round brush, and begin by wetting the entire paper with clean water. Pick up some medium-value Prussian blue, and start at the top of your paper. Pressing the barrel of the brush to the page, move the brush horizontally from edge to edge, moving down the paper as you go. This gradient should only extend until just past your first mountain peak, not all the way down the paper, as we'll need the white of the paper to create our fog.

Once you're satisfied with your gradient, let the entire paper dry.

STEP 3: THE DISTANT PEAKS

Let's create our first mountain peak! This one is farthest away from the viewer, so it will need to be the lightest in value. Using a size 6 round brush, pick up light-value Prussian blue, and follow the outline of your sketch (photo 1). Quickly clean off your brush, and pick up a bit of clean water. Run this wet brush along the bottom of your previous Prussian blue brushstroke. The Prussian blue paint will naturally spread into the clean water, eliminating the hard edge of the previous brushstroke. Extend your clean water strokes on either side of your mountain peak and downward for an inch or two (2.5 to 5 cm).

This will give the paint room to spread out without creating a new hard edge, as the clean water will dry clear. If you find your paint is spreading out and extending too far, just add more clean water, and extend the wet area another inch or two (2.5 to 5 cm).

Let this peak dry completely before continuing on to the next one.

Repeat this whole process for the next mountain peak but with a slightly more saturated Prussian blue (light to medium value). You can even drop a little bit of that same value Prussian blue along the top edge of your mountain peak, letting the paint naturally spread around throughout the clean water you've applied.

Working Quickly: You need to work quickly when softening your brushstrokes! If your first stroke begins to dry, you'll have a difficult time dragging pigment down into the clean water. See the two small photos below. In figure A in the photo below, the paint stroke was allowed to dry before clean water was applied. You can see that some of the pigments were activated, but a hard line was still left behind. In figure B, clean water was applied to the stroke before it could dry, resulting in a soft blend without any hard edges. It pays to work quickly in watercolor!

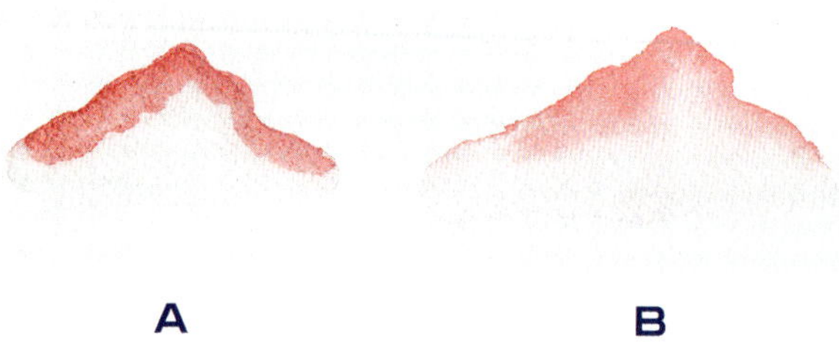

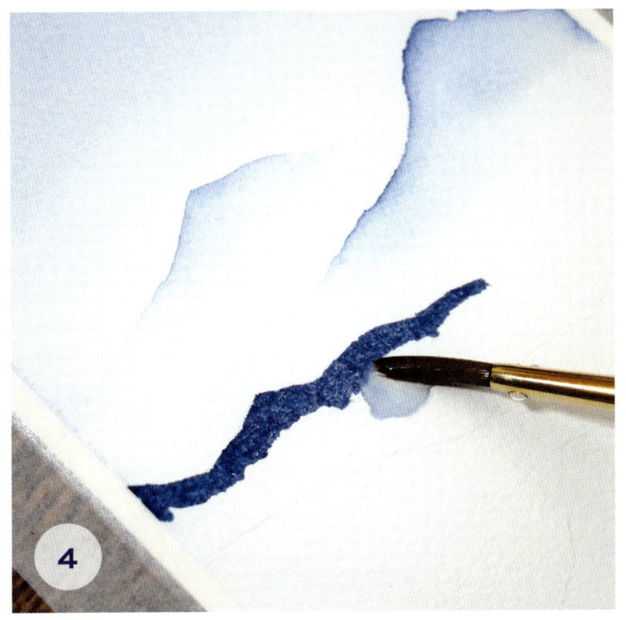

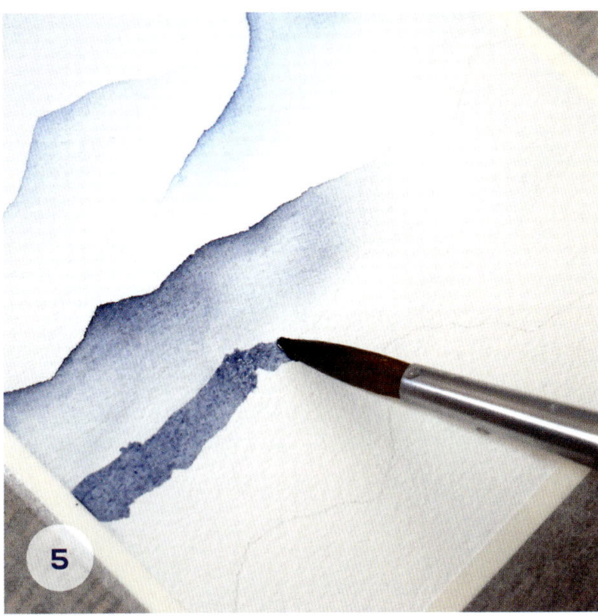

STEP 4: THE MIDDLE-GROUND PEAK

As we move down the page and paint the mountains closer to the viewer, we need to increase the saturation of each peak. For this third peak, we're going to switch to indigo. Using a medium-value indigo, repeat the process from Step 2. This time, once you've used a clean, wet brush to soften your initial stroke, extend that clean water for another 2 inches (5 cm) downward. Pick up some medium-value indigo again, and touch in a few drops of paint in the wet area below the top edge of the peak. You can use your brush to spread the paint around a little bit, but make sure to leave some white space. If you don't leave some white space, you'll lose the illusion of fog. For this type of painting, less is more. Leave plenty of white space. You can always add another layer later if you wish to increase the saturation of your colors.

Again, let this dry completely before moving on to the next peak.

STEP 5: THE FIRST FOREGROUND PEAK

Switch to a larger round brush for this next step; I used a size 10 here. For this next peak, mix up some slightly more saturated indigo than the previous step, and begin the same process, this time extending the brushstroke all the way across the paper (rather than the hill dissolving into the fog again). Turn your brush vertically so that the tip of the brush is pointing toward the top of the paper. Using the point of the brush, create a few dips and bumps in the hill to mimic the tops of trees in the distance. Then, repeat what you've been doing previously by using clean water to soften the edges and drag the paint down. This time, you can extend the clean water all the way down to the bottom of the page.

Same as in the previous step, pick up some medium-value indigo, and drop in some color, leaving white space to create fog. While your paper is still wet, you can even drop in clean water on your paint, letting the paint bloom naturally. This creates some interesting textures!

Let this mountain dry completely before moving on.

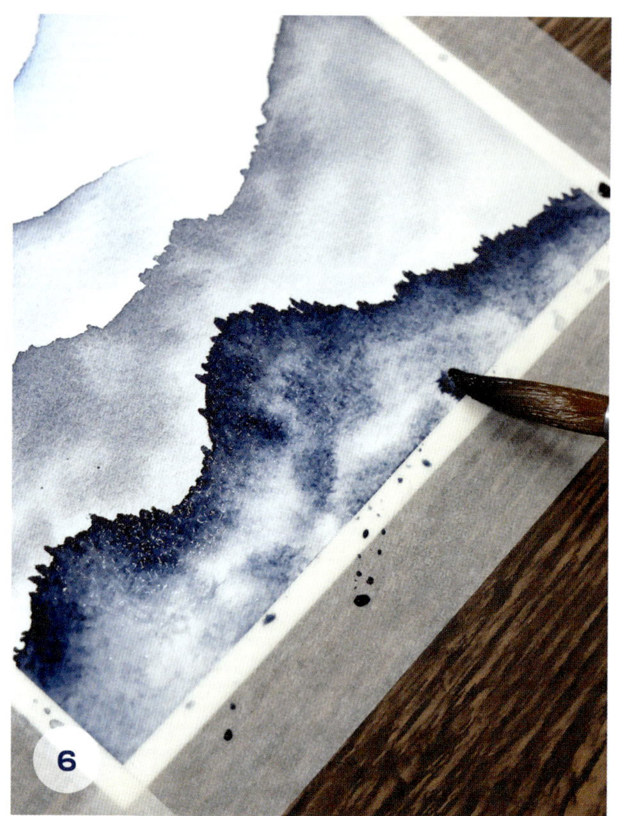

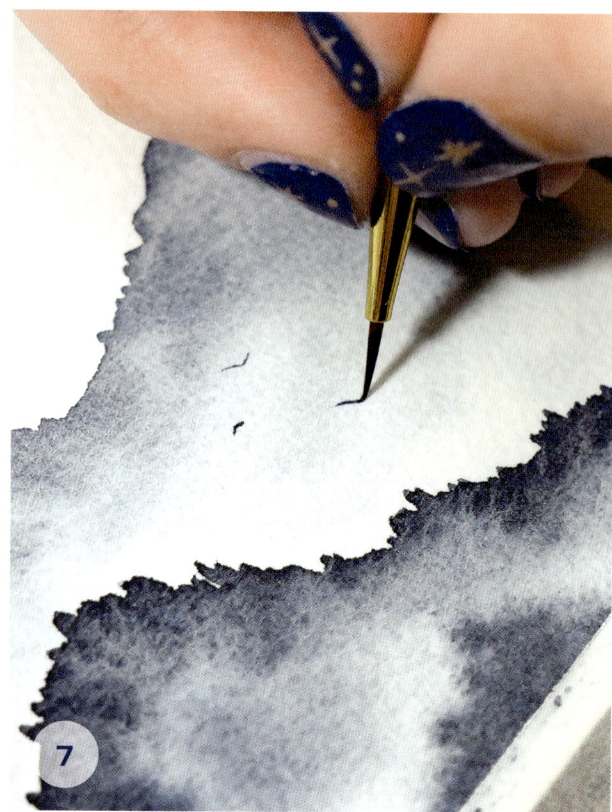

STEP 6: THE SECOND FOREGROUND PEAK

Now, let's paint our last mountain in our scene. Using the same brush, pick up dark-value indigo, and repeat the process from Step 4, this time creating more treetops than the previous mountain. After all, this mountain is far closer to the viewer and, therefore, we'll be able to see a bit more detail. Soften the edges again with clean water, and extend it all the way down to the bottom of the paper. Like in previous steps, dab in a few drops of dark-value indigo, and let the paint work its magic! You can also drop in some clean drops of water while your wash is still wet to create subtle blooms in the paint.

STEP 7: THE BIRDS

Time for some finishing touches! Using our size 2 brush, let's add a few bird silhouettes in between the two mountain peaks closest to the viewer. Keep the birds varied in size and shape, some distant and some closer, all rising from the foggy trees below. For more on how to paint birds, see page 40.

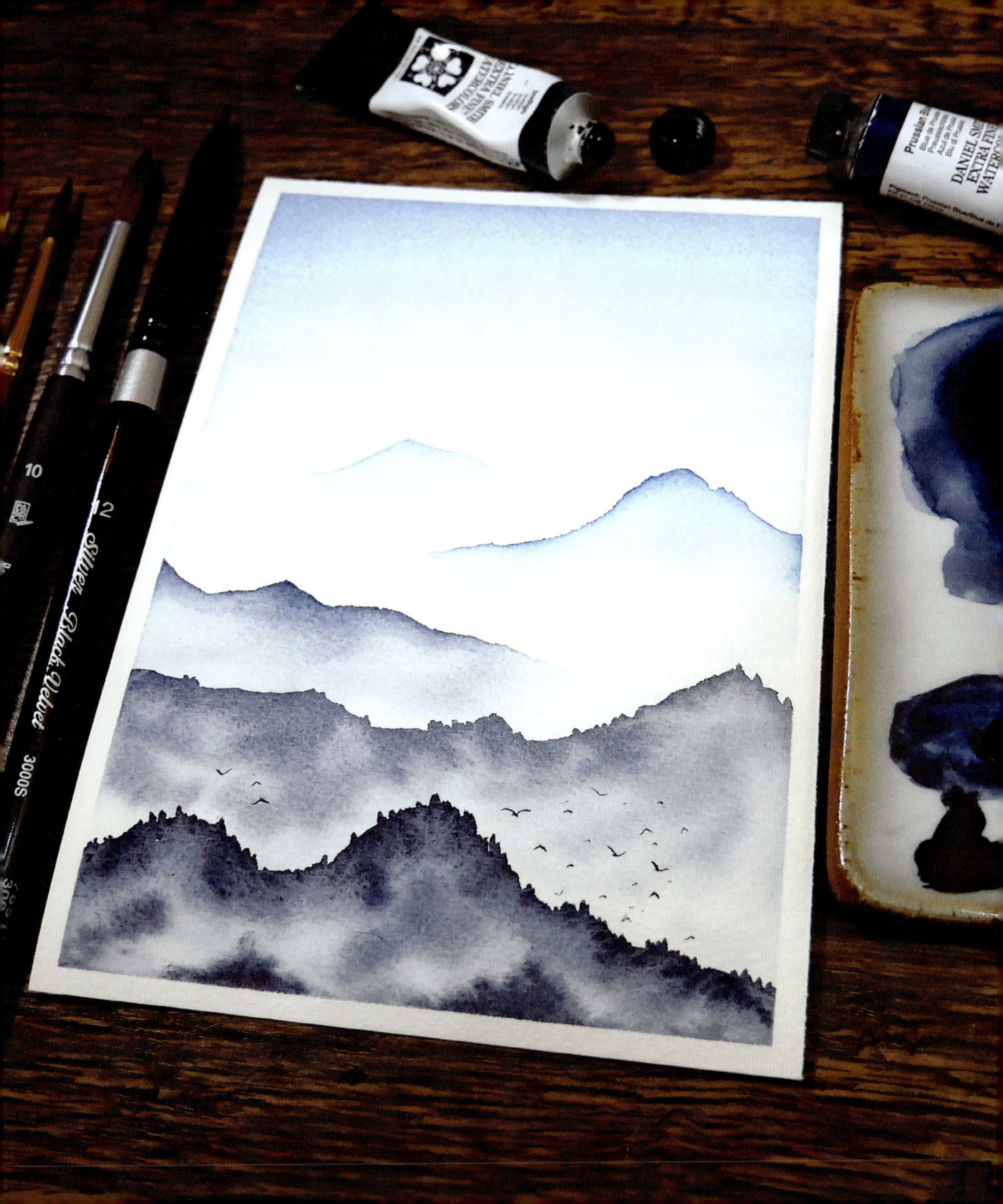
10
Silver Black Velvet
3000S

THE LONE PINE

Before the sun kisses the earth, a lone pine sits on the edge of a lake in the early morning: solitary, yet strong and unyielding. In this painting, let's explore creating contrast that draws in the eye of the viewer.

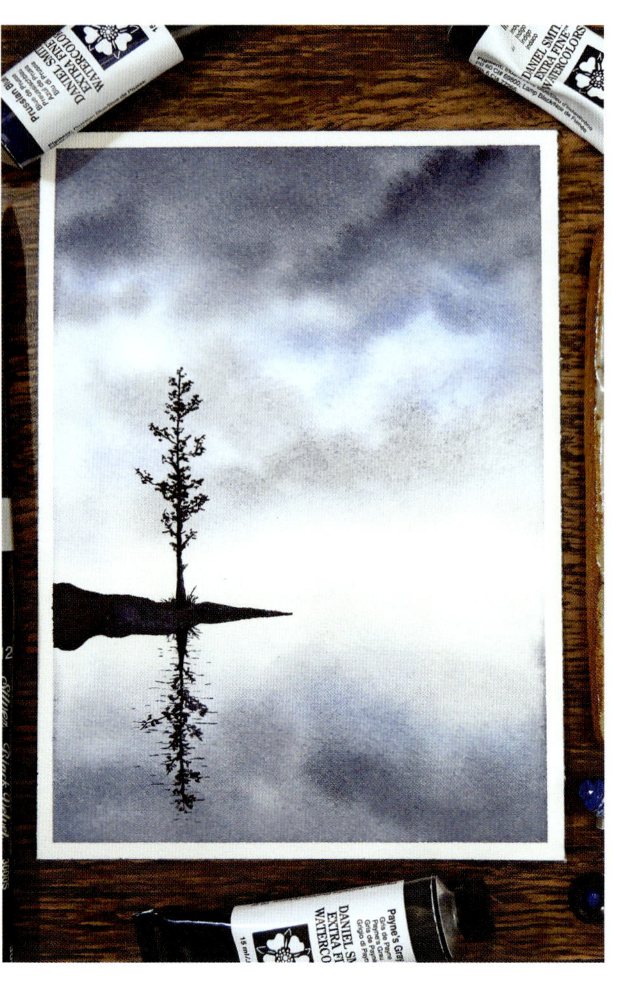

MATERIALS

Paints: cobalt blue, Prussian blue, indigo and Payne's gray

Brushes: sizes 12 and 2 round

Paper: 5 x 7-inch (13 x 18-cm) cold-pressed watercolor paper

Painter's tape (or washi tape)

Paper towels (or a rag)

Ruler

Pencil and kneaded eraser

SWATCHES

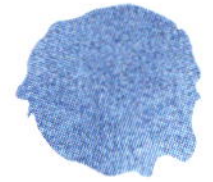

Cobalt Blue

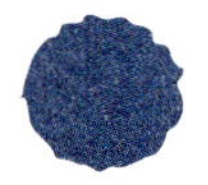

Prussian Blue

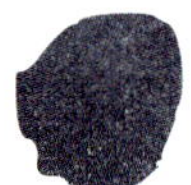

Indigo

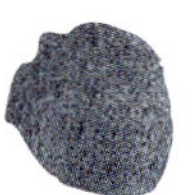

Payne's Gray

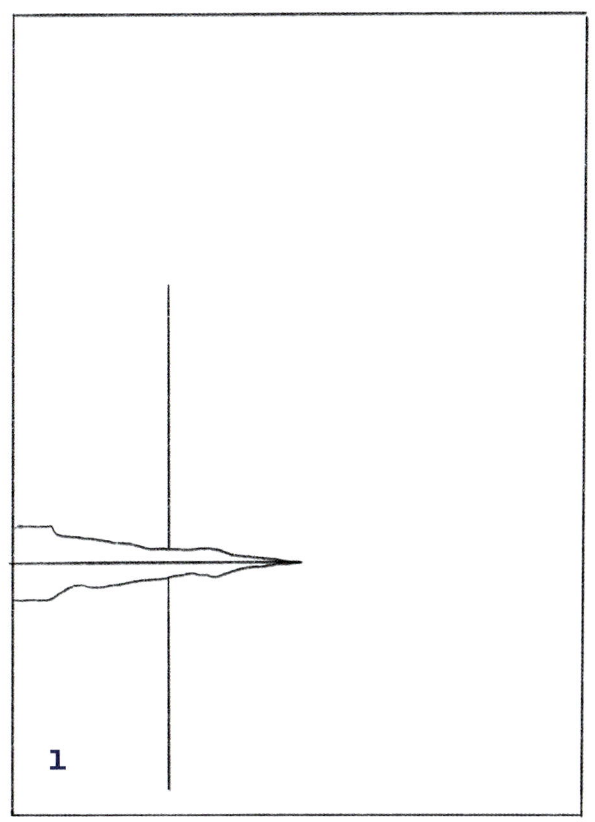

STEP 1: THE SKETCH

For this piece, let's start out with a very simple sketch. Grab your pencil and ruler, and draw a straight, horizontal line about one-third of the way up from the bottom of the paper. I made my line approximately 2 inches (5 cm) long. We're aiming to create a gentle hillslope that meets the edge of our lake (refer to the sample sketch). This is our piece of land that juts out into the lake. Now, turn your ruler vertically, and let's draw the skeleton of our pine tree. A little over halfway into our piece of land, make a light vertical pencil line that's approximately 1½ inches (3.8 cm) tall from the base of the land up. Extend that line about 1½ inches (3.8 cm) below the land line for the pine tree's reflection. This line is just our guide for the pine tree, so don't worry about it being perfect.

STEP 2: THE FIRST WASH

Take your size 12 round brush, and wet the entire paper with clean water. Pick up some medium-value cobalt blue, and begin lightly dabbing your brush in the first one-third of your sky portion. Paint a few wispy strokes, and leave some white space in various sections. Additionally, leave white space right along your horizon line, and let the paint naturally bleed down. By doing this, we're creating the effect of mist in the distance. Let the watercolors work their magic.

Using that same value of cobalt blue, paint a few loose strokes in the top one-thirdish of your water reflection portion. The reflection doesn't need to be exact, but we do need to give the illusion of the misty sky being reflected in the still water.

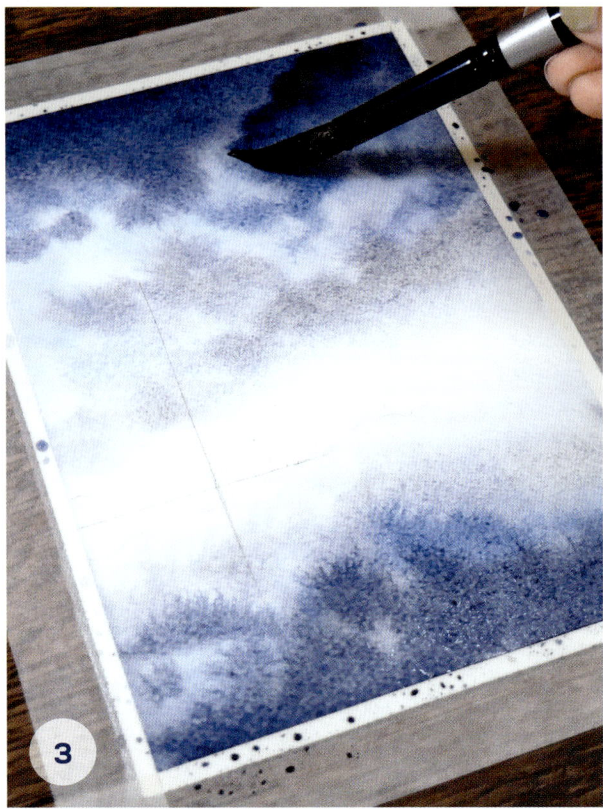

Before your paper dries, clean off your brush and pick up medium-value Prussian blue. Use the same loose strokes above the cobalt blue in the sky and below the cobalt blue in the water. Dab a bit of your Prussian blue within the white spaces you left before, letting the paints naturally mix together.

Lastly, do the same with indigo, filling in the last one-third-ish of the sky and the water. Let the entire painting dry. We're going to build up another layer of mist next to intensify our colors.

STEP 3: THE SECOND WASH

Once your entire painting is dry, wet the entire thing once more with clean water using your size 12 round brush. Make sure to start applying your clean water in the lightest section of your painting, and then work outward (in this case, start applying clean water at our horizon line). This will keep the lightest sections of your painting from becoming too muddy with the other colors.

For this layer, start out with a light-medium value of Payne's gray. Lightly dab in some darker clouds in the cobalt blue section of your sky. Keep your brushstrokes light and somewhat random, sometimes simply dabbing on paint and other times stroking your brush in short bursts. Do the same in the water portion of your painting. One of the keys of painting mist is keeping your brushstrokes loose. Being too rigid or falling into patterns will diminish the realism (and magic!) of your piece.

Clean your brush and pick up some Prussian blue, adding a few more wispy clouds and dabs of color in the sky portion above the Payne's gray you just added. Do the same in the water portion, but this time below the Payne's gray.

Lastly, let's intensify our indigo. Pick up some medium-dark value of indigo, and create some clouds in the upper portion of the sky. Pressing the barrel of your brush into the paper, move it in a slight "swirly" motion to mimic the round swells of clouds. Since we're doing this wet-on-wet, expect some of that color to bleed out. This will soften the stroke naturally, giving our cloud a faraway, misty quality. Next, add that same value of indigo to the bottom of your water portion.

Let the entire painting dry.

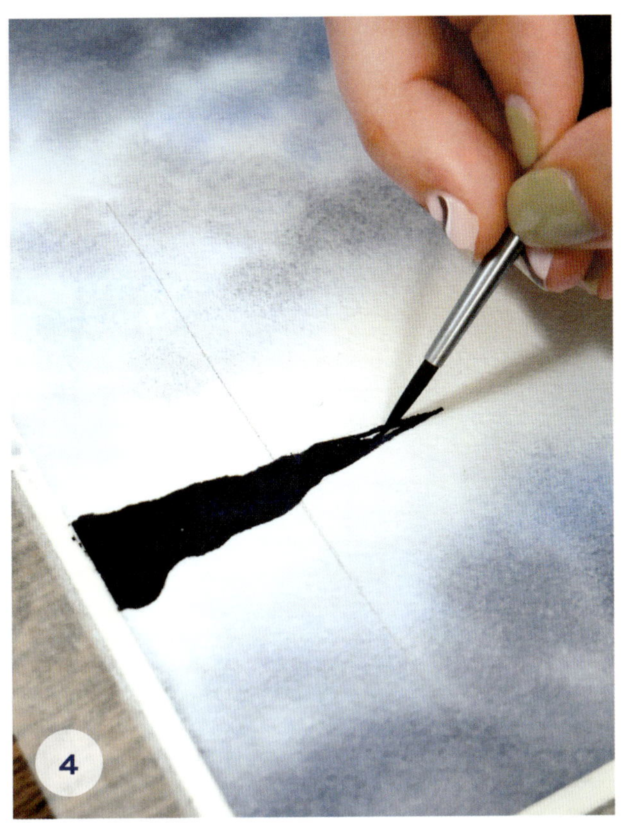

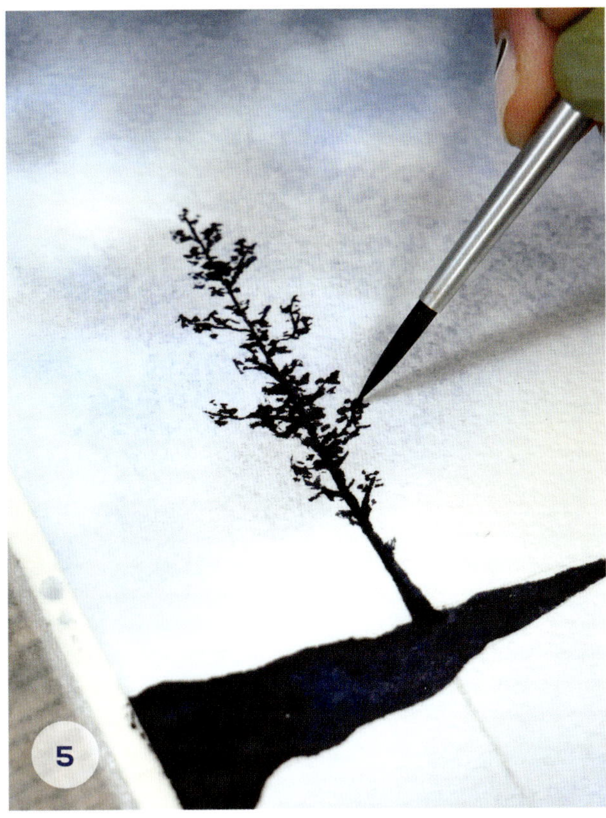

STEP 4: THE LAKE'S EDGE & TRUNK OF THE PINE

Switch to your size 2 round brush. Pick up some dark-value indigo, and begin filling in the silhouette of our land jutting out into the lake. Whatever you paint for the land, make sure you paint it for the reflection. We're aiming to create a mirror image in the still water.

Next, follow your pencil sketch, extending a skinny, vertical line of dark-value indigo up. This is just the trunk of our tree, something for us to build upon.

STEP 5: THE PINE DETAILS

Now, let's add some detail to our lone pine! For this pine, I used a combination of the "blobby" method (see page 39) and the "branch" method. Using the tip of your brush, create small lines angled up toward the sky at the top of the tree. Branches at the top of pine trees tend to grow nearly straight up toward the sky, as they are new growth reaching for the sun! Branches toward the middle of the tree may still angle up but at less of a steep angle, as they're older and need to reach out first, and then up, for sunlight (they get shaded from higher branches).

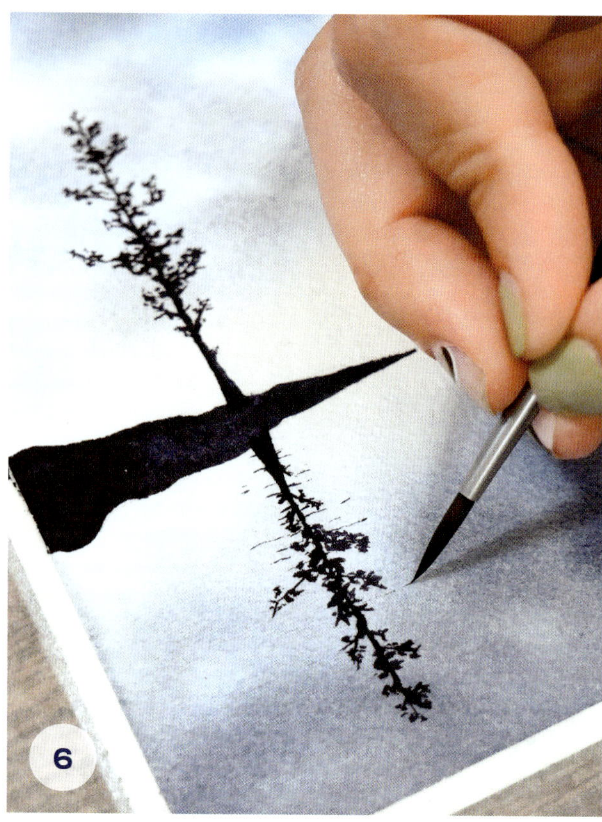

Add little blobs at the end of and around the branches you create, leaving some open space in some places so you can see the "skeleton" of the tree. Create some thicker branches and bunches of pine needles toward the center of the tree and less toward the bottom. With this pine tree sitting out alone on the edge of a lake, it most likely gets buffeted by wind a lot, meaning branches may often break off! Therefore, this lone pine is a little sparser and skinnier than some of the other pines we'll paint in the book. Yet, it still stands strong!

The dark values and wet-on-dry technique of the lone pine contrast beautifully with the misty background, drawing in the eye of anyone viewing your painting.

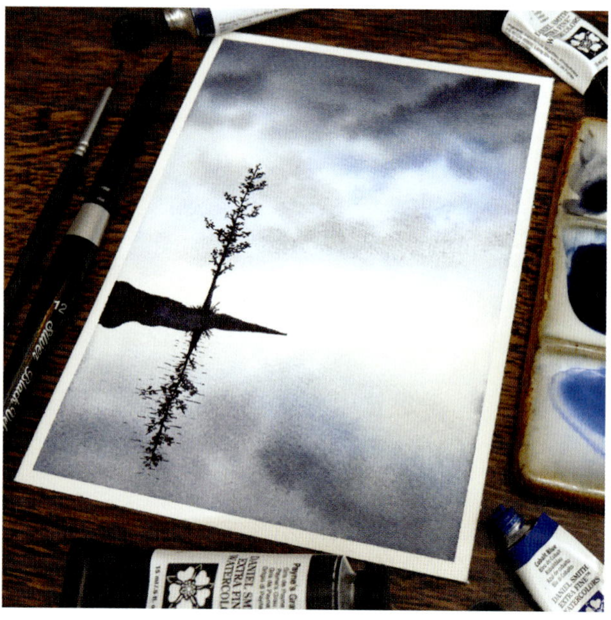

STEP 6: THE REFLECTION & FINAL TOUCHES

Let's add the reflection of our pine in the water. Start again by painting the trunk of the tree. This time, I started my branches from the "bottom" of the tree to the "top." I did this so I could see where I was going along the trunk. Keep referring to what you painted above as you add branches and pine needle clusters, aiming to create a mirror image. It doesn't need to be 100 percent perfect, but it needs to resemble the same overall shape as the one above.

Now, let's add in some details and final touches! Using that same size 2 round brush and indigo color, lightly paint some horizontal lines in various lengths along the reflection of our pine. Though our lake is pretty calm, adding in these tiny ripples will help indicate that this is water. Additionally, let's add some clumps of grass growing at the base of our pine tree as a final touch. Adding in a few sprigs of grass will help to "ground" the tree in the painting.

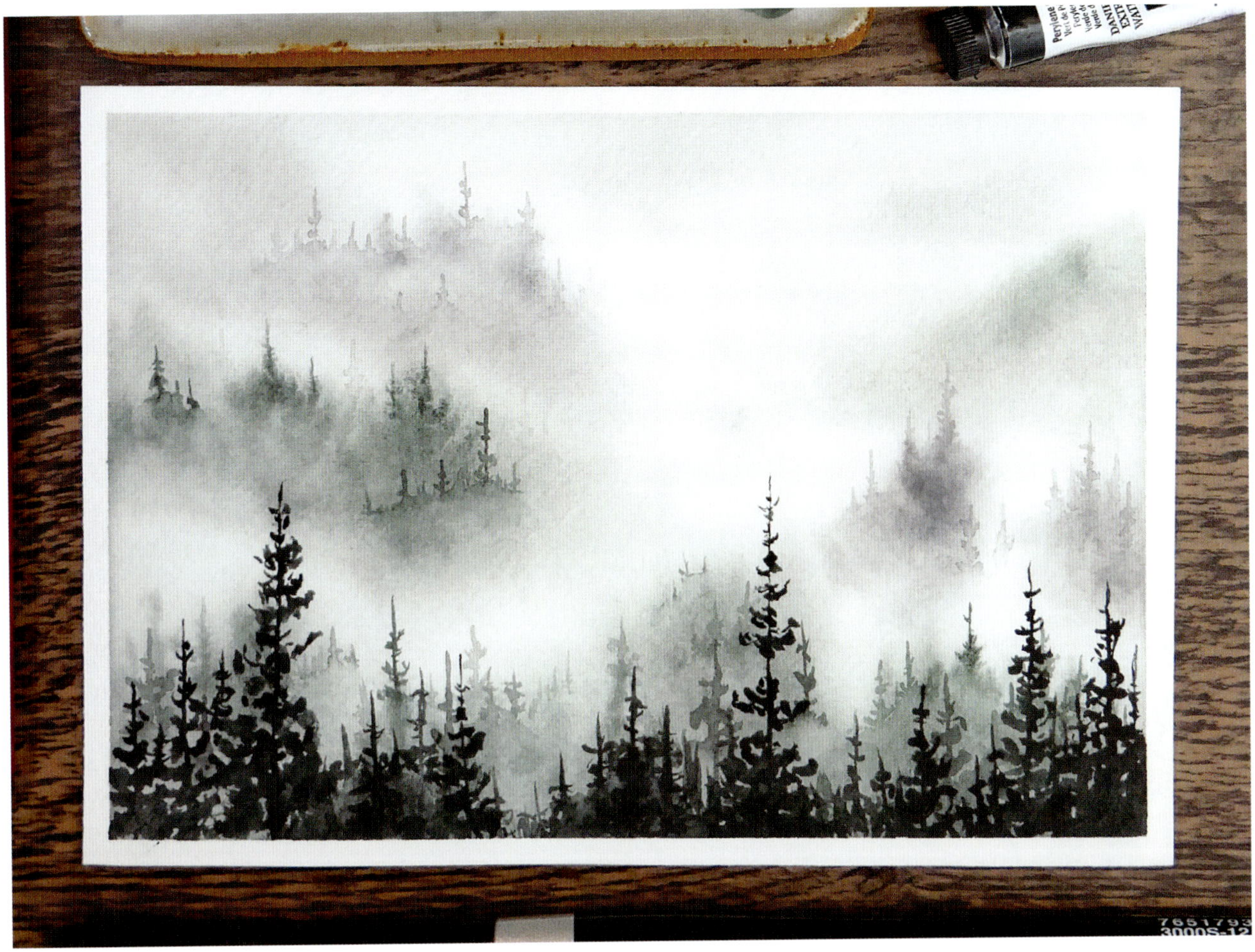

FOGGY FOREST

The sun has not yet risen to burn away the lingering fog of the early morning, meaning this forest is bathed in clouds. There's something mysterious about this sleeping forest. Let's capture this moody scene on paper using a combination of the wet-on-wet and wet-on-dry techniques.

MATERIALS

Paints: Neutral Gray (page 28) and perylene green

Brushes: sizes 12, 6 and 2 round

Paper: 5 x 7-inch (13 x 18-cm) cold-pressed watercolor paper

Painter's tape (or washi tape)

Paper towels (or a rag)

SWATCHES

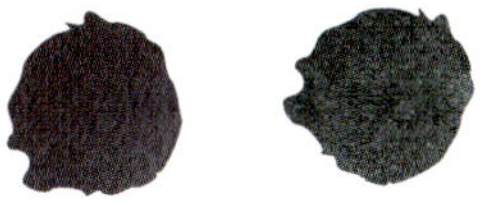

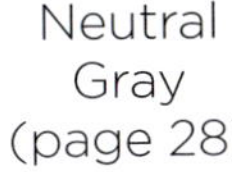

Neutral Gray (page 28)

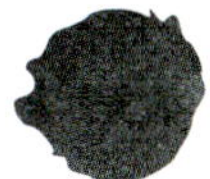

Perylene Green

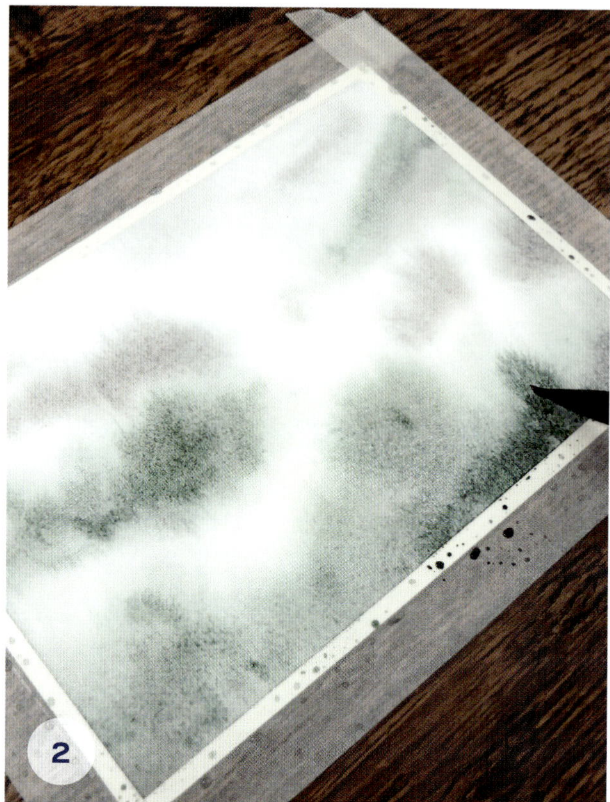

STEP 1: THE FIRST WASH

Using a size 12 round brush, wet the entire sheet of paper with clean water. Then, pick up some light-value Neutral Gray, and add a few small strokes to the top of your paper. Clean off your brush, and then add in some light-value perylene green strokes a bit farther down your paper. Let the paint spread out naturally, creating those magical soft edges watercolor is so well known for. Make sure to leave white space between these strokes! We'll need that white space to act as our fog.

Continue with perylene green along the bottom of your paper, stretching all the way across horizontally. Try your best not to paint perfectly straight lines but, rather, strokes that swell and dip as a forest naturally would. Drop in some Neutral Gray among some of the perylene green, again for variety and interest. Once you're satisfied with the first wash, let the entire paper dry.

We'll be adding more color in the next layer, so no need to worry if your colors aren't as saturated as you wish them to be. One of the important aspects of mist/fog paintings is layering.

STEP 2: THE SECOND WASH

Once you've let your paper completely dry, wet the entire thing once more with clean water. It's time to build up color/depth with the next layer. Repeat the same process as Step 1, adding Neutral Gray and perylene green where you placed it before, letting the paint spread out across the wet paper on its own. Remember: You can always lift some paint with a clean, "thirsty" brush if paint travels somewhere you don't wish it to.

Work quickly because you'll need to move on to the next step before your paper dries completely.

STEP 3: SHAPING THE FOGGY TREES

For this next step, we should be working with damp paper, not as wet as it was for the previous steps. Hopefully, by the time you've completed Step 2, your paper will not be as glossy as it was. The reason we want the paper to be a touch drier than previously is because we don't want our paint to spread out quite as much. This is all about water control.

If your brush or paper is too wet, the paint will spread out dramatically. If your paper is leaning more toward damp and your brush isn't dripping with water and paint, your brushstrokes will only bleed slightly. This means that with damp paper, you can still be fairly precise with your strokes while still achieving a softened stroke rather than hard edge (for more information on the wet-on-wet technique, see page 20).

Using this technique, we're going to begin to shape our misty pines. Switch to a size 6 round brush, and pick up some medium-value perylene green. Make sure your brush isn't dripping with the paint, otherwise it will spread out too much once it hits the paper. If needed, dab your loaded paintbrush on a paper towel to remove any excess moisture. Then, paint vertical strokes of perylene green, mimicking pines, in the areas you've already placed the color in previous layers. Vary the height of the vertical strokes and even skip over certain areas. Perhaps there is more fog there and it further obscures details. As mentioned previously, variety is important in landscape paintings because nature is random! Repeat the same vertical strokes in any areas of gray.

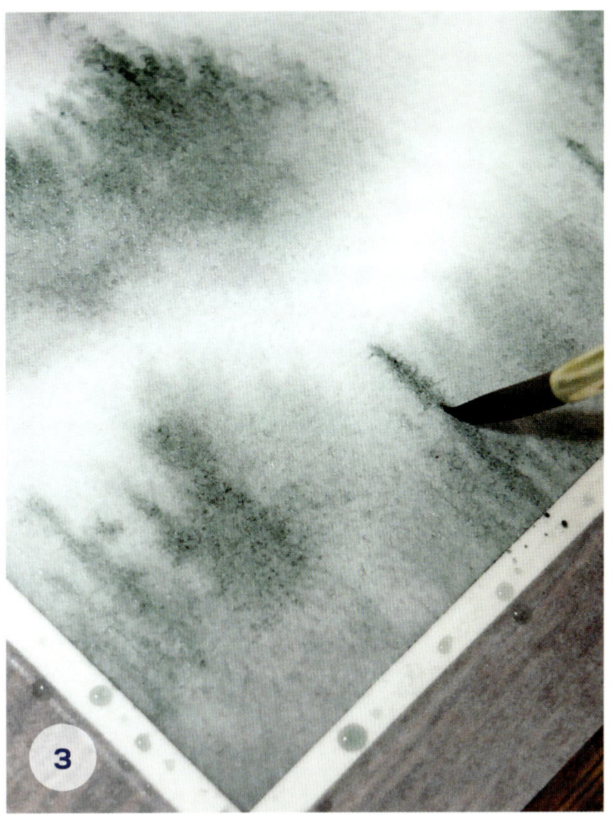

STEP 4: ADDING IN DISTANT TREES

Let's begin adding trees to the lightest-value areas. For this step, it's important to match the color values already on your paper. Make sure to test your paint color on a scrap sheet before applying it to the paper—that way you can adjust the color of the paint accordingly.

Using a light value of Neutral Gray and a size 2 round brush, add some pine tree tops using the blobby technique (see page 39). We don't want to paint entire trees but rather just the tops—most of the trees are obscured by fog. Before your treetops dry, clean off your brush, remove excess water on a paper towel so that it's just damp and soften the bottom edge of your treetops, making it look as though the rest of the tree dissolves into the fog below.

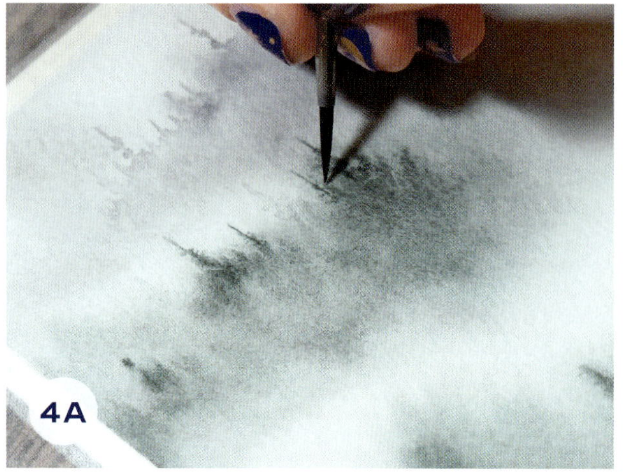

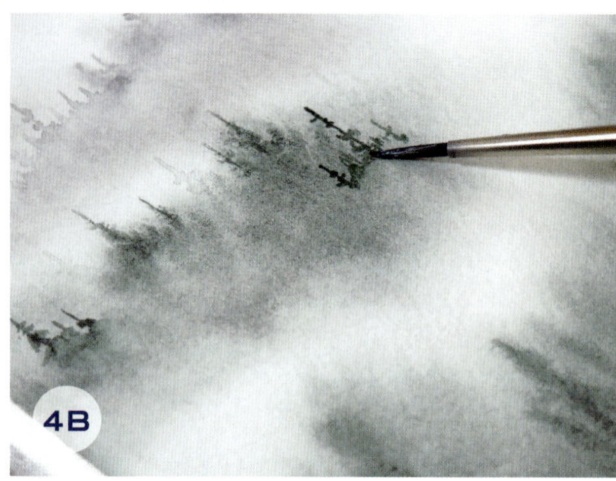

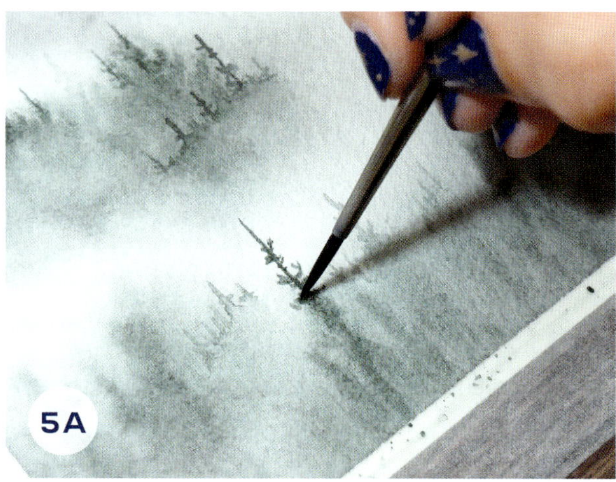

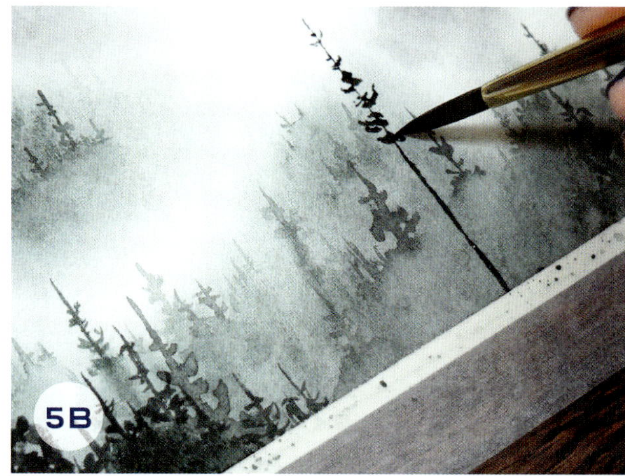

Alternatively, if you have another round brush handy, you can keep that one clean of paint and use it for softening edges only rather than switching back and forth with one brush. I often do this and find it saves time and energy!

Repeat this same process with the perylene green sections, painting a few treetops and then softening the bottom of the tree into the mist. I like to use some of the misty, blurry treetops from Step 3 as a base for some pine trees, as shown in photo 3. Don't forget: Trees in the distance will appear smaller and of lesser color value, so don't use saturated colors quite yet.

STEP 5: ADDING IN FOREGROUND TREES

As you move closer to the bottom of the paper, paint your trees with increasing saturation/value and with more detail. Continue to check your color value on a scrap sheet before adding it to your painting. For foggy forests, matching the color value of the tops of the pines to the mist beneath is essential for cohesion.

The trees directly in the foreground should be a dark value of perylene green, as they're closest to the viewer and least obscured by fog. Switch to a size 6 round brush for these closer, larger trees, and continue using the blobby technique to create them.

MISTY LAVENDER FIELD

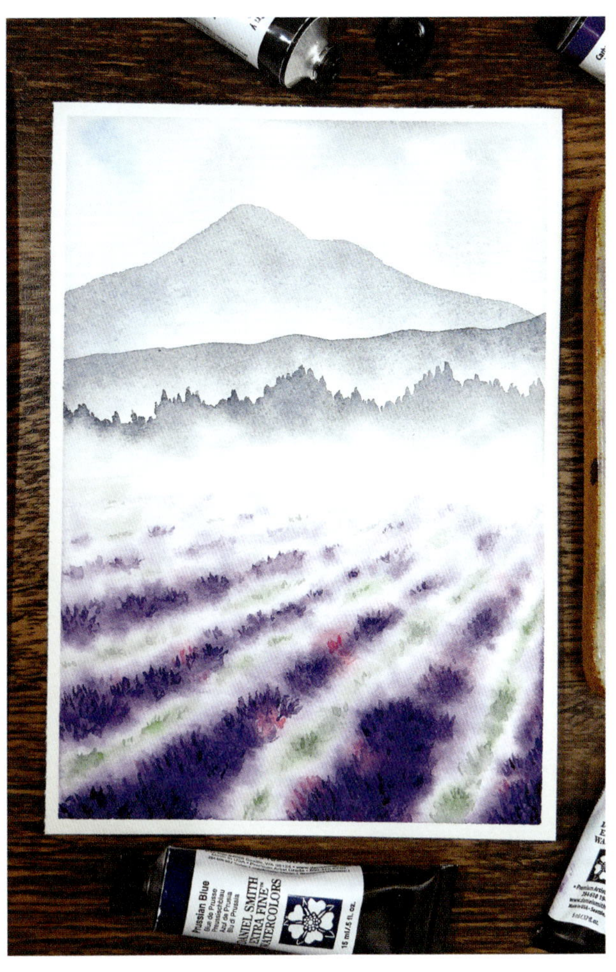

Rows upon rows of lavender plants bloom here in this field. A morning mist has settled over the flowers, coating everything in a fine dew. In fact, the mist this morning is so thick that it obscures the distant forest, shrouding its trees in mystery. In this painting, we'll learn how to use one-point perspective to make our landscape look three-dimensional.

MATERIALS

Paints: Payne's gray, Prussian blue, carbazole violet, perylene green, opera pink and hooker's green

Brushes: sizes 12 and 6 round

Paper: 5 x 7–inch (13 x 18–cm) cold-pressed watercolor paper

Painter's tape (or washi tape)

Paper towels (or a rag)

Ruler

Pencil and kneaded eraser

SWATCHES

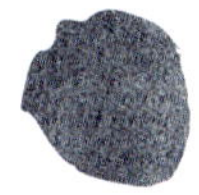

Payne's Gray

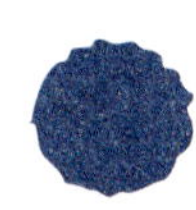

Prussian Blue

Carbazole Violet

Perylene Green

Opera Pink

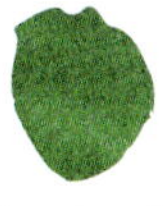

Hooker's Green

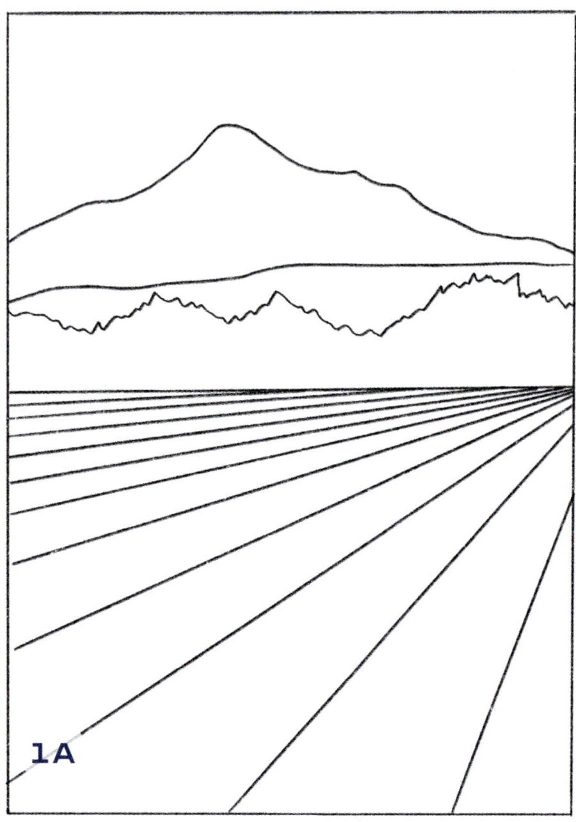

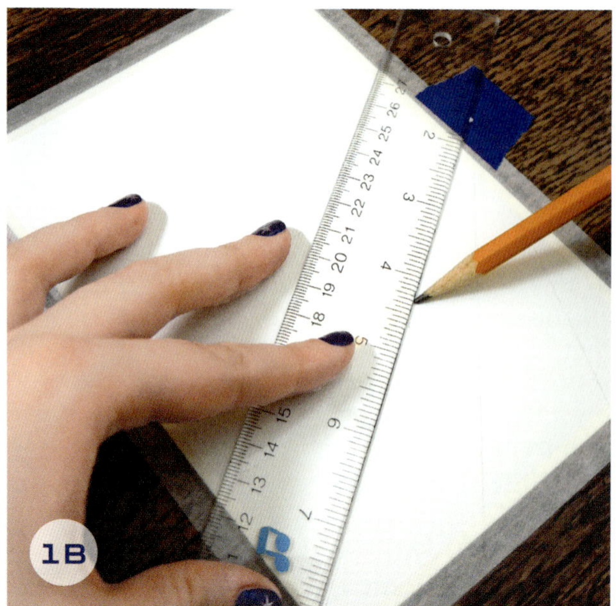

STEP 1: THE SKETCH

In order to make it appear as though our rows of lavender fade into the distant horizon, we'll need to use one-point perspective. One-point perspective is a method of drawing used to make things appear smaller as they get "farther away," all converging on a single point called a vanishing point. Essentially, it's a technique artists use to create three dimensions on a flat surface.

You'll need a ruler or another straight edge for this method. Grab a small piece of painter's tape, or a Post-it® note, and stick it on the right-hand side of your paper, a little over halfway up. With a pen, draw a small dot—the vanishing point. Pick up your ruler, place it on your vanishing point and draw a horizontal line all the way across the paper. This is your horizon line.

Now, we need to sketch out our rows of lavender. Rotate your ruler as if it were a hand on a clock, with your vanishing point as its center. In order to create proper one-point perspective, all of your lines must pass through the vanishing point. Begin sketching out rows using this method, making sure to place the wider, larger rows closer to the bottom right-hand corner of the paper. If we're using the clock metaphor, the ruler would be in the 7 o'clock position, moving forward in time to 8 o'clock and 9 o'clock. As you rotate your ruler around, the rows must be skinnier and skinnier as you approach your horizon line. These rows are farther away from the viewer and, therefore, will be smaller. Don't worry too much about the sizes of your rows nearest the horizon line. Because our field is covered in mist, we won't paint much detail here anyway.

Once you're done adding in your one-point perspective lines, lightly sketch in a taller mountain, a smaller hill and the shape of a distant forest.

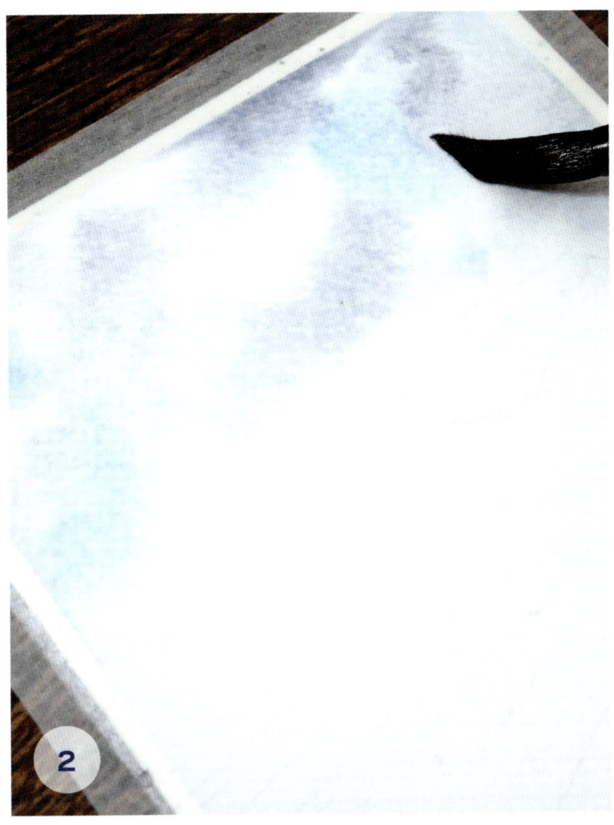

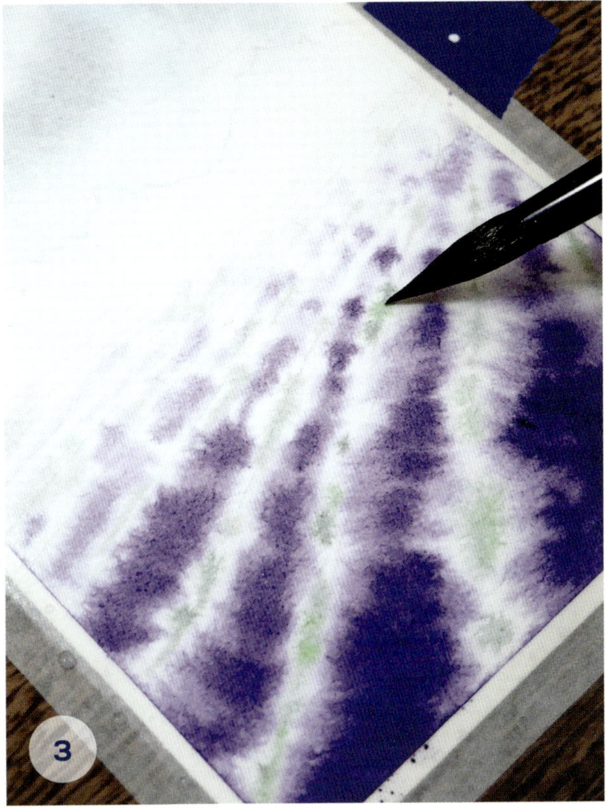

STEP 2: THE SKY (LAYER 1)

Like our other foggy pieces, we'll be relying on the white of the paper to create the fog/mist. So, throughout this process, make sure to leave plenty of room!

Begin by wetting the entire paper with clean water. Once glistening, pick up your size 12 round brush. It's a misty morning, and the sun hasn't broken through to burn away the moisture in the air; therefore, our sky will be full of light gray and vague blue tones. Paint in strokes of light-value Payne's gray and light-value Prussian blue, allowing the strokes to mix the paint on the paper. Add pigments above and slightly below the tallest mountain, and be sure to leave some white spaces in the sky. This white space will help the morning sky appear cloudy and diluted of color.

STEP 3: THE LAVENDER FIELD (LAYER 1)

Before your paper dries, switch your attention to the bottom half of the paper where the lavender field is. Load up your size 12 round brush with medium-value carbazole violet, and begin dropping pigment into your rows, following the perspective lines. Add in carbazole violet using both brushstrokes and dropping pigment. Dropping pigment off your brush will form rounded blobs, mimicking the rounded shape of a lavender bush.

Leave plenty of white space in between your rows of violet! Not only will the pigments naturally spread on the paper, filling in some of that white space, but we will also be adding in some perylene green as well in a few moments. Plus, we need that white space to act as the mist!

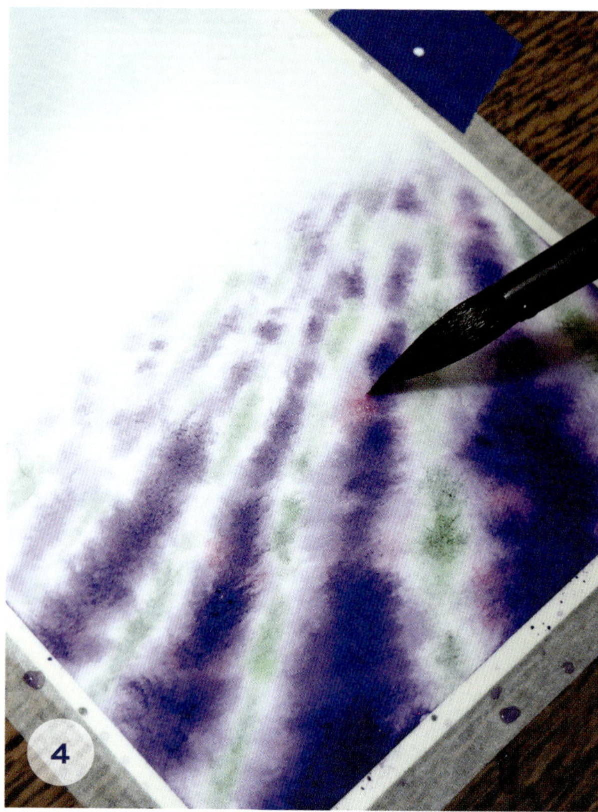

To keep a realistic perspective, the color values of the carbazole violet need to decrease as they approach the horizon and the vanishing point; therefore, the areas with the highest values of colors (or most color saturation) will be the bottom right-hand corner. The top left-hand corner at the horizon line should have next to no pigment. Remember: Mist and fog reduce visibility until objects and colors altogether vanish in the distance. We need to recreate that illusion with clever use of color value.

So, once you've added carbazole violet to your many rows, quickly clean off your brush and grab some light-value perylene green and repeat the same process, this time painting small lines of perylene green in between the rows of violet. Again, don't fill in the entire space. Leave some white of the paper showing through.

Lastly, for added color variety, clean off your brush, load it up with light-value opera pink and drop the pigment onto the page in a few different places. I enjoy adding a little bit of pink because it brings some warmth into an otherwise cool-tone painting.

Let this entire layer dry before continuing on.

STEP 4: THE LAVENDER FIELD (LAYER 2)

As is typical with another layer of paint, let's build up color values, depth and luminosity. Rewet the entire paper with clean water, making sure to add clean water at the horizon line (where the least amount of pigment is) and then expanding outward.

Once your entire paper is wet, let's repeat the process of painting the lavender field. Load up your size 12 round brush with a darker value of carbazole violet, and paint in/drop in the pigment within the rows, following the perspective lines. Same as before, leave plenty of space in between your rows, and decrease the value of your violet color as you approach the horizon line and vanishing point.

After adding in carbazole violet, clean off your brush and add light-value perylene green in between the rows. For added color variety, I also dropped in just a little bit of light-value hooker's green, just to shake things up! Don't go overboard with this addition, but instead use it as a subtle way to add interest to your painting.

Let this layer dry before moving on.

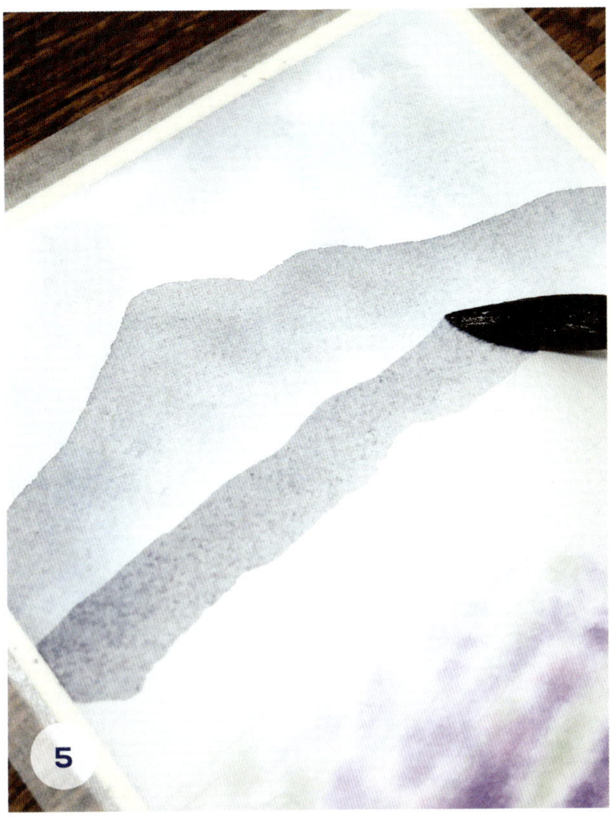

STEP 5: THE MOUNTAINS

For our distant mountains, we'll be using techniques you learned in the Misty Mountains project (page 92). Specifically, we will use a damp brush to soften the edge of our brushstroke, dragging the pigments downward in a gradient until they vanish.

So, load up your size 12 round brush with light-value Payne's gray, and paint in the farthest mountain, following your sketch from earlier. Then, quickly clean off your brush, dab off any excess water on a paper towel and drag the clean, slightly damp brush on the bottom edge of your brushstroke, watching as the pigments travel into the clean water. Extend this clean water until the pigments vanish altogether, and no harsh edges will appear when dry. Let this mountain dry completely before painting in the next one.

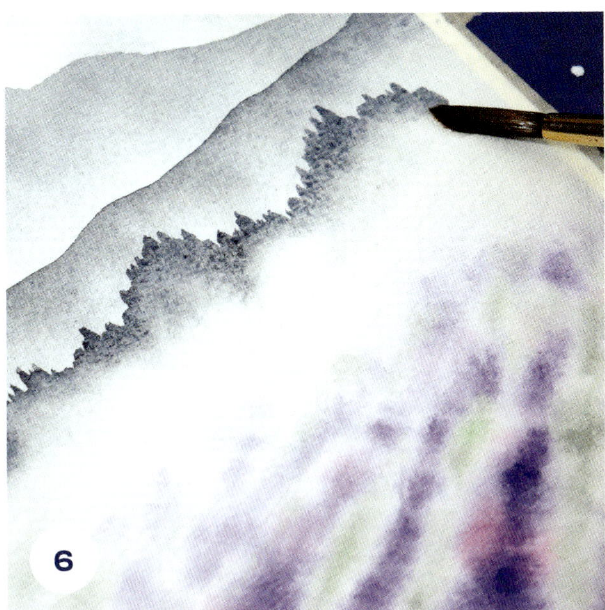

Once dry, paint in your second mountain/hill using the same method, this time with a slightly darker value of Payne's gray but still very light. These mountains are distant and mostly obscured by morning mist, so they should not be extremely saturated. Let this second mountain/hill dry as well.

STEP 6: THE DISTANT FOGGY FOREST

Lastly, switch to your size 6 round brush for the distant forest. Like in previous projects (Winter Morning Sunrise, page 41, or Misty Mountains, page 92), we'll use the shape of our round brush to our advantage, using the pointed tip to depict the tops of distant trees. In order to soften our stroke, however, we'll need to work in smaller sections. If you attempt to paint the entire forest in one go, by the time you reach the other side of the paper, the treetops you painted first will likely be dry, and their edges will not soften.

That said, once you add in a few treetops, use a clean, damp brush to soften the edges of that section, and then repeat this process until your misty forest stretches across the entirety of your paper. Let dry.

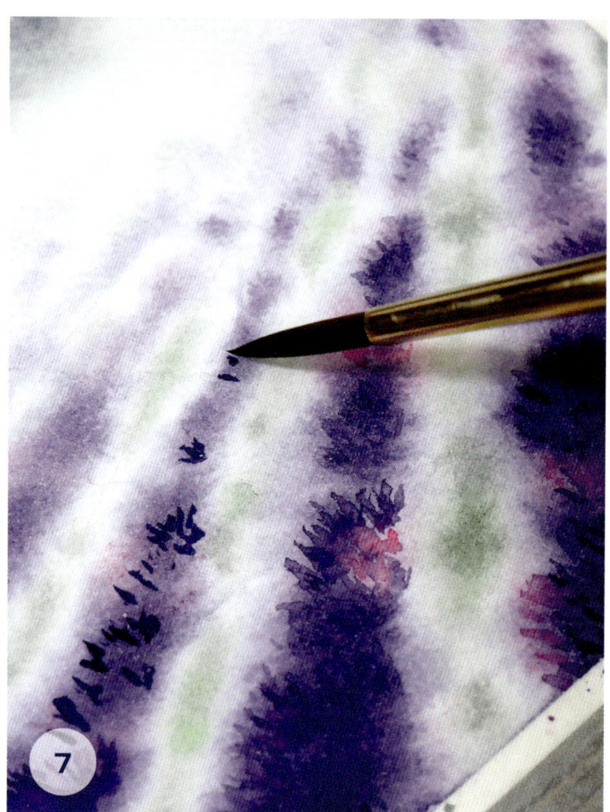

STEP 7: THE LAVENDER DETAILS

Time to add in some final details, specifically the tops of lavender flowers. Using your size 6, or smaller, round brush, load it up with various values of carbazole violet. Similar to how we used the pointed tip to create treetops, we'll also use the small tip to create the tops of lavender flowers. Press just the tip of your brush into the rows of lavender, leaving tiny flower tops behind. Once you've added a few flowers, clean off your brush, dab it off on a paper towel until it's damp and then use that damp brush to soften a few of the strokes you just made. This back and forth of adding a few flowers and then using a light wash of water to soften/blend some of them adds to the illusion of mist settled over the field. Because mist isn't completely opaque, we're bound to see a few details here and there as the mist moves.

Continue this process of painting in details with perylene green and opera pink, following the same rules as before: darker values in the bottom right-hand corner, closer to the viewer, and lighter values as you approach the horizon line and vanishing point. Throughout this process, take several moments to reevaluate your painting to see if it's complete. Like painting waves (see Tempest Sea, page 79), the process of adding flowers and final details can easily bridge into overworking your painting. In many cases, less is more. The more detail you add, the less your lavender field is covered in fog. The key here is to suggest details rather than painting all of them.

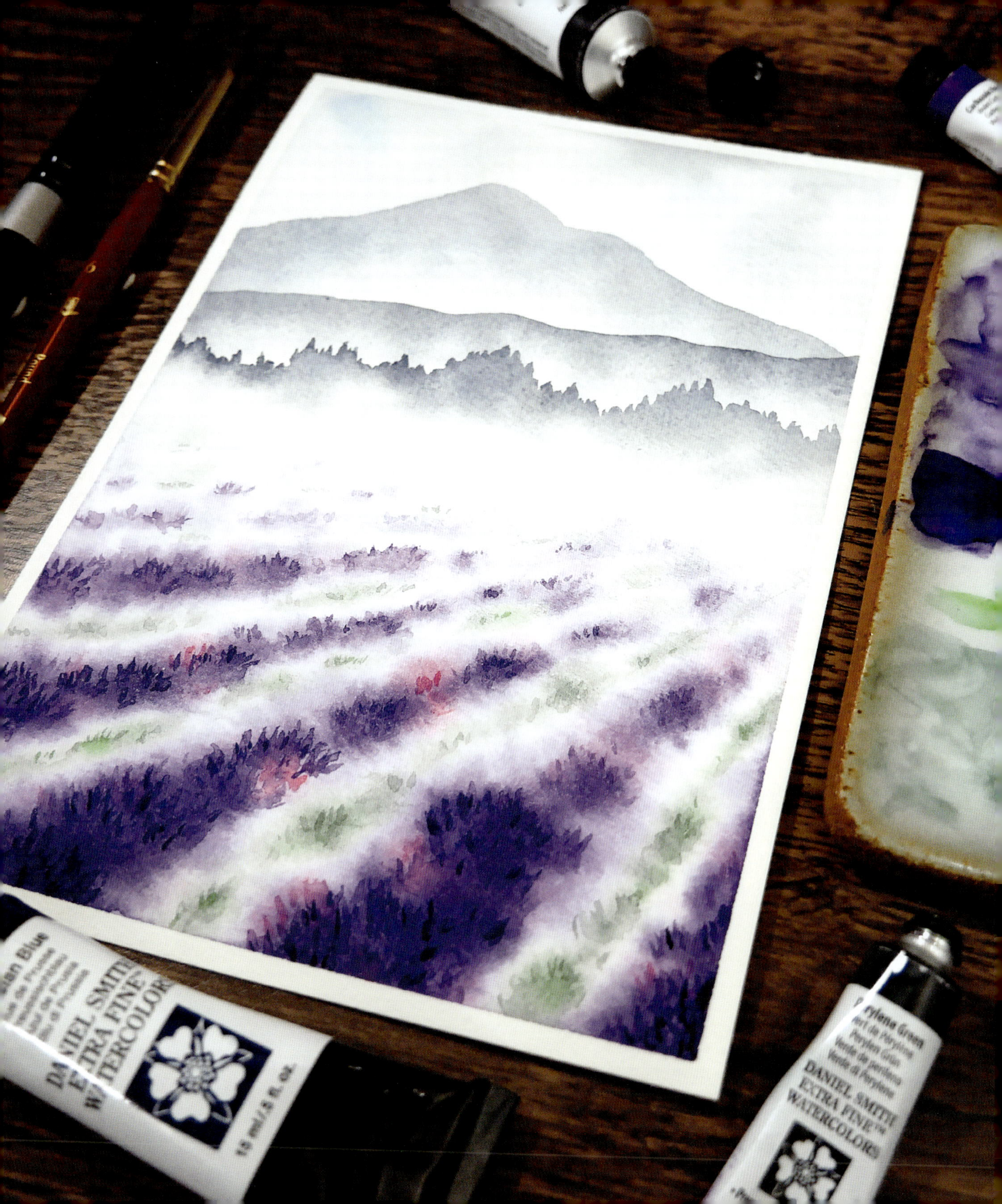
DANIEL SMITH
EXTRA FINE
WATERCOLORS
DANIEL SMITH
EXTRA FINE
WATERCOLORS

RAINY MORNING IN THE ADIRONDACKS

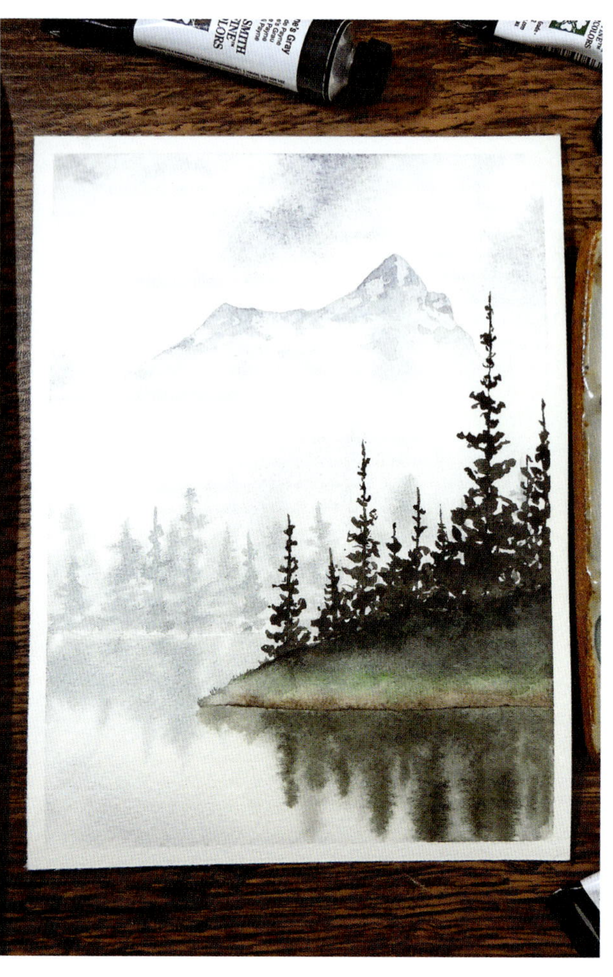

You've spent the weekend camping by a lake in the mountainous region of the Adirondacks, the United States' largest state park. The loons have just begun their eerie calls, and the cool fog still hangs low, obscuring most of the mountain in the distance. To capture this moody, yet peaceful, scene, we'll need to mix some colors that fit the ambience we're going to capture.

MATERIALS

Paints: Payne's gray, Sea Sage (page 28), Pewter (page 29), burnt umber, hooker's green and perylene green

Brushes: sizes 12, 6 and 2 round

Paper: 5 x 7-inch (13 x 18-cm) cold-pressed watercolor paper

Painter's tape (or washi tape)

Paper towels (or a rag)

Ruler

Pencil and kneaded eraser

SWATCHES

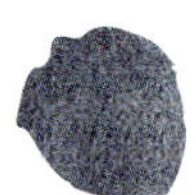

Payne's Gray

Sea Sage (page 28)

Pewter (page 29)

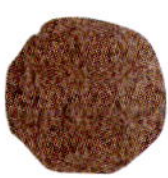

Burnt Umber

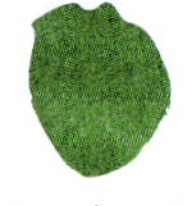

Hooker's Green

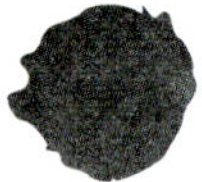

Perylene Green

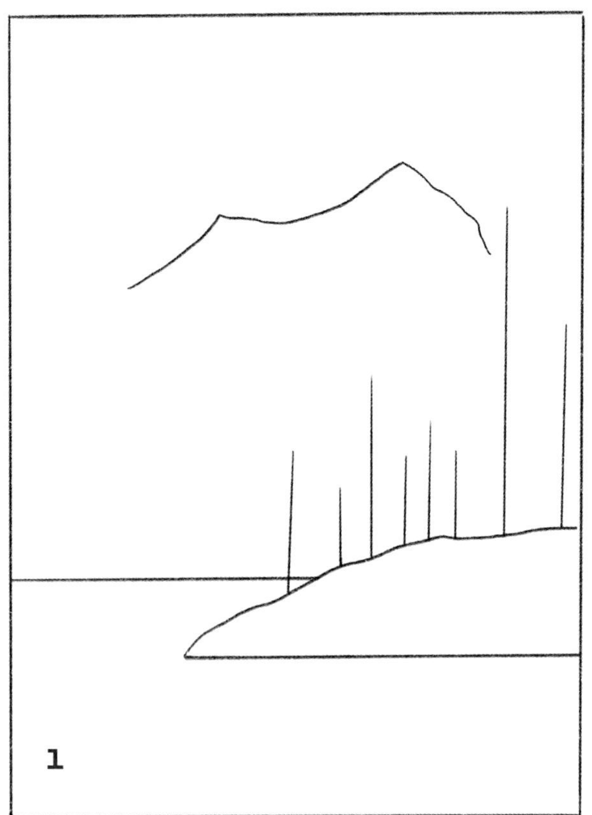

STEP 1: THE SKETCH

Grab your ruler and sketch in a horizon line one-third of the way up from the bottom of the paper. Roughly an inch (2.5 cm) below that horizon line, use your ruler to sketch another line that extends two-thirds of the way across the paper, starting from the right-hand side. From that line, sketch a small hill, using your ruler to sketch out the skeletons of the future pine trees. Lastly, lightly sketch a mountaintop in the top one-third of the paper.

STEP 2: THE GRAY SKIES

Begin by picking up your size 12 round brush and wetting the entire sky portion of your paper with clean water. Dip your brush into some light-value Payne's gray, and add a few wispy strokes of it throughout the sky portion. Leave plenty of white space.

Before your wash dries, pick up some medium-value Payne's gray with the same brush, and drop in some color at the top of your paper, mimicking gray rain clouds far above in the sky. Let the pigments spread out naturally so that everything remains soft.

Let this entire wash dry before moving on.

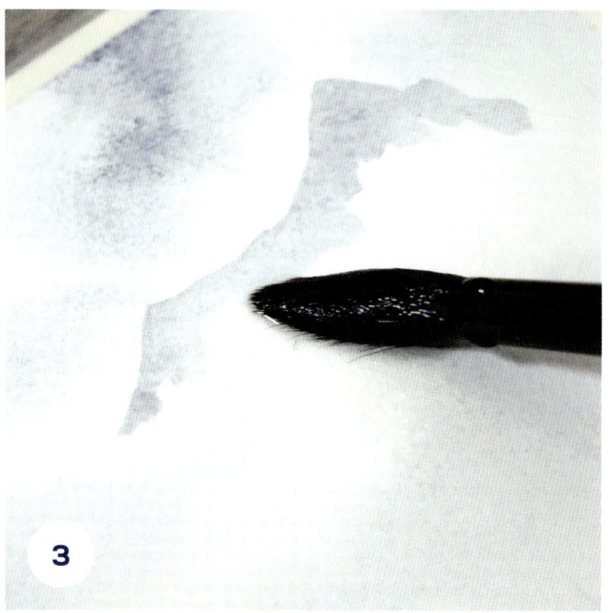

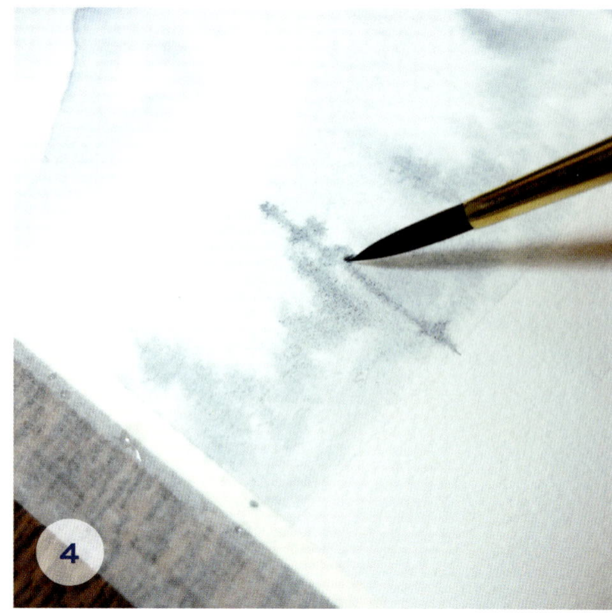

STEP 3: THE MOUNTAIN PEAK

Now, it's time to add in our mountain, peeking out of the fog blanketing lower elevations. Again, using your size 12 round brush, pick up light-value Payne's gray, and paint a mountain peak near the top of your paper. We're not going to be painting the entire shape of the mountain but rather just the top, very similar to how we painted our mountains in Misty Mountains (page 92). Like Misty Mountains, we'll be using clean water to soften the edges of our brushstroke and drag the pigments down.

Next, clean off your brush, pick up some clean water and apply that clean water to the edge of the still-wet Payne's gray you just applied. Soften the hard edge of your stroke with the clean water. Extend that clean water all the way until the top of your lake (the horizon line).

We'll later return to our mountain peak to add finishing details toward the end of our painting process.

Now, before your painting dries, move on to the next step. If your paper has mostly dried in some or all areas, wait for it to finish drying completely. Once it is dry, apply clean water from the top of the lake to the mountain peak but no farther. This will ensure our mountain peak remains a crisp line.

STEP 4: THE DISTANT, MISTY PINES

While your wash has begun to dry at this point, it should still be just damp. Meaning, the paper is no longer glistening as brightly but rather has absorbed a bit of the water. If your paper is still soaking wet, wait about a minute before beginning the process below.

To paint our distant, misty pines, we'll need to prevent our wet-on-wet brushstrokes from exploding across the paper, hence why we want our paper damp, not soaking. Pick up some light- to medium-value Sea Sage with your size 6 round brush. When you believe your paper has the right amount of moisture, touch your loaded brush to either the bottom left or bottom right corner of this section above the lake, and observe how much the paint spreads. If the paint explodes across the paper, wait a few moments and try again. If the paint spreads out only slightly, you're good to go!

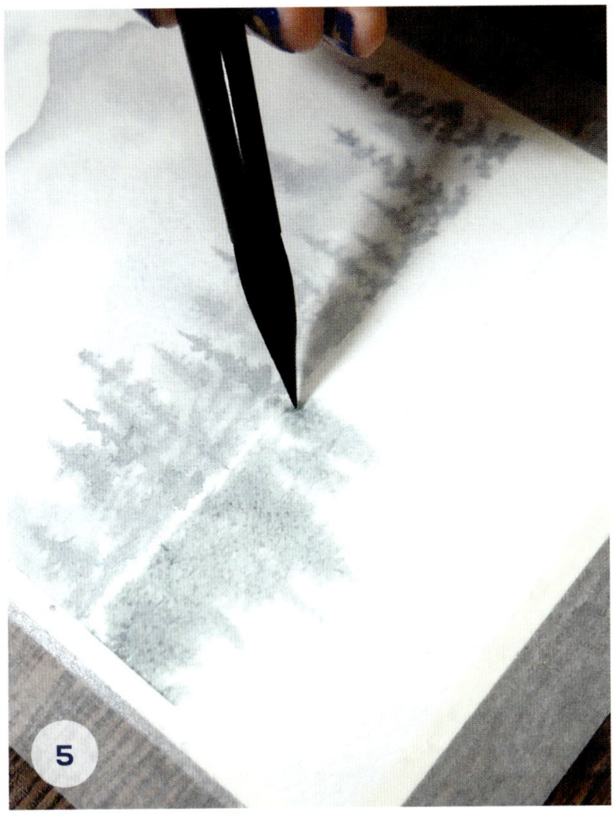

Begin to paint the suggestion of trees along the lake's edge in the distance. Hold your brush almost vertically so the point of it can create the tops of your blurry trees. Since these trees are obscured by mist and far away, don't worry about the details too much.

Keep adding tree shapes with light- and medium-value Sea Sage as your painting continues to dry. As your paper dries, you'll notice that the pigments you're applying will spread out less and less. Use this to your advantage! Begin to paint pine trees with the blobby technique (see page 39), suggesting more detail. These trees will have a more treelike shape and may even have some hard edges. That's okay! They're closer to the shoreline of the lake, less hidden than their counterparts in the fog.

Moisture Control: An important note here! The key to avoiding blooms during the process of painting while your paper dries is to avoid substantial differences in moisture. Don't apply a dripping wet brush to damp paper. Instead, when you load your brush with fresh paint, dab it off on a paper towel before applying it to your paper. Match the moisture of your paper with your brush, and you'll have much better luck at avoiding blooms.

Once you're satisfied with your misty, distant trees, wait for everything to completely dry before moving on.

STEP 5: THE DISTANT PINES' REFLECTIONS

On this still morning, the lake reflects the shapes of our tree line. So, pick up your size 12 round brush, and apply clean water to the lower half of your painting, from the lake's edge downward. Immediately, pick up some light-value Payne's gray, and apply one stroke of it to the bottom left-hand corner of the painting, reflecting some of the gray clouds in the sky above.

Then, clean off your brush, and pick up some light-value Sea Sage, and wait a few moments for your paper to absorb some of the clean water you just applied. Like in the previous step, we don't want the pigment to explode across the paper. We need the wet-on-wet technique's softness, not its chaotic nature.

Once your paper is damp, begin to paint the reflection of pine trees on the water. Again, use the tip of your brush to your advantage, painting the tips of the pine trees with the tip of your brush. Use vertical brushstrokes, placing the tip of your brush where the tip of the reflection would be, and then draw your stroke upward, lifting your brush where the lake's edge would be.

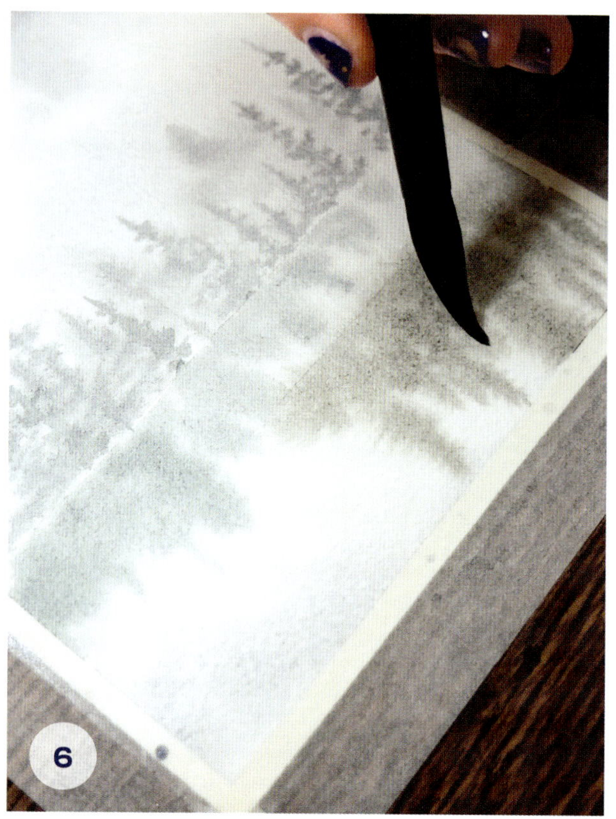

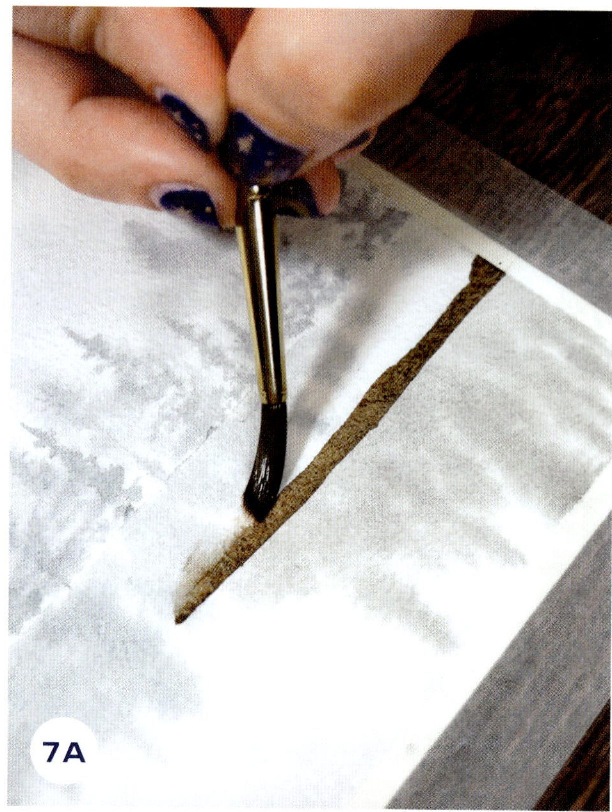

STEP 6: THE FOREGROUND PINES' REFLECTIONS

Before your wash dries, let's add in some tree reflections for our little island in the foreground. Pick up some light-value Pewter, and begin the same process. This time, extend the reflections all the way to the bottom of the page, as they'll actually extend off the page due to their size. We'll later intensify the color of these reflections, but it's always great to add a base layer to build off of.

Let this layer dry completely.

STEP 7: THE BASE OF THE ISLAND

Time to add in some foreground elements! Load up your size 6 round brush with some medium-value burnt umber and then, following your sketch, paint a line to create the base of the island. Before your brushstroke dries, clean off your brush and pick up some clean water. Then, apply that clean water to the top edge of the burnt umber, dragging that pigment upward and softening its edge. Clean off your brush again, pick up some medium-value hooker's green and immediately apply that paint to the top edge of your previous brushstroke with clean water. The hooker's green will blend downward into that clean water, softening any hard lines.

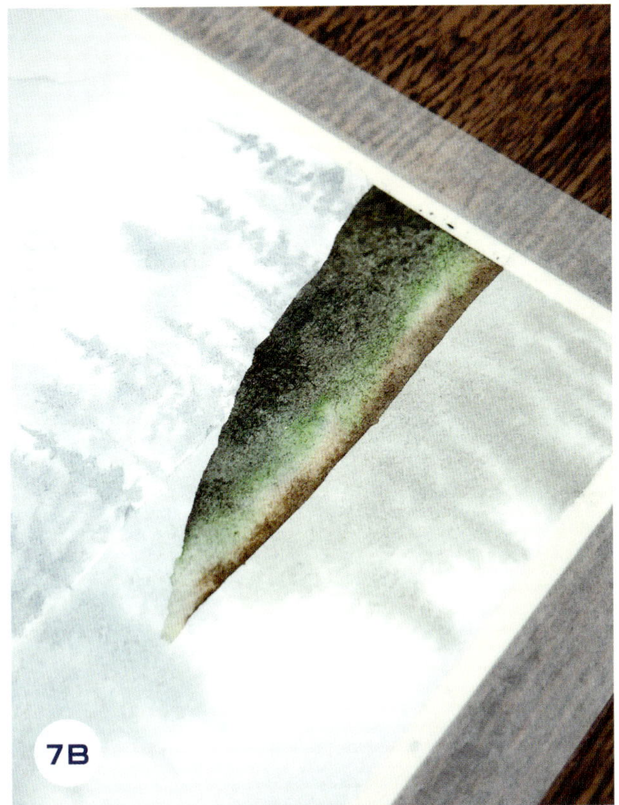

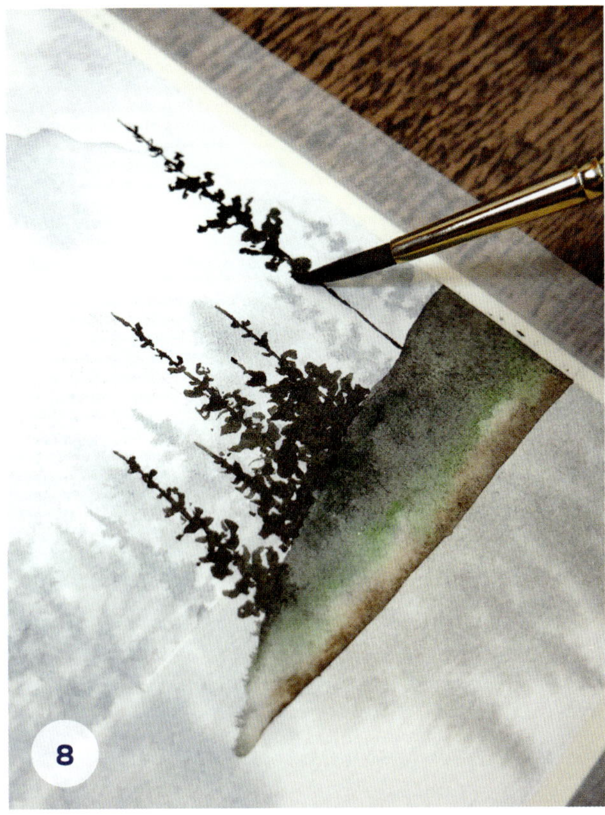

Next, before that stroke of hooker's green dries, pick up some dark-value perylene green with your brush, and repeat the process again. Perylene green is the last color we'll apply to the base of the island, so use this to fill in the rest of the base. When done, your little island should look like the one in photo 7B. Let dry and then move on to painting the pine trees.

STEP 8: THE ISLAND TREES

Using your size 6 round brush, begin painting various pine trees with a dark-value Pewter, using the blobby technique. Vary the shapes and sizes of the trees on the island for realism.

Additionally, you can add a few very small brushstrokes at the island's edge to create some sprigs of grass. Try your best to match the value and color of the island's base. That way, your brushstrokes will make the grass appear natural and like they belong.

Let the entire island dry before continuing on.

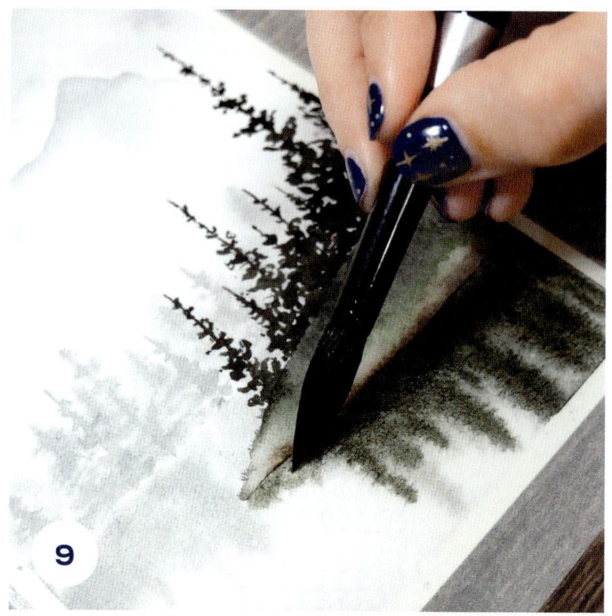

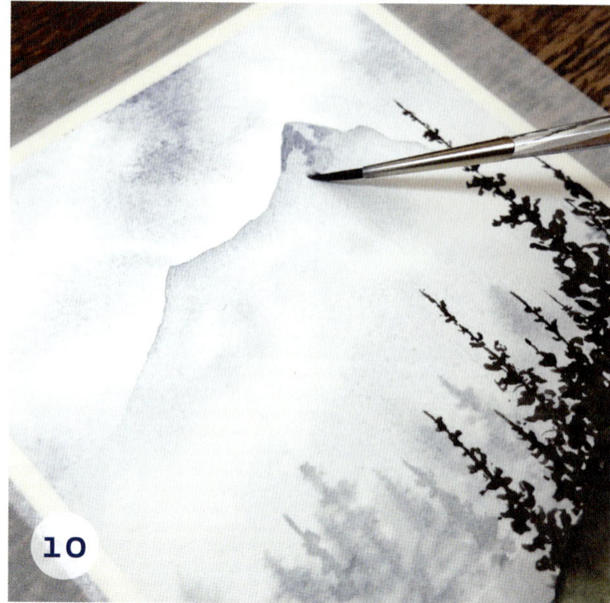

STEP 9: INTENSIFYING FOREGROUND REFLECTIONS

Let's intensify the colors of the reflections of our little pine tree-covered island. For this, grab your size 12 round brush, and apply clean water at the bottom edge of the island, extending that clean water right to the bottom of the paper. Wait a moment or two for your glistening wet page to become damp. Then, pick up some dark-value Pewter with your brush, and repeat the process of painting reflections. Try to match the size and length of the pine trees on your island—that way your reflection appears accurate and real.

Once complete, let dry and then move on to the final step.

STEP 10: MOUNTAIN DETAILS

Right now, our mountain peak is just an outline and, if you're satisfied with how it looks, call your piece finished. When I took a step back and looked over my painting, I found that the mountain needed just a few suggestions of details in order to cement it in my landscape.

Using your size 2 round brush, grab some light-value Payne's gray, and paint in a few shadows and crevices in the mountain's peak. There's no particular science to adding textures to mountains, but I find that looking up some mountain images on Pinterest is a great way to view how they may look and how the shadows might behave. You should only add marks and texture along the mountain's peak and right below—you won't be able to see these details on the portion of the mountain that is obscured by morning fog. Nonetheless, as you paint downward, use an even lighter-value Payne's gray to paint any textures that are along the cusp of where the fog begins to obstruct.

Try not to overwork the details here. Though this mountain peak rises above the fog, giving us a beautiful view, add a few textures and then step back to observe the piece as a whole. Just like our Tempest Sea project (page 79), it can be easy to get lost in finishing details and forget to view the entire picture. So, make sure to take breaks, step away and return with fresh eyes.

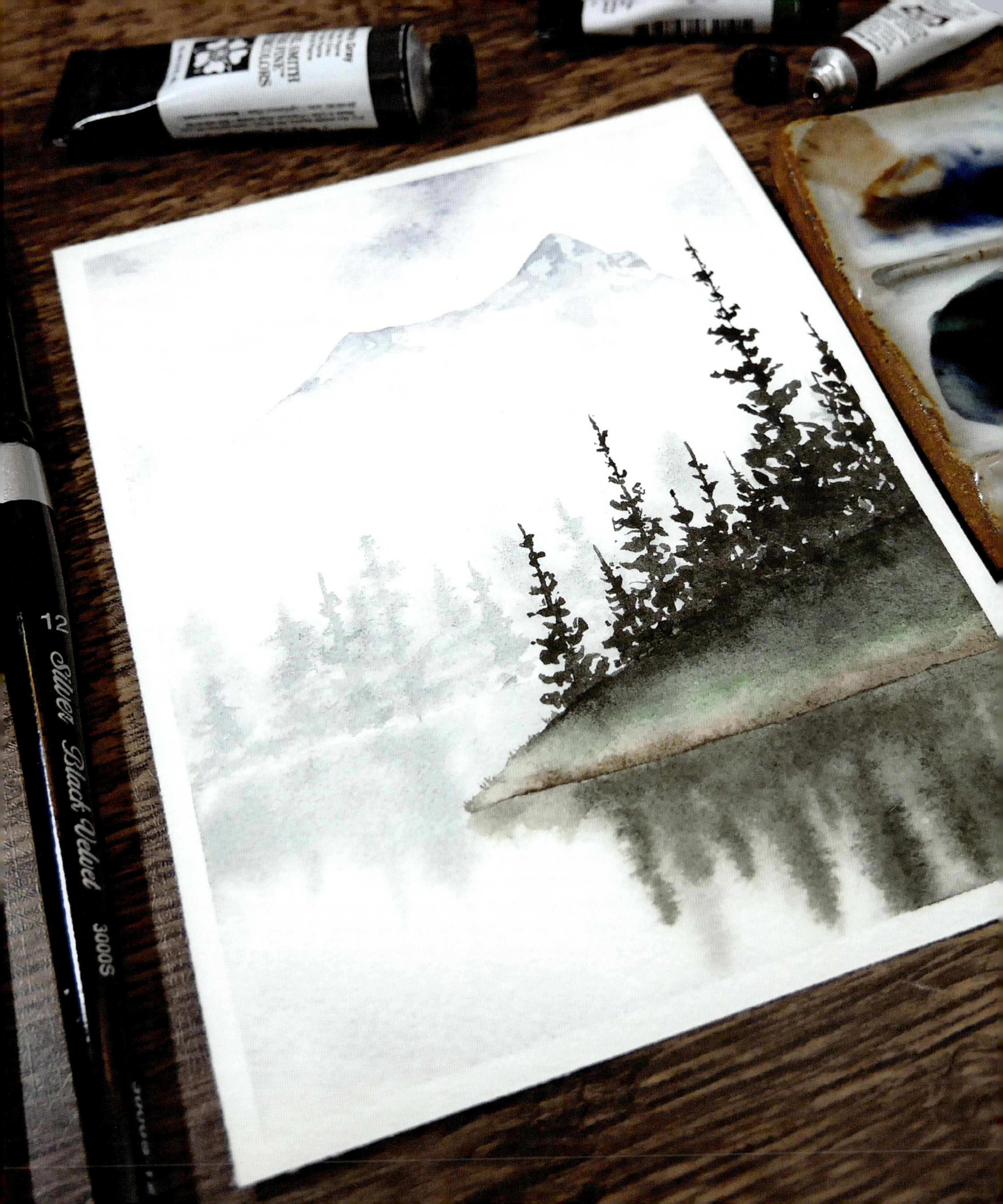
12
Silver Black Velvet
3000S

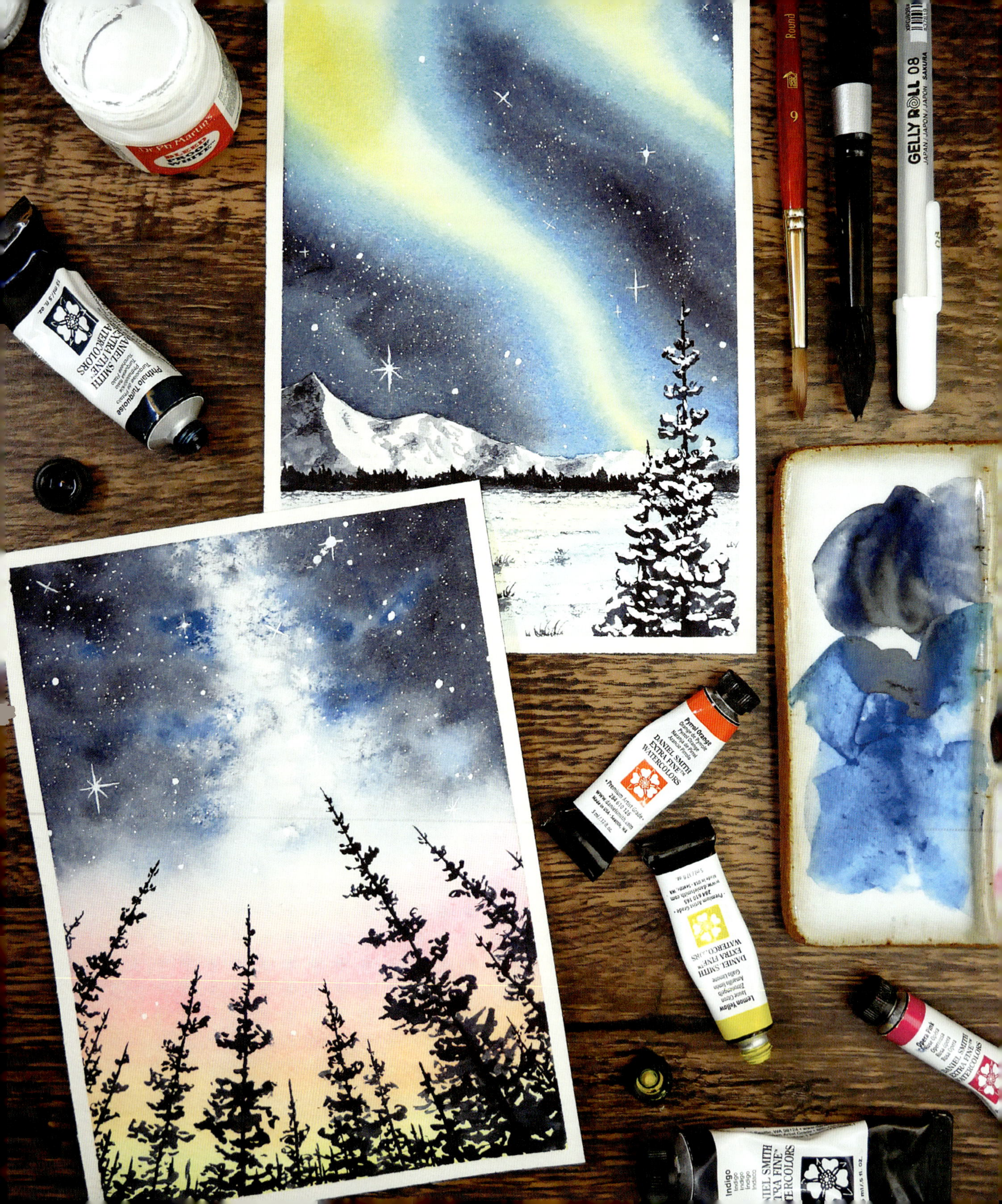

Dr. Ph. Martin's
Round
GELLY ROLL 08
SAKURA
DANIEL SMITH
EXTRA FINE
WATERCOLORS
Pyrrol Orange
Indigo

Never-Ending NIGHT SKIES

When the sun disappears for the night, the moon and stars come out to play. I have harbored a fascination with the stars from a very young age—watching meteor showers on the roof with my older brother, staying up late to catch lunar eclipses and learning how to identify constellations with friends. My watercolor journey started here, with a desire to paint the night sky I so dearly love. In this chapter, we'll create monochrome galaxies, paint the moon and capture the brilliance of night on paper.

A vast sea of stars
Shining down from the heavens
Mirroring our souls

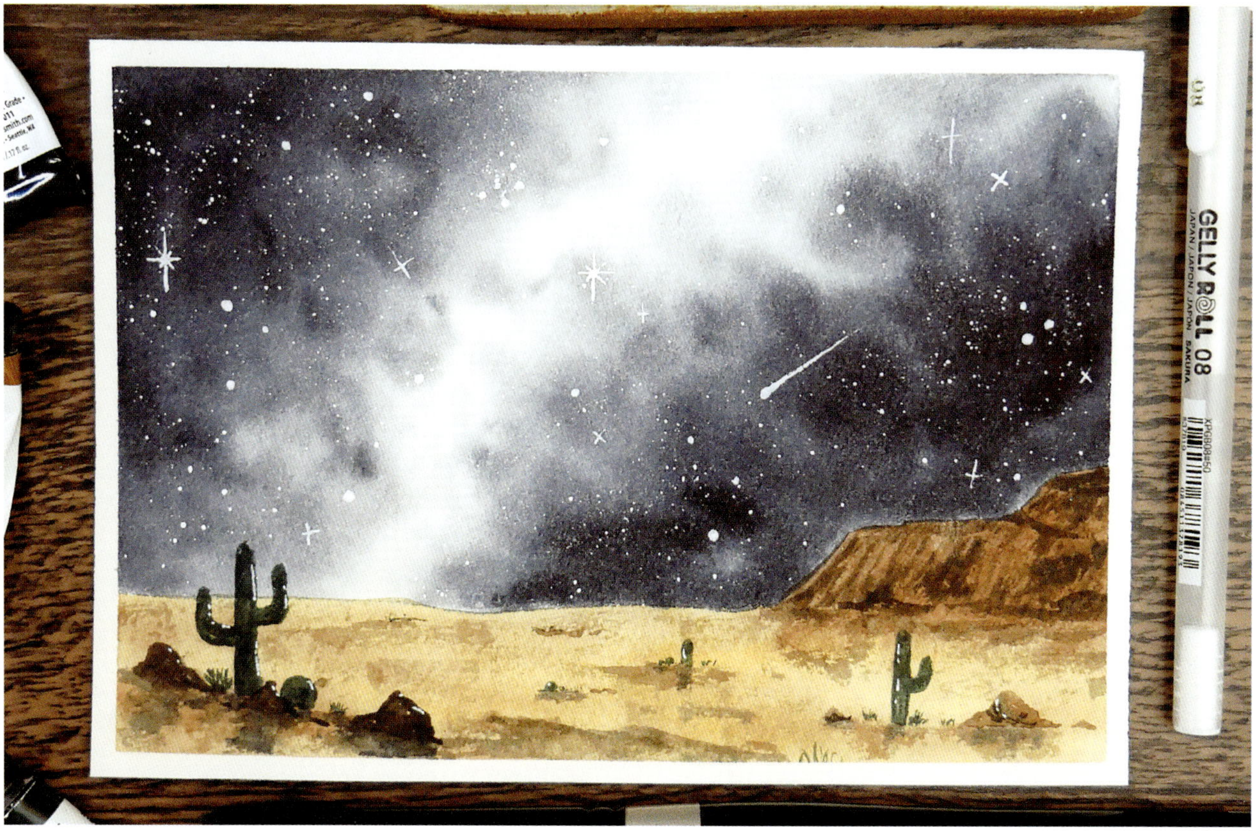

MILKY WAY OVER THE DESERT

There is perhaps no better place to stargaze than in the desert. Away from light pollution and the noise of cities, clear desert nights provide a glimpse at what our skies once looked like before electricity lit our homes. No wonder our ancestors used the stars to guide and inspire. Let's capture our galaxy, the Milky Way, on paper by using a monochrome sky that illuminates the desert rocks and sand below.

MATERIALS

Paints: indigo, yellow ochre, burnt umber, perylene green and Neutral Gray (page 28)

Brushes: sizes 12, 10, 6 and 2 round

Paper: 5 x 7–inch (13 x 18–cm) cold-pressed watercolor paper

Painter's tape (or washi tape)

Paper towels (or a rag)

Pencil and kneaded eraser

White gouache and/or white gel pen

SWATCHES

Indigo

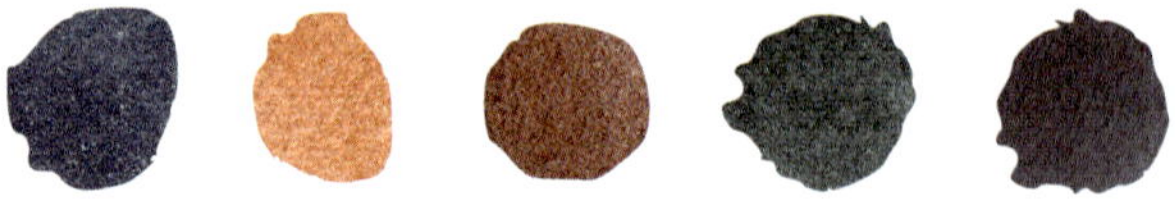

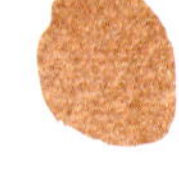
Yellow Ochre

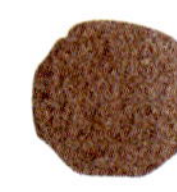
Burnt Umber

Perylene Green

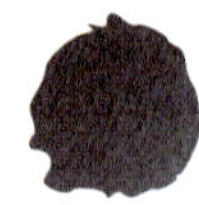
Neutral Gray (page 28)

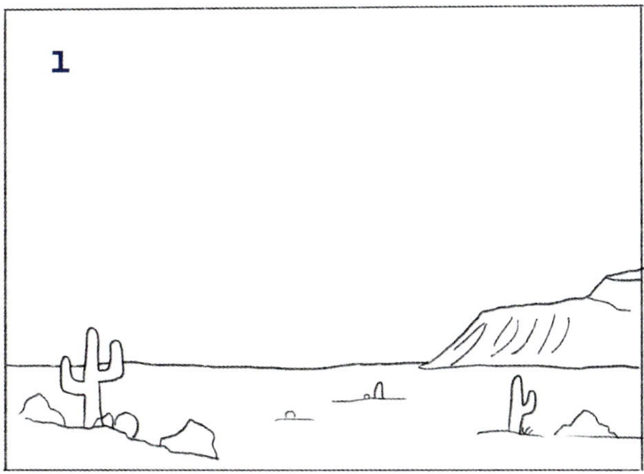

1

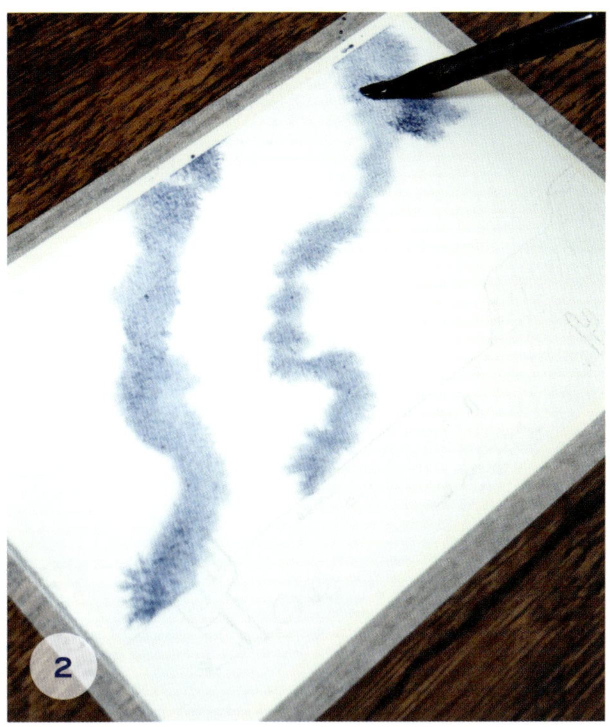

2

STEP 1: THE SKETCH

This is a fairly simple sketch. Across the bottom one-third of your paper, draw your horizon line. It doesn't need to be perfectly straight; in fact, a slight wobble to your line will add to the realism of your piece. On the right-hand side of your horizon line, let's draw in a simple rocky hill one may find in the deserts of western North America. Next, sketch in a few cacti, some shaped like the typical cactus everyone thinks of and others round. You can also sketch in a few rocks and lines to denote land features.

STEP 2: OUTLINING THE MILKY WAY (LAYER 1)

One of the reasons watercolors create such intense and luminescent galaxies is due to their transparent nature. In order to achieve that effect, we'll be relying on the powers of layering! So, as always, start with light values and build up.

That said, begin by using a size 12 round brush to wet the entire sky portion of your paper. Make sure to leave the bottom desert portion dry. We don't want our indigo paint to travel there. I always begin a galaxy painting by outlining the white luminescent portion of the galaxy. So, once your paper is nice and glossy, pick up some light-value indigo, and begin painting in a loose, slightly wobbly stroke, starting from the horizon line and working your way up to the top of your paper. Then, repeat the same motion on the other side, leaving white space in between your two indigo strokes.

In order to create depth within the sky, the white space of your galaxy should be skinnier near the horizon line and wider at the top, almost like the galaxy is expanding as it grows closer to the viewer. This creates the illusion of the galaxy appearing over the viewer's head. This is very similar to the idea of one-point perspective (discussed in the Misty Lavender Field project on page 107). By utilizing perspective, we can create the illusion of three-dimensional depth on flat paper. Pretty cool, right?

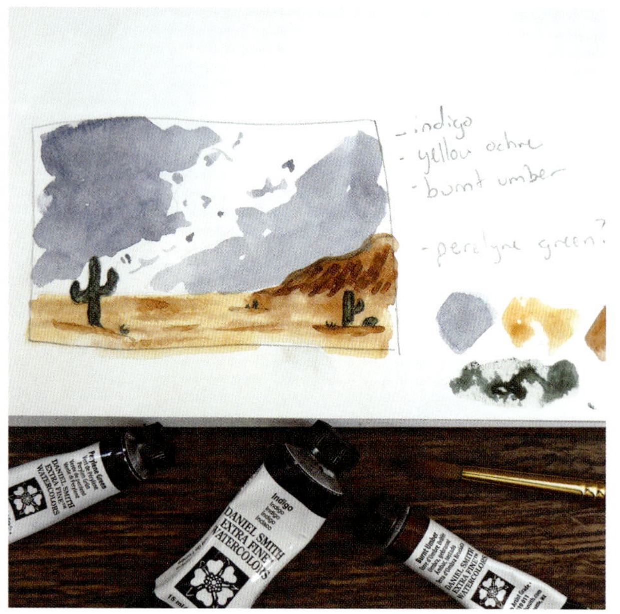

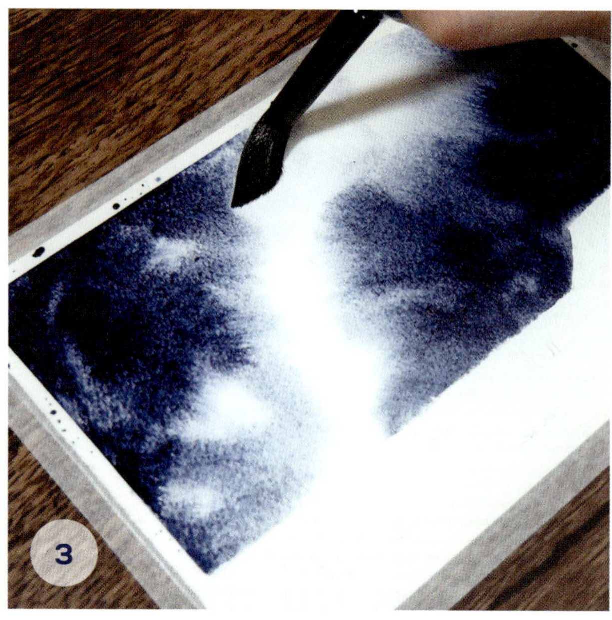

Composition Planning: A helpful tip for planning your composition is to quickly sketch it on a scrap sheet of paper. The reason I don't sketch out a galaxy's composition on the actual painting is because I don't want pencil lines to show up in the sky. But, if you're like me, having a plan in place makes me feel more confident going into my actual creation. For reference, I included the original composition thumbnail I drew in my sketchbook! Thumbnail sketches are also great for planning out colors, as you can see I did here.

STEP 3: BUILDING UP VALUES (LAYER 1)

Once you have the white portion of your galaxy outlined, we need to fill in the rest of our sky before our paper dries! Pick up some medium-value indigo with your size 12 round brush, and begin dropping in color, surrounding your outlined galaxy. Leave little portions of white space as you go (more white spaces closer to the galaxy and less as you move farther from it). This adds variety, interest and texture. The more variety and texture you can add to your galaxy, the more visually complex and pleasing it will be.

As you move toward the corners of your paper, add more pigment to your indigo until you're working with a dark value. The darkest portions of your sky should be in the corners of your paper, while the brightest should be near your galaxy. The darker corners and brighter galaxy center will draw the eyes of our viewer into the painting.

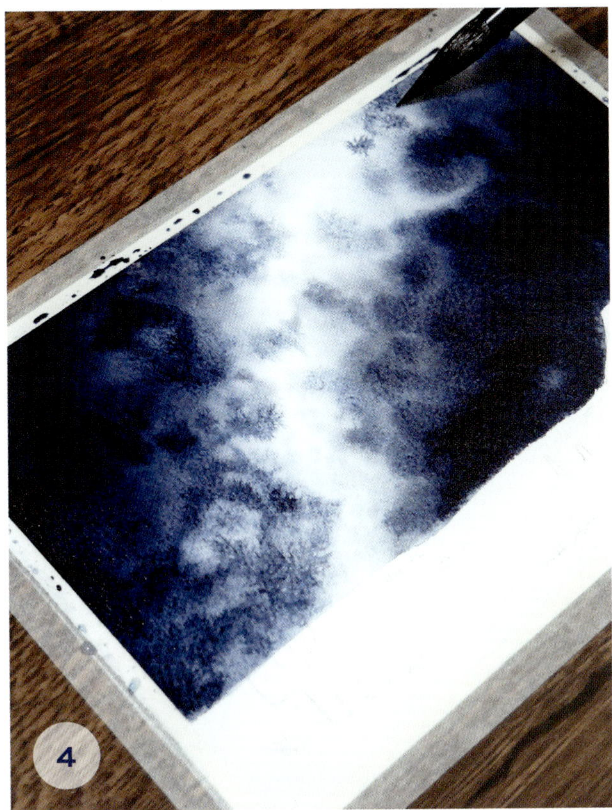

Before your paper dries fully, clean off your brush, dab it on your paper towel to make it thirsty and return to your painting. Lift a few areas of paint to create some highlights and additional white luminescent areas. You can also do this if you feel your indigo paint has encroached too closely to the white portion of your galaxy.

Let dry.

No worries if your galaxy doesn't look how you envisioned right now! My first layer of a galaxy always tends to look like a mess. You'll need at least one more layer before the pieces start to fall into place. Trust the process and continue on!

STEP 4: CREATING LUMINOSITY (LAYER 2)

For your second wash, wet the entire sky portion of your paper again with clean water. Once your sky is wet, pick up some light- to medium-value indigo, and begin dropping in color near and within the white luminescent section. For the most part, let the paint spread out naturally, but feel free to add a few swoopy, loose brushstrokes here and there. Then, repeat the steps of the first wash, darkening the value of your indigo as you move away from the white luminescent portion of your galaxy. You can even drop in some medium- or dark-value indigo into your white section, letting the pigments spread to mimic the dark dust portions of our Milky Way galaxy.

This second wash is all about adding textures and building upon what's already there. So, my best suggestion is to play with the paints! Add in some indigo, drop in some clean water to push the wet pigments around, lift some of those pigments with a thirsty brush to create highlights—play! Painting galaxies with watercolor requires purposeful playfulness. Don't be afraid to make some mistakes here and there. You can always lift up mistakes with a paper towel or thirsty brush.

I used two layers for this galaxy, but if your sky still isn't where you want it, wait for it to dry and add another layer of indigo, repeating the same process. For most of my galaxy pieces, I add between two and four layers, depending on the level of complexity I wish to achieve. There isn't necessarily a wrong answer for how many layers you can use, but always stop and evaluate how your painting looks in between each layer.

Let your sky dry completely before moving on.

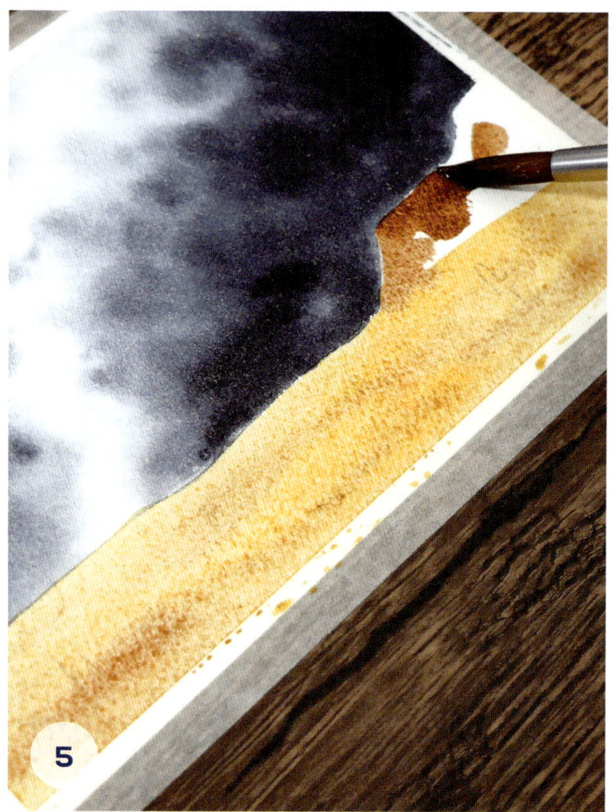

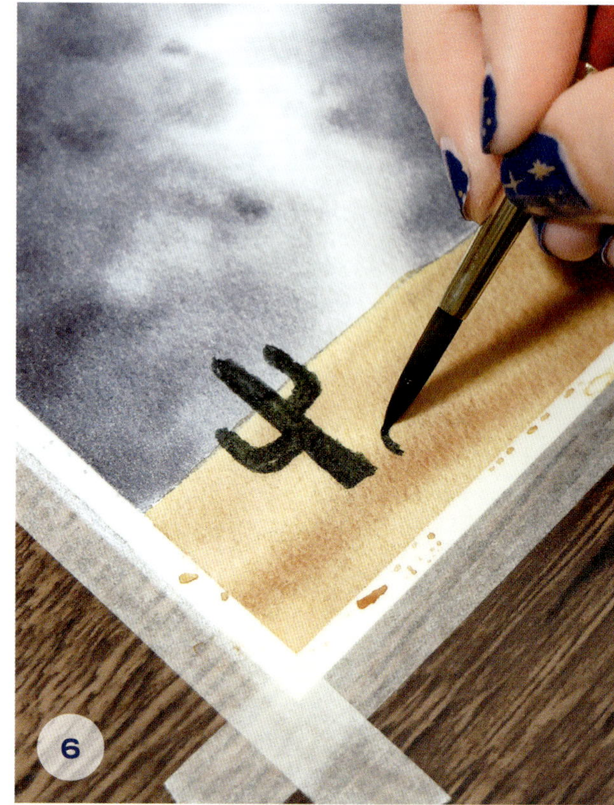

STEP 5: THE DESERT

For creating our desert sand and rocks, we'll need a base layer of yellow ochre and burnt umber. So, using your size 10 round brush, apply a wash of medium-value yellow ochre across your desert portion. Mix in some strokes of medium-value burnt umber, too, letting the paints mix naturally as you stroke them across the paper.

For the rock formation in the distance, load up your brush with some medium-value burnt umber, and apply it to that section. Ideally, your yellow ochre wash should still be wet, as we want the color of the rock formation to blend into the desert.

Let this wash dry and then move on.

STEP 6: THE CACTI

Time to add some life to this barren landscape! Using a size 6 (or smaller) round brush, pick up some dark-value perylene green, and begin painting cacti. Add in one or two cacti with arms closer to the foreground of your painting, as well as a few smaller, circular/ball-shaped cacti nearby. Additionally, you can add in a few scrubs of grass with the tip of your brush near your cacti.

Continue adding in a few cacti in the middle ground, adjusting the size and color value according to how far away from the viewer they are. The cacti closest to your viewer should be the most saturated in color, while the cacti farther away will be of a lighter-value perylene green.

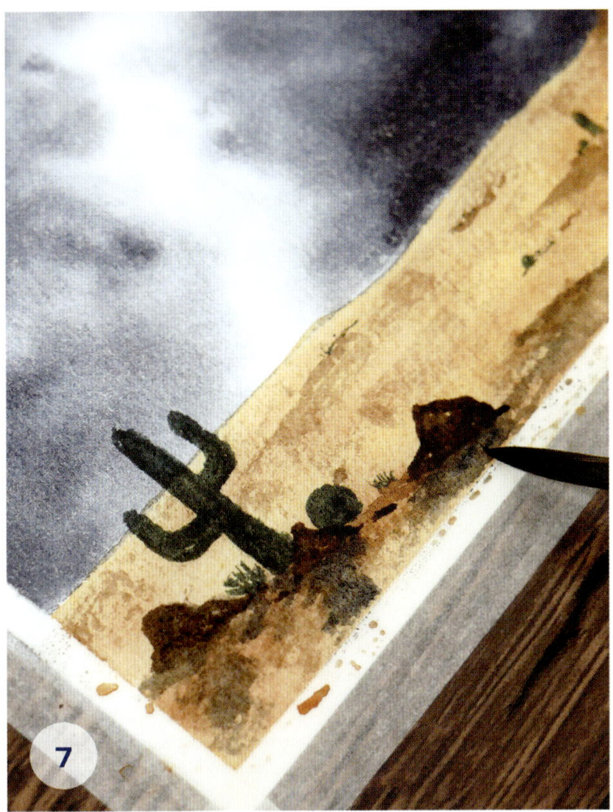

STEP 7: THE ROCKS & TEXTURES

While these cacti are drying, we can shift our attention to adding rocks and other details. For example, our rock formation in the distance could use some more interesting textures. Clean off the same brush, and pick up some dark-value burnt umber. Paint in some skinny, diagonal lines in the rock face to suggest rocky slopes, as well as horizontal, dry brushstrokes along the base to ground it.

Then, using a similar value of burnt umber, add in a few rocks near your cacti. The rocks should be angular in shape but fairly flat on the bottom. This suggests they're rising out of the sandy ground below.

Next, add some texture to your desert landscape by using the dry-brushing technique (see page 46 for more information). Again, apply medium and dark values of burnt umber with the dry-brushing technique in horizontal strokes across your desert, paying special attention to the strokes beneath your cacti. The strokes beneath your cacti can have more paint and be of a darker value—doing so will help ground the cacti, as well as provide some shadows.

Following that, add in a few more rocks to the bottom left-hand corner of your painting, where the nearest cacti is to the viewer. Use a dark-value burnt umber or, even better, mix a touch of indigo into your burnt umber, creating a shade of dark brown (similar to the color Barn Wood). This dark shade of brown will make your rocks appear shadowed, which, in this case, makes sense, since it's nighttime!

Another tip for realism is to paint some of those rocks in front of your cacti. It's a small detail but something that can make your painting stand out. If you place every single rock along the same line, it tends to look unrealistic and flat. Placing overlapping objects within your painting adds a touch of three dimension that can make a huge difference in the overall presentation.

Lastly, pick up some medium-value Neutral Gray, and add some more dry brushstrokes below these dark rocks and cacti to create additional shadows.

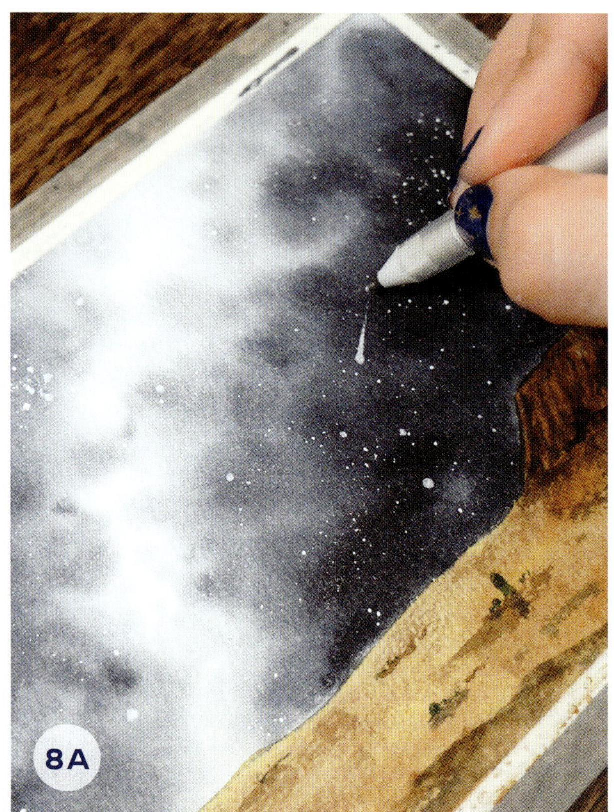

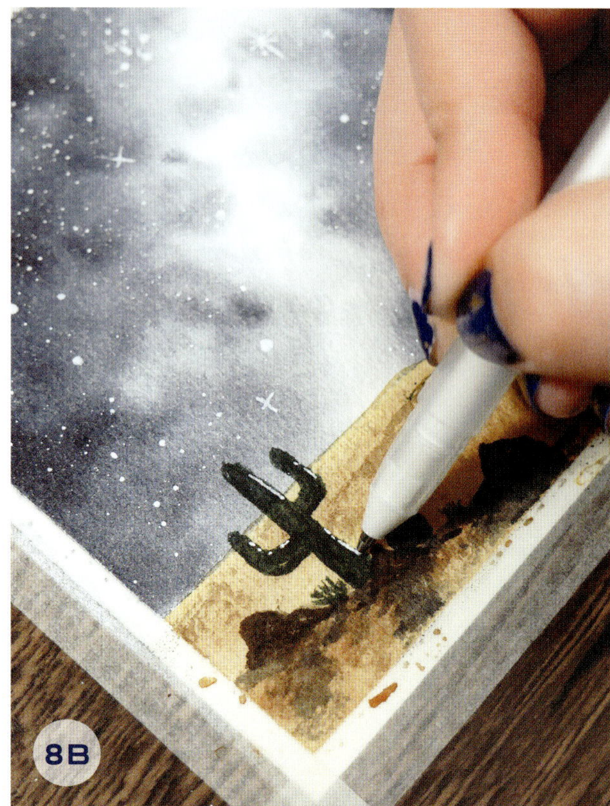

STEP 8: THE STARS & FINAL DETAILS

The final step for a galaxy painting is nearly always what ties the entire thing together: the stars. In my experience, even a galaxy that I'm feeling unsure about always looks better after the addition of stars. For the stars, use the spatter technique discussed on page 58 and white gouache, with your size 2 brush.

Once you have a random spatter of stars across your galaxy, wait for them to dry completely before adding in further details.

One of the things that brings a lot of magic to a galaxy painting is a shooting star! For a shooting star, create a small dot with your white gel pen. Then, quickly swipe your pen up at a diagonal angle. The key here is to be fast with your movement. That speed is what will create the tapered edge of the shooting star.

My suggestion is to practice a few of these on a scrap sheet before adding them to the painting —that way you can get a feel for it.

I always create a few additional stars with my gel pen, too, making them a bit larger than the stars I created with the splatter technique. I do this for further variety. After all, some stars are a lot larger in the sky than others. Also, with my white gel pen, I'll draw in a few twinkling stars. These are simply a circle with either a cross through it or compass-like lines for extra twinkle. Some smaller twinkles/sparkles don't need a dot in the middle, so add in some small "X" marks or "+" marks scattered across the sky too.

For some last highlights, add a touch of white along the edges of your cacti and rocks, demonstrating the light of the starry sky reflecting off these surfaces.

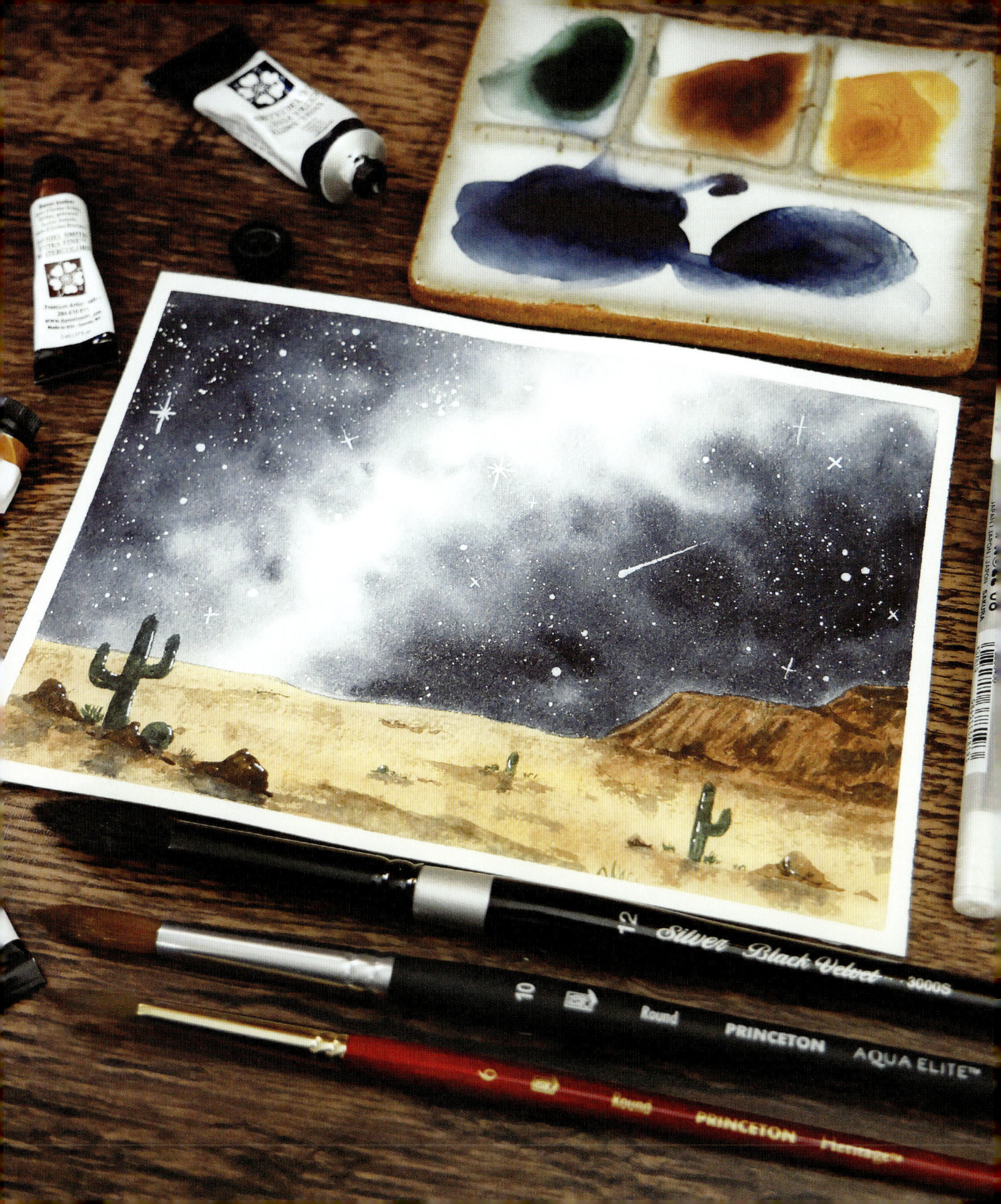
12 Silver Black Velvet 3000S
10 Round PRINCETON AQUA ELITE
Round PRINCETON Heritage

NIGHTTIME IN THE TOWERING FOREST

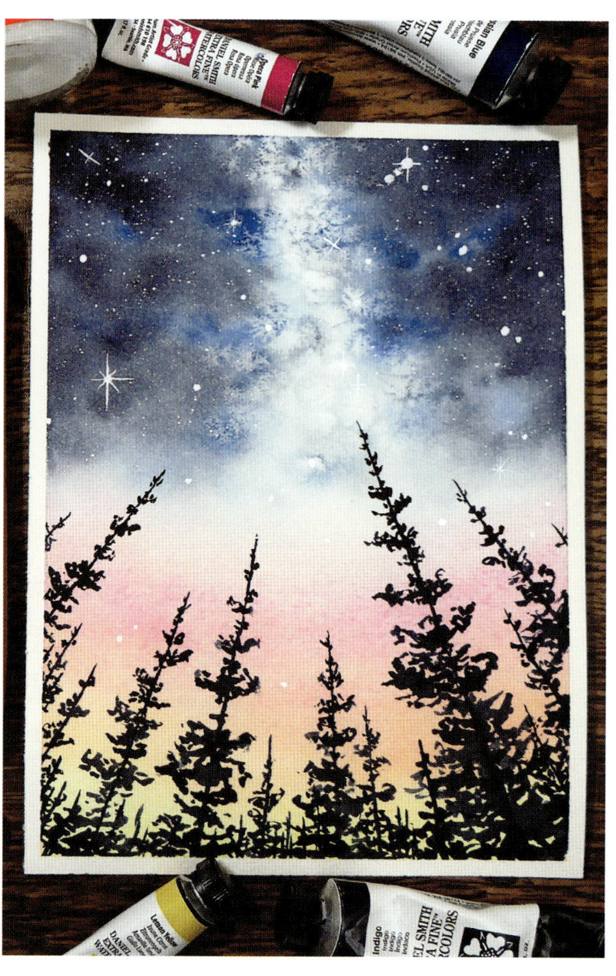

The sun has disappeared beneath the horizon, leaving brilliant colors in its wake as night slowly spreads. You take a moment to breathe, glance up and view the magic above the towering pines. In this painting, let's discover how the use of rock salt can add incredible texture to our galaxy sky.

MATERIALS

Paints: lemon yellow, pyrrol orange, opera pink, Prussian blue and indigo

Brushes: sizes 12 and 2 round

Paper: 5 x 7-inch (13 x 18-cm) cold-pressed watercolor paper

Painter's tape (or washi tape)

Paper towels (or a rag)

Ruler

Pencil and kneaded eraser

White gouache and/or white gel pen

Rock or kosher salt

SWATCHES

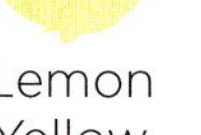

Lemon Yellow

Pyrrol Orange

Opera Pink

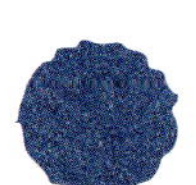

Prussian Blue

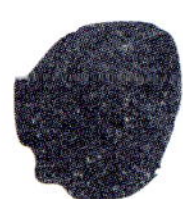

Indigo

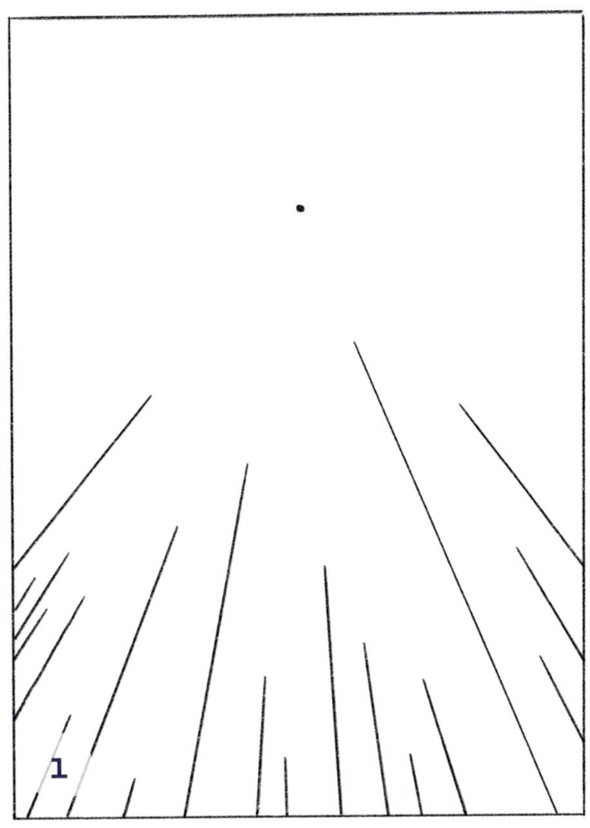

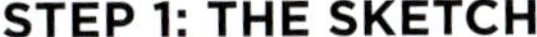

STEP 1: THE SKETCH

Like the project Misty Lavender Field (page 107), we'll be employing the use of one-point perspective in this painting to make it appear like the pine trees are towering overhead. I love using perspective in pieces like this because, when viewing the piece, it feels as though I've stepped into the painting.

For this sketch, place your vanishing point in the center of your paper, about one-third of the way down from the top. For a more severe perspective, place the point lower; for a less severe perspective, place the point higher on the paper.

Then, using a ruler, draw in straight lines of various sizes, the "skeletons" for your future pine trees. Make sure your ruler passes through the vanishing point every time you draw a line.

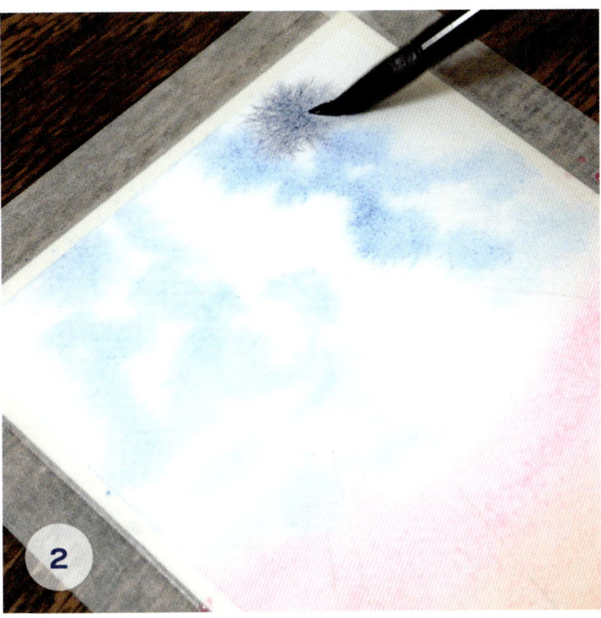

Once your sketch is complete, you can lighten your pencil marks with a kneaded eraser if need be, but, for this piece, I suggest leaving the marks a bit darker than other projects in this book. We'll need to be able to see these pencil marks to paint our pine trees in the correct perspective.

STEP 2: THE FIRST LAYER

For this piece, we'll be combining a gradient sunset and a galaxy sky, all using the wet-on-wet technique and strategic layering.

That said, start off by wetting the entire paper with clean water. Once glistening, use your size 12 round brush to apply a sunset gradient, starting with lemon yellow on the bottom, pyrrol orange in the middle and opera pink on the top. My suggestion is to use light or medium values for all three colors, as we'll be adding saturation with each layer. This three-color gradient should stop about halfway up the paper.

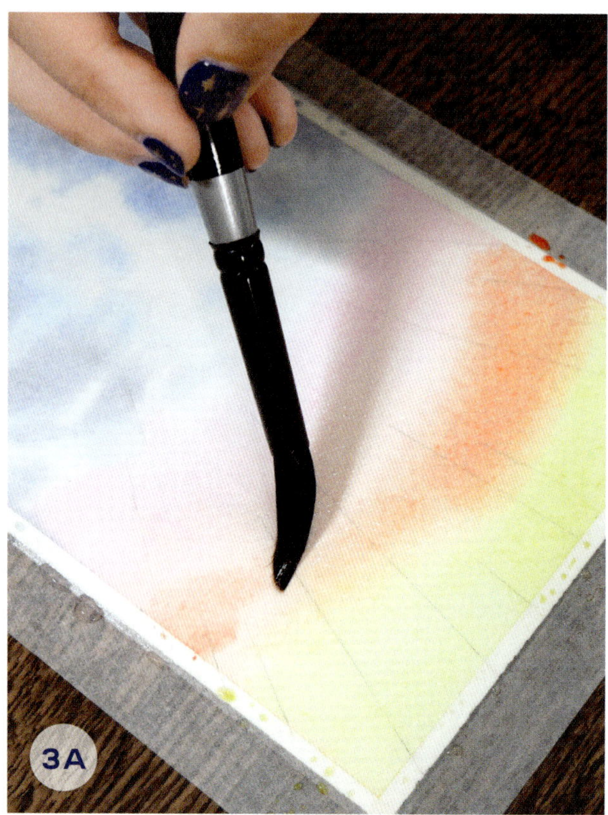

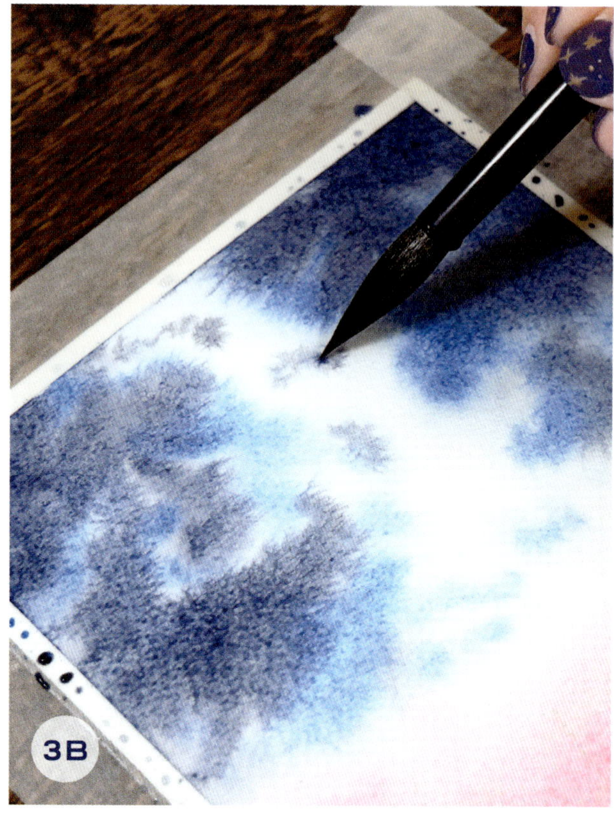

Then, starting from the top of the paper, let's outline the white portion of our galaxy. Using the same brush, apply light-value Prussian blue to the paper with loose strokes, leaving plenty of white space in the middle of the paper and in between strokes. We'll need that white space to create luminosity. Then, clean off your brush, and apply light-value indigo surrounding and in between your Prussian blue. Like in the project Milky Way Over the Desert (page 124), the use of indigo surrounding our galaxy and in the corners of our painting creates depth.

Another key here is to leave a portion of white space just above the opera pink. This prevents the opera pink and Prussian blue from mixing too much and creates an additional glow that our galaxy rises out of.

Let this layer dry completely, and then move on to the next step.

STEP 3: THE SECOND & THIRD LAYERS

Because of watercolor's transparency, the key to creating vibrancy and depth in galaxies is the use of multiple layers. So, let's repeat the steps of the first layer. Rewet the entire paper, and add the same colors in the same spots.

In the galaxy sky, paint in more Prussian blue and indigo, increasing the values. Drop in some Prussian blue and indigo in the white portion of your galaxy sky, replicating the dust of the Milky Way band.

Let this layer dry completely. Then, repeat the entire process again for a third time. Once you've painted your third layer, move on to the next step before your paper dries!

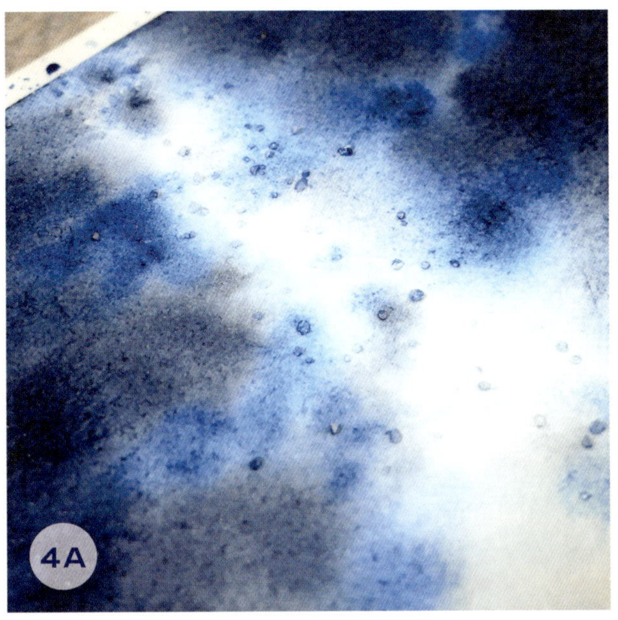

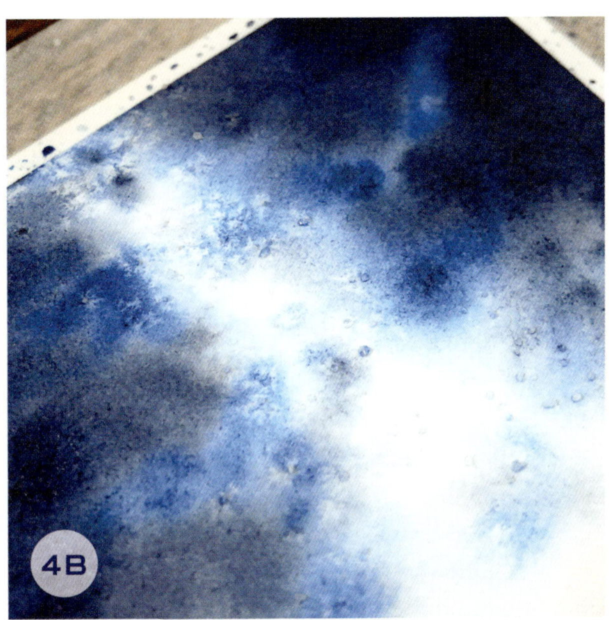

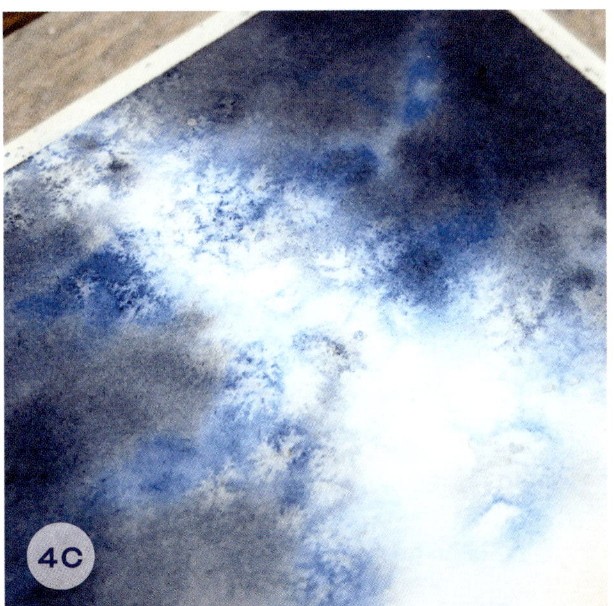

STEP 4: THE SALT

Salt reacts rather uniquely to watercolor paint and creates textures perfect for galaxies! While your paper is still wet, drop in a few pieces of rock or kosher salt in the white section of your galaxy, and sit back and watch the magic! Don't remove the salt until your paper has completely dried.

Salt acts as a "resist" of sorts, pushing the pigments away to create a lighter spot around the salt grain. Different sizes of salt will create different effects, so feel free to experiment with table salt, sea salt, kosher salt and more! Moreover, different paper textures will also impact the salt texture you achieve. When you paint on cold-pressed paper, the pigments fall into the rougher texture, and the paper almost acts like a sponge. When you paint on hot-pressed paper, the pigments tend to float on the surface for a longer period of time before absorbing into the paper. Due to this, the salt effect on hot-pressed paper will be lighter, with more paper showing, compared to the effect on cold-pressed or rough paper.

When your paper has dried completely, remove the salt by rubbing it away with your finger.

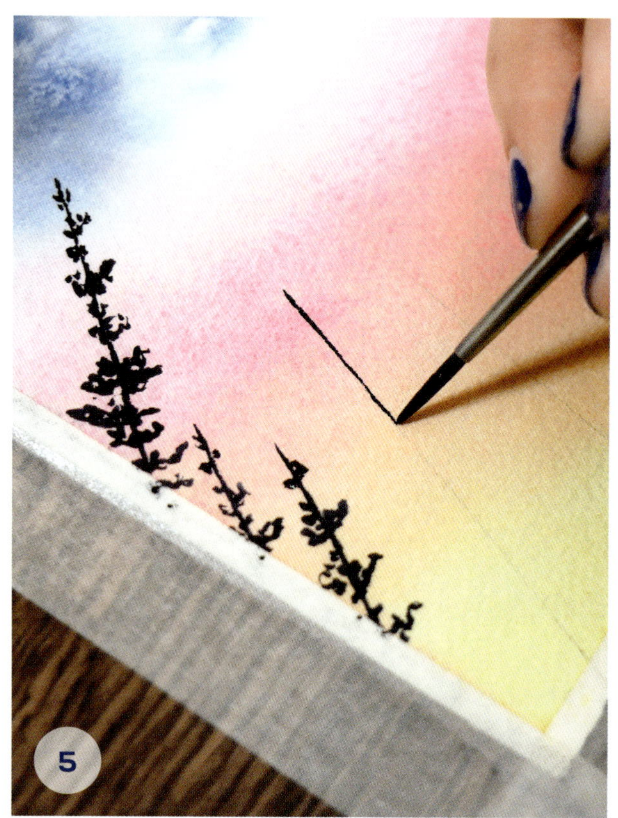

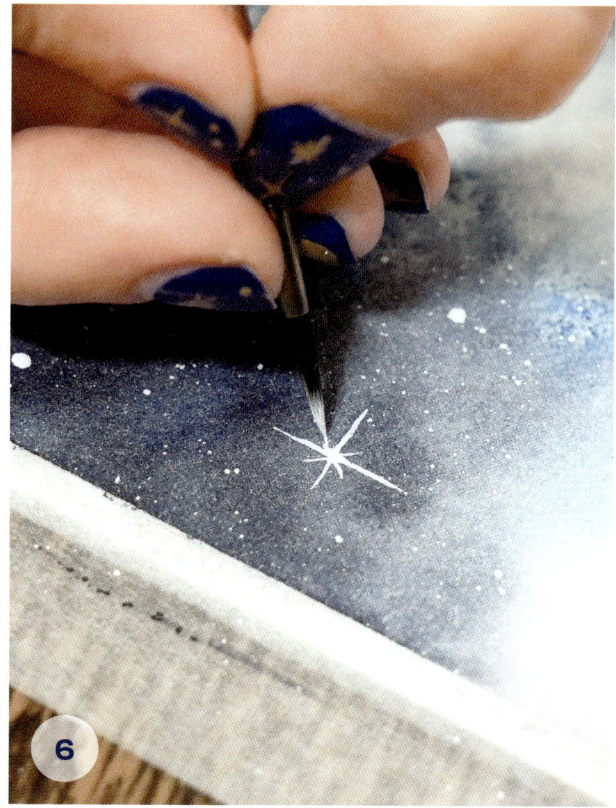

STEP 5: THE TREES

Time to add in our towering forest! Using your size 2 round brush, load up some dark-value indigo, and begin painting pines of various sizes using the blobby technique (see page 39). Make sure to follow your pencil marks from the beginning, as they should be visible beneath your sunset gradient. Following these sketches will ensure that you achieve the proper perspective.

STEP 6: THE STARS

The final step in any galaxy painting: Let's add in the stars! Cover up any portions of your piece where you don't want stars with scrap pieces of paper, and then use the spatter technique to add in your stars (for more information, see page 58).

Once you have a spattering of stars, load up your size 2 round brush with white gouache, and add in a few extra stars of varying sizes. In galaxy pieces where I've used salt, I love to add in a few stars in those light sections left behind by the salt grains. The texture surrounding the white dot from the salt makes it look as though it's glowing. Additionally, add in a few twinkling stars as well! For realistic-looking stars, make sure your "compass lines" are of varying lengths. I also added in a couple of stars within the sunset gradient—these are brighter stars in the sky that can shine through the fading light of the sun.

DANCING NORTHERN LIGHTS

Aurora borealis, or the northern lights, is proof that magic exists on earth. I believe this is one of the phenomena that comes to mind when people think of dazzling night skies. I certainly do! It's a dream of mine to see the northern lights in person one day, but, for now, I'll have to settle with recreating the magic with watercolors. To paint this, we'll rely on the wet-on-wet technique to create soft blends in between colors and strategic paint strokes to illustrate depth.

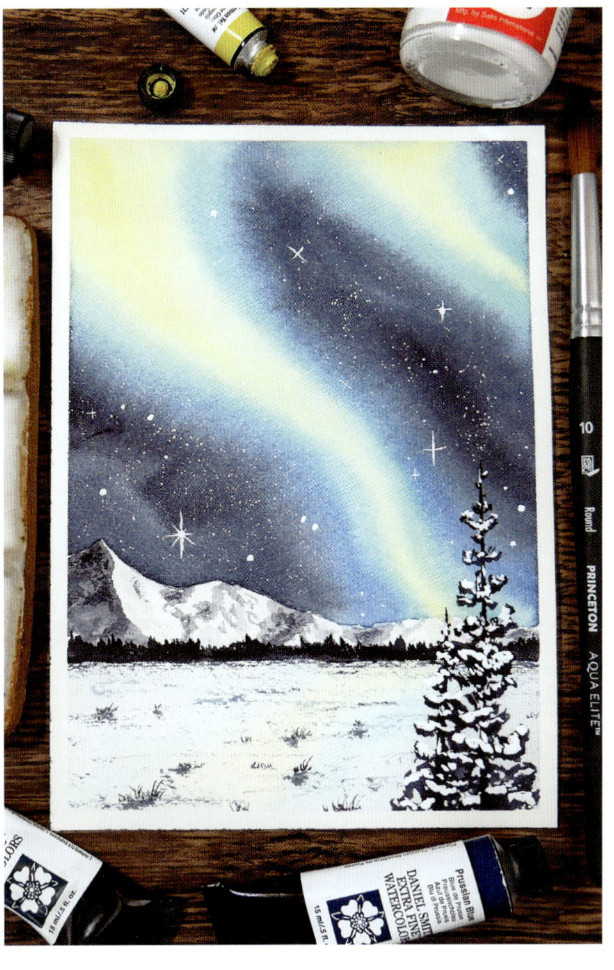

MATERIALS

Paints: lemon yellow, phthalo turquoise, Prussian blue and indigo

Brushes: sizes 10, 6 and 2 round

Paper: 5 x 7–inch (13 x 18–cm) cold-pressed watercolor paper

Painter's tape (or washi tape)

Paper towels (or a rag)

Pencil and kneaded eraser

White gouache and/or white gel pen

SWATCHES

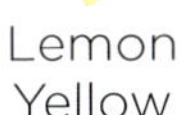
Lemon Yellow

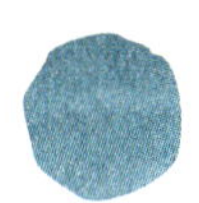
Phthalo Turquoise

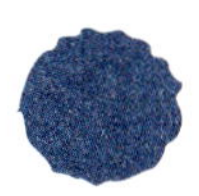
Prussian Blue

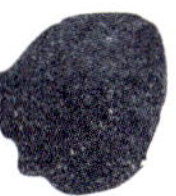
Indigo

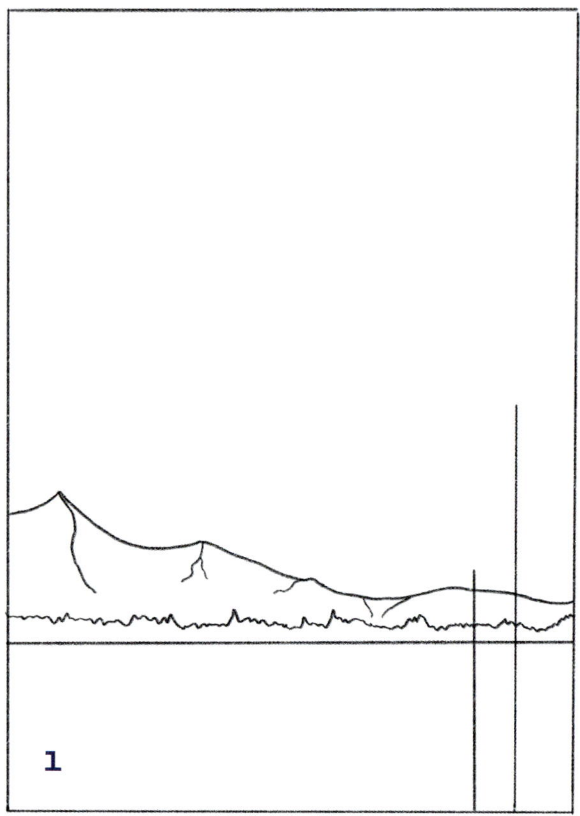

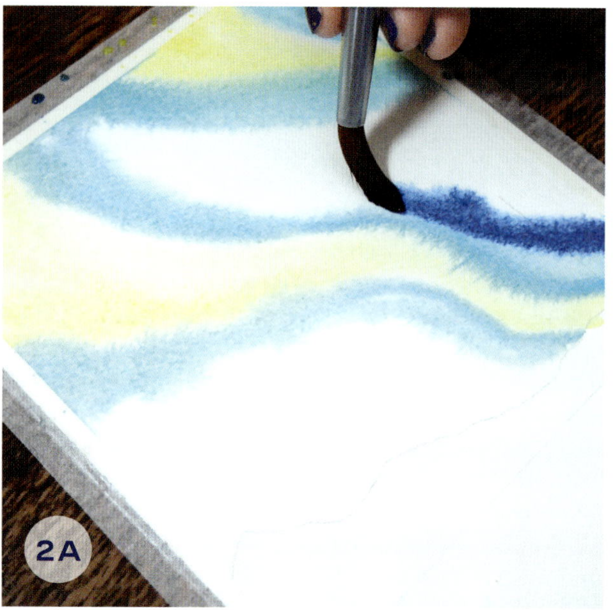

STEP 1: THE SKETCH

Our sketch for this piece is very simple. We're just going to outline the mountains, the snowy field and a place for a few pine trees.

STEP 2: THE NORTHERN LIGHTS

Watercolors are a perfect medium for painting the northern lights. Their transparency allows us to build up vibrancy and depth, and the wet-on-wet technique creates soft, natural blends between the colors.

So, let's begin with our first wash. Wet the entire sky portion of your paper with clean water. Grab your size 10 round brush, and load it up with medium-value lemon yellow.

Then, starting directly above your mountains in the bottom right-hand corner, paint a stroke of lemon yellow, extending it all the way up across your page into the top left-hand corner. This stroke should curve and bend, as if it's dancing. Don't paint a straight line! As with our Milky Way Over the Desert project (page 124), we need to create the illusion of depth here. So, your stroke of yellow closer to the mountains should be thinner and then become wider as it moves up the paper.

Add in another stroke of lemon yellow in the top right-hand corner, applying the same principles of depth here too. The northern lights should look as though they're getting larger as they get closer to the viewer. Once you've applied your lemon yellow, clean off your brush, and pick up some light-value phthalo turquoise. Paint the phthalo turquoise along the outsides of your lemon yellow, letting the pigments naturally mix on the wet paper. If you wish to smooth out the boundaries further, you can take a clean, slightly damp brush and run it along the edges where the two colors meet.

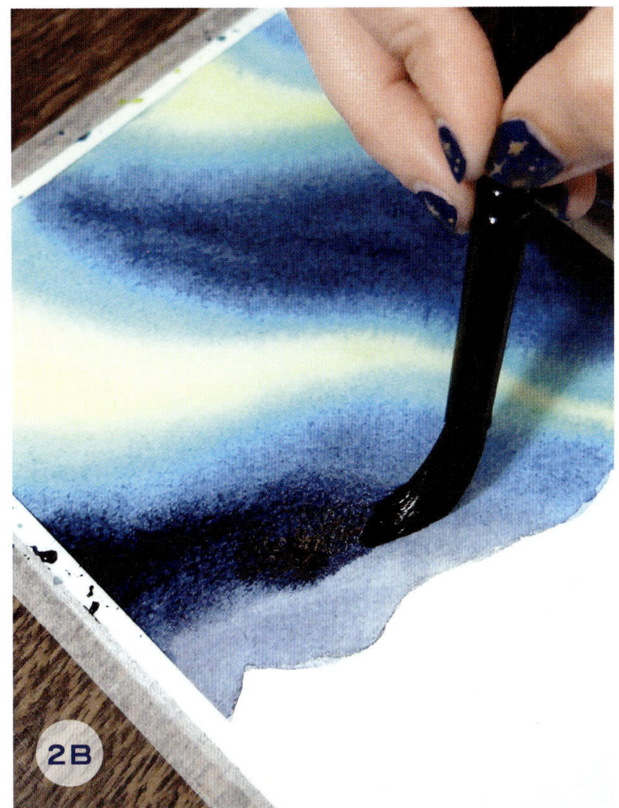

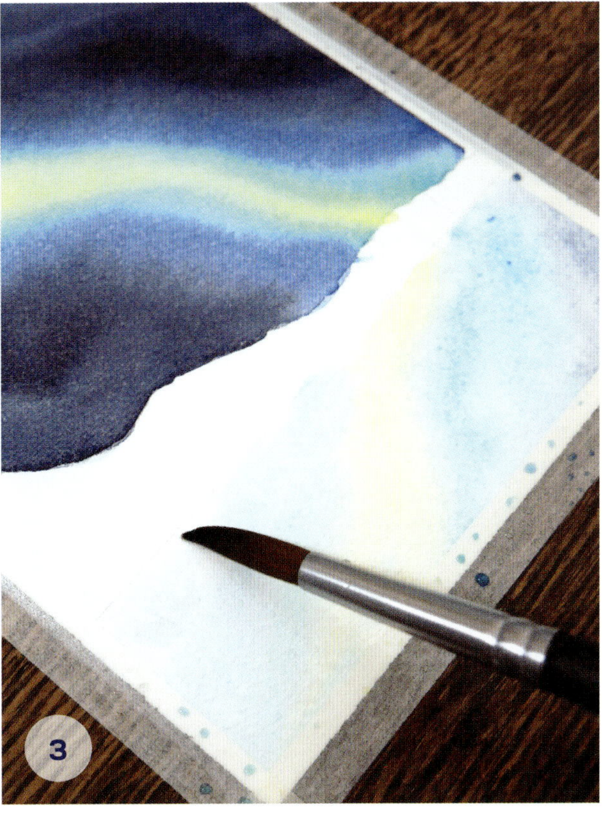

Once you've added phthalo turquoise, clean off your brush and add the next color: medium-value Prussian blue. Again, let those pigments mix together on the wet paper, smoothing out the blend with a clean, damp brush if needed. Lastly, use a medium-value indigo to fill in the rest of the sky. Once dry, the colors will appear soft and blended.

Let this layer dry completely.

Let's intensify the saturation of our colors with a second wash of paint. Wet the entire sky portion of your paper again with clean water, applying clean water first to the yellow segments and then moving outward. This will keep your lemon yellow pure and vibrant. Once glistening again, repeat the steps of the first wash, using medium or dark values of the paints. Again, once satisfied, let the painting dry completely.

STEP 3: THE SNOWY FIELD

A field covered in snow like this one will more than likely reflect the colors of the northern lights above; therefore, we will need to paint a light wash of colors to show that. With a size 10 round brush, wet the entire snow field portion with clean water, and start adding in paints to reflect what you've done in the sky. Use the steps from painting the northern lights, starting with a light-value lemon yellow and then surrounding that with light-value phthalo turquoise, light-value Prussian blue and, lastly, light-value indigo.

This layer should not be too saturated with color, as snow's reflection capabilities only go so far. Let dry and then move on to painting the mountains.

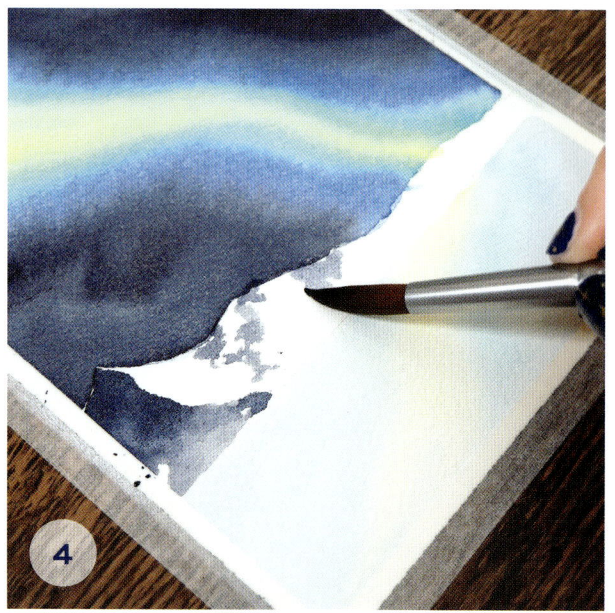

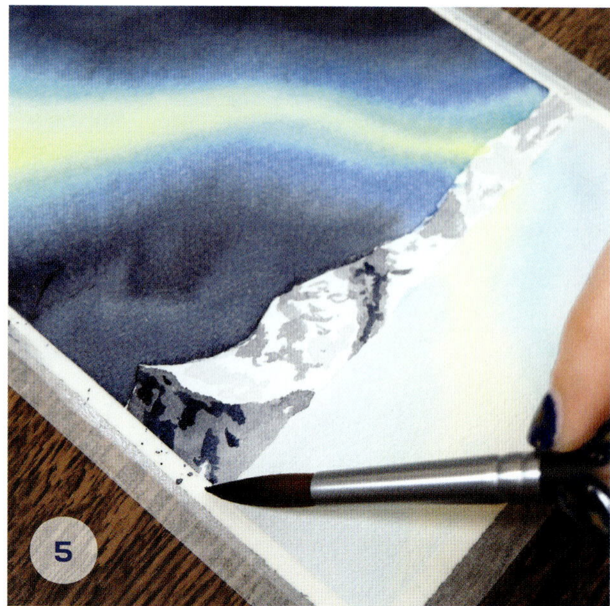

STEP 4: THE MOUNTAINS (LAYER 1)

It's time to give our northern lights something to shine over, specifically a mountain range. Unlike in previous projects where we simply used a flat wash to paint our mountains, we're going to create snow-covered peaks with rocky outcrops. Staying in tune with watercolor painting, we'll be breaking things down into multiple layers.

Let's begin by adding a few washes of light-value indigo, demonstrating the shadows of the distant mountains. In the mountain on the left, add a wash of indigo that bisects it completely. This will create a shadowed side of the mountain, the side facing away from the northern lights high above the mountain range. From there, work your way across the range, adding shadows of various sizes and shapes as you go. You can even vary the value of your indigo wash, adding a very light mix in brighter areas and a darker mix where you would imagine shadows or a rock face to be.

Let these shadows dry.

STEP 5: THE MOUNTAINS (LAYER 2)

In this next layer, use a darker-value indigo wash, and apply more shapes within the shadows you've already created. Additionally, this is a great place for using the dry-brushing technique (see page 46), as the textures dry brushing can create make for fantastic rocky outcrops.

Since these mountains are far off in the distance, you don't need to add a ton of details. Rather, you simply need to suggest where the rocky outcrops and shadows are.

When I first began watercolor painting, mountains were a scary subject for me. I didn't believe I could correctly place the shadows and would constantly overthink every single brushstroke. But I'll let you in on a little secret: There are no right or wrong answers to painting mountains. Nature is wild and unorganized. Your lines don't need to be perfect; your shadows don't always need to make sense. Mountains were carved by the wind, forced upward from the ground over thousands of years. They are untamed and unruly. It's okay for your paint strokes to reflect that.

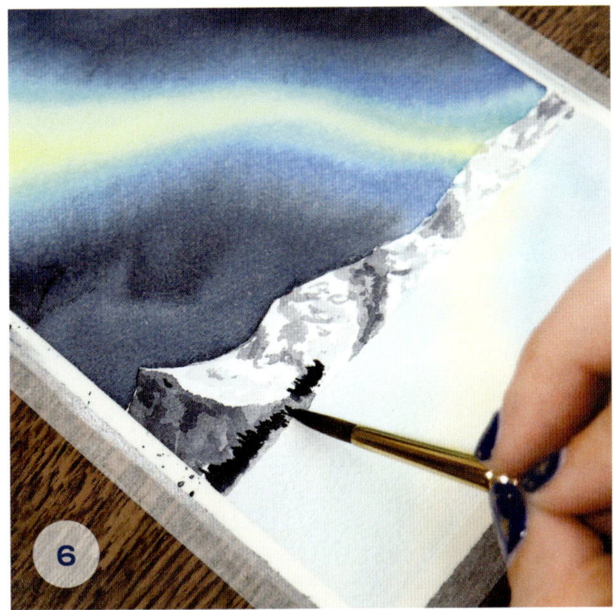

My best advice for painting mountains is to simply try it. Tackle the subject head-on but with a curious mind. And when you're done, identify what you like and what you don't like, and then carry that knowledge with you into your next painting.

STEP 6: THE DISTANT FOREST & SNOWY DETAILS

Once your mountain range is dry, let's add in some more details. Use your size 6 round brush to pick up some dark-value indigo. Using the pointed tip of the round brush, add in a distant line of trees along the base of the mountain. This line of trees should stretch across the entire paper.

Once you've completed your distant forest, clean off your brush, and pick up some light-value phthalo turquoise. Using the dry brush technique, let's add some textures to our snow field. Swipe your brush horizontally to create said textures.

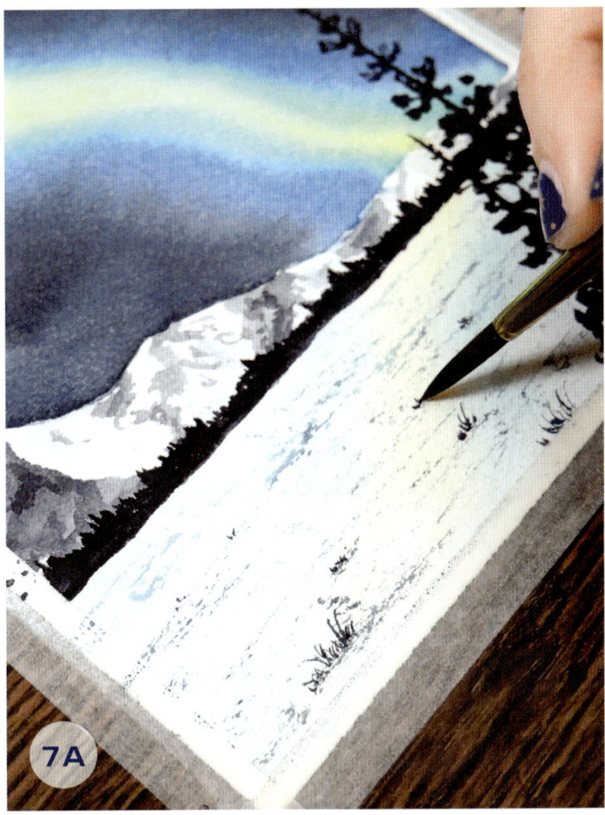

Clean off your brush, and then pick up some light-value indigo, repeating the same horizontal dry brushstrokes.

Let dry.

STEP 7: THE SNOWY PINE TREES & GRASS

Our snowy scene wouldn't be complete without some snow-covered pines! Load up your size 6 round brush with dark-value indigo and, using the blobby technique on page 39, paint in the two pine trees we outlined in our pencil sketch. While you're waiting for these two trees to dry, add in some various grass patches peeking up through the snowy field, also with dark-value indigo. With a wide-open field like this one, the wind is bound to blow some of the snow away, exposing the scraggily grass beneath.

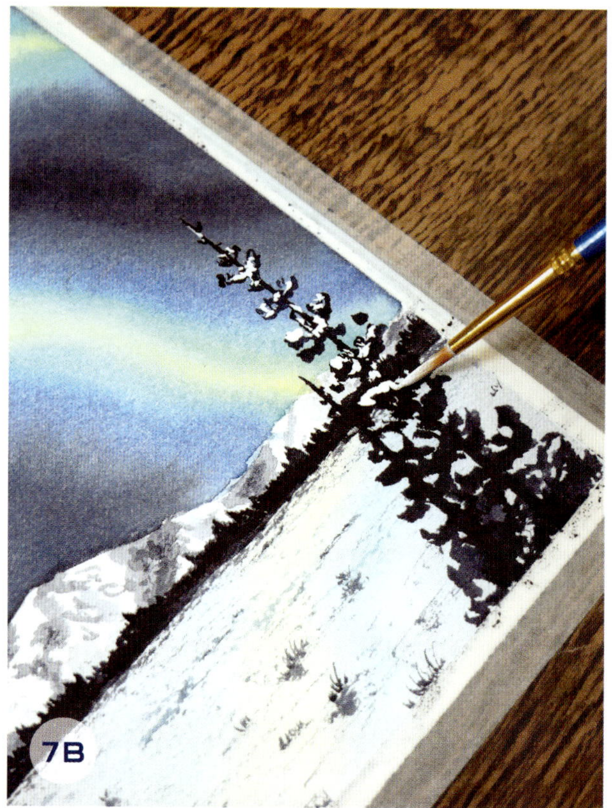

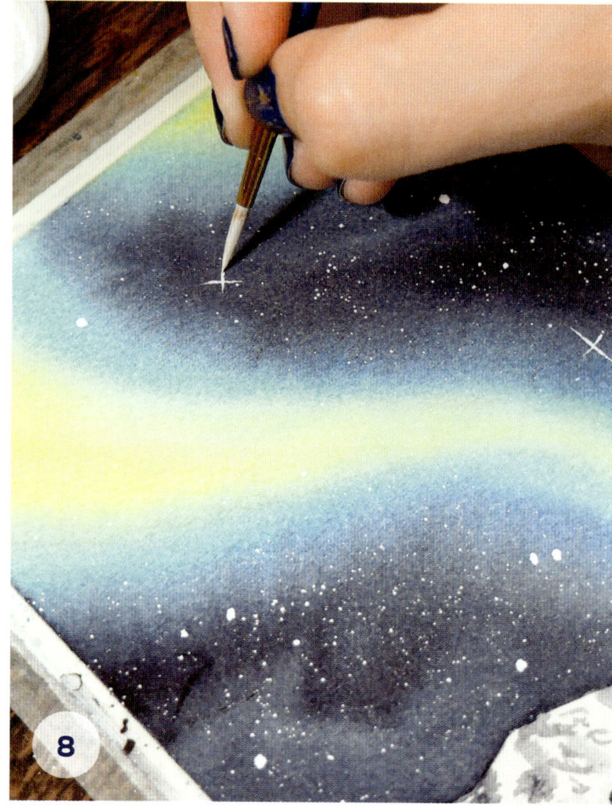

Once your pines are dry, load up some white gouache on a small brush (I used a size 2), and begin adding snow to the pine branches. To add realistic-looking snow, add white blobs on the top parts of the pine branches, as the snow would be sitting on top. Just like how we created the trees with random blobs, your snow should also reflect that.

STEP 8: THE STARS

Our night sky wouldn't be complete without a smatter of stars! Cover up the sections of your painting you don't want spattered with white gouache, and then begin using the spatter technique to add in your stars (see page 58). Don't forget to add in a few twinkling stars with your brush or white gel pen, too.

RISING FULL MOON

A warm ocean breeze caresses your hair, the sounds of calm waves breaking in the distance. The air is salty and tall grass tickles your skin as you step forward on the sandy path down to the beach. Glancing up, you see the full moon in all its glory, its light cutting through the darkness of night and reflecting off the ocean's surface. Let's capture the moon and its glow on paper using masking fluid and a circular gradient.

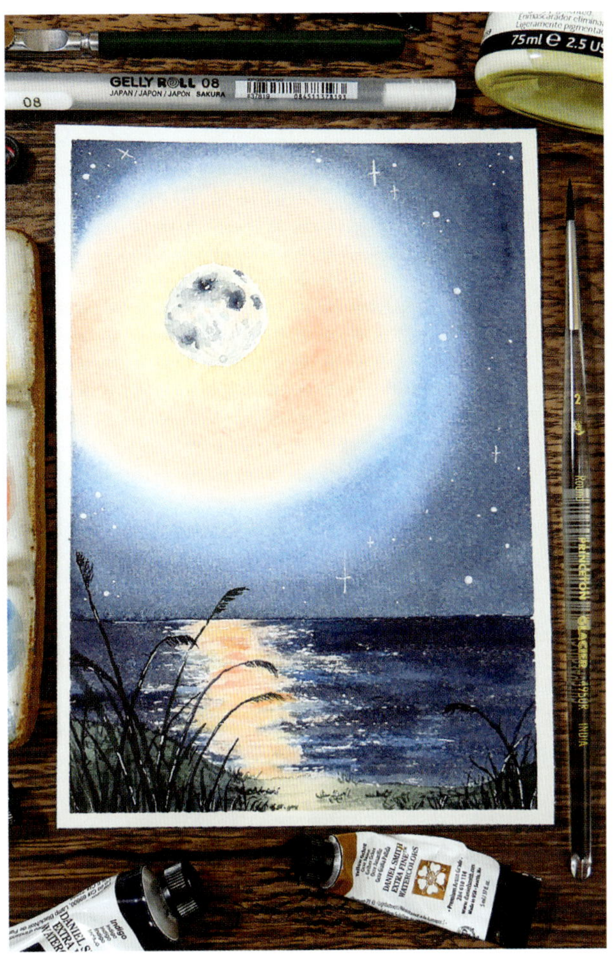

MATERIALS

Paints: yellow ochre, Pastel Orange (page 28), Prussian blue, indigo and perylene green

Brushes: sizes 12, 10 and 2 round and small liner

Paper: 5 x 7–inch (13 x 18–cm) cold-pressed watercolor paper

Painter's tape (or washi tape)

Paper towels (or a rag)

Ruler

Pencil and kneaded eraser

White gouache and/or white gel pen

Masking fluid and ruling pen (or another applicator)

A drawing compass, bottle cap or washi tape roll

Something to sketch a circle with

SWATCHES

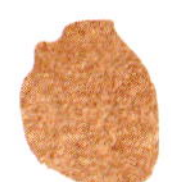
Yellow Ochre

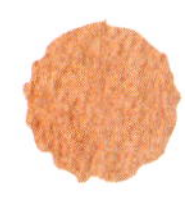
Pastel Orange (page 28)

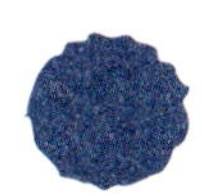
Prussian Blue

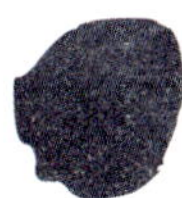
Indigo

Perylene Green

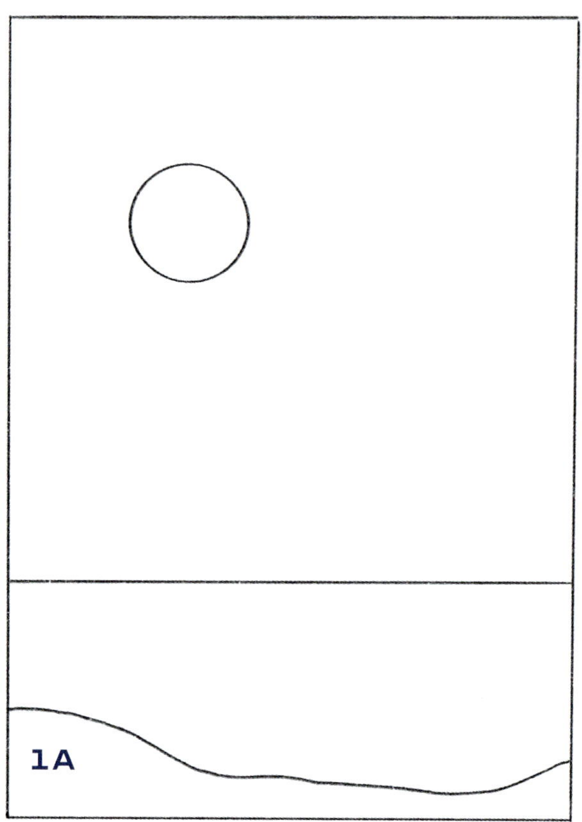

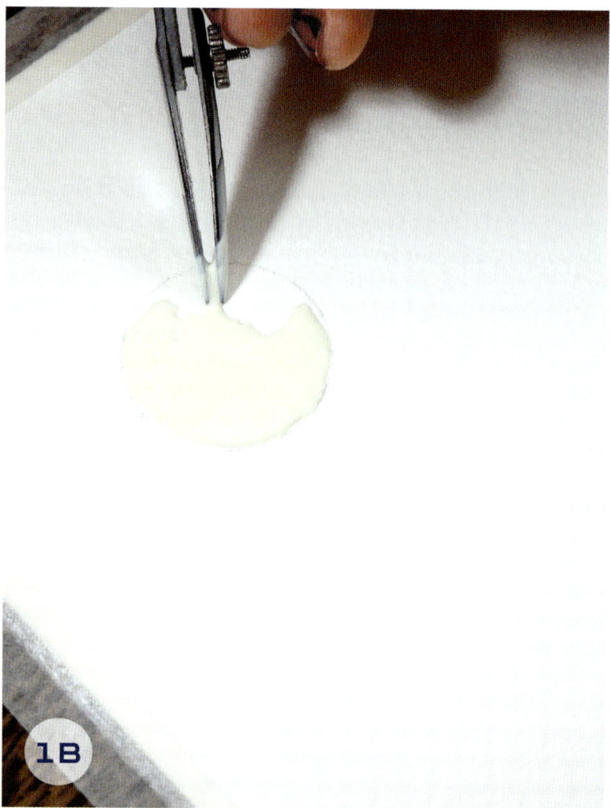

STEP 1: THE SKETCH & MASKING FLUID

Grab your ruler, and pencil in a horizon line about one-third up the paper from the bottom. From there, sketch in a small hill that dips down in the middle and rises back up closer to the edge of the paper. Now, grab whatever tool you'll use to sketch in your moon. You can use a variety of circular objects. In the past, I've used bottle caps or an old roll of washi tape, but my father recently gifted me his old set of drawing compasses. They're a fantastic and versatile tool and create perfect circles, so if you have access to one, try it out!

Once you're done with your sketch, use a kneaded eraser to lighten up your pencil marks. Since our moon will be light in color, you don't want dark, harsh pencil lines showing up.

Next, pick up your masking fluid, and begin applying it to your moon. Fill in the entire circle, as we want our moon to remain white. Later, we'll be applying details to our moon, but for the ease of keeping paint off of the area, we'll rely on our masking fluid (for more details on masking fluid, see page 22).

Let your masking fluid dry completely before you begin the next step. Make sure to test it by lightly touching your finger to the surface.

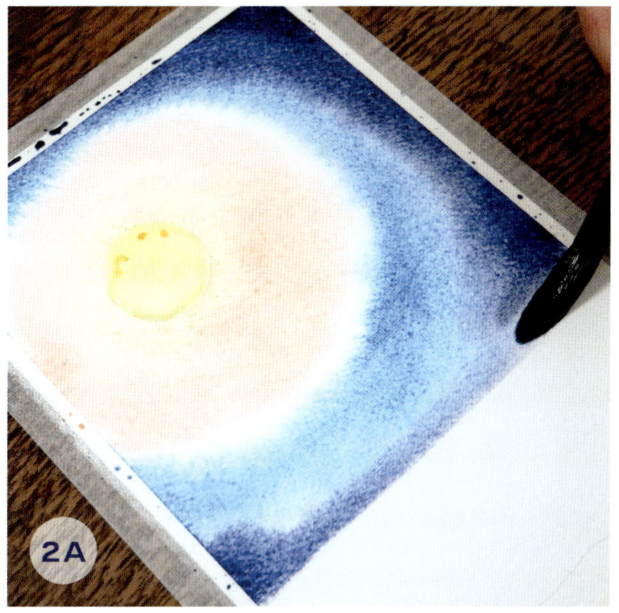

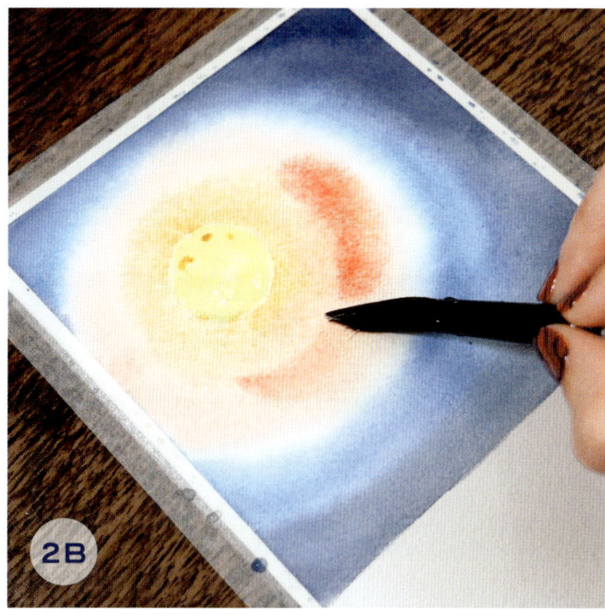

STEP 2: THE GLOWING SKY

In order to create the warm glow around the moon, we'll need to create a gradient of yellow ochre, Pastel Orange, Prussian blue and indigo.

Start out with wetting the entire sky portion of the paper with clean water. Then, load up your size 12 round brush with medium-value yellow ochre. Paint this yellow ochre around your moon. Since we covered our moon with masking fluid, there's no need to worry about avoiding it! You can paint right over the masking fluid with your paint and it will repel off.

Next, load up your brush with medium-value Pastel Orange, and repeat the same process, this time painting around the yellow ochre ring. Let the colors naturally blend into one another—their edges blurring and softening. Clean off your brush, and then load it up with medium-value Prussian blue. Unlike the yellow ochre and Pastel Orange, Prussian blue will not mix well with our warm tones.

That said, we can still create a gradient here, but you will need to be careful as you apply your paint. Paint your Prussian blue around the orange, keeping a small amount of the white of the paper in between. The pigments will naturally spread out, blurring into each other without drastically mixing and becoming muddy. If you want to soften and blend this edge further, run a clean, damp brush along the edge of the two colors. It's important not to overwork this area, otherwise you'll risk muddying the colors.

Lastly, use your brush to apply medium-value indigo around your Prussian blue circle. These two colors blend well due to being analogous in nature, so you don't need to worry about muddying them as you paint along the boundary.

Let this layer dry completely, and then repeat the same steps with a second wash to further saturate the colors. Start with yellow ochre, and then work your way outward until you finish up with indigo again.

Let dry and then reevaluate your colors to see if you wish to apply another layer or not. When you're ready and your paper is dry, move on to the next step.

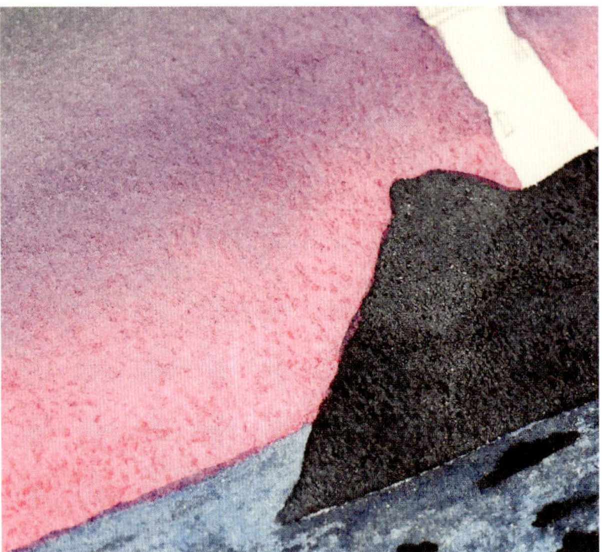

Granulation: Throughout this book, you may have noticed a few of your paints "granulating." Granulation in watercolors is the effect you get when pigment particles clump together rather than evenly spreading across the surface, creating an almost speckled texture. Generally, the finer the particles in the pigment, the less they granulate. For example, man-made pigments—which tend to be very fine and evenly sized, such as the pigments that make up phthalo turquoise—will create a very smooth wash. On the other hand, natural pigments, such as the ones that make up opera pink, will granulate. Pictured above is a photo from the project Sunset Shift at the Lighthouse (page 52), which features two granulating colors, opera pink and Payne's gray.

Many watercolorists use granulation to create added textures, such as rough bark on trees or rust on cars. If you want to see if your tube of paint will granulate, look up the color online. Many watercolor paint makers will indicate whether that specific color will granulate or not.

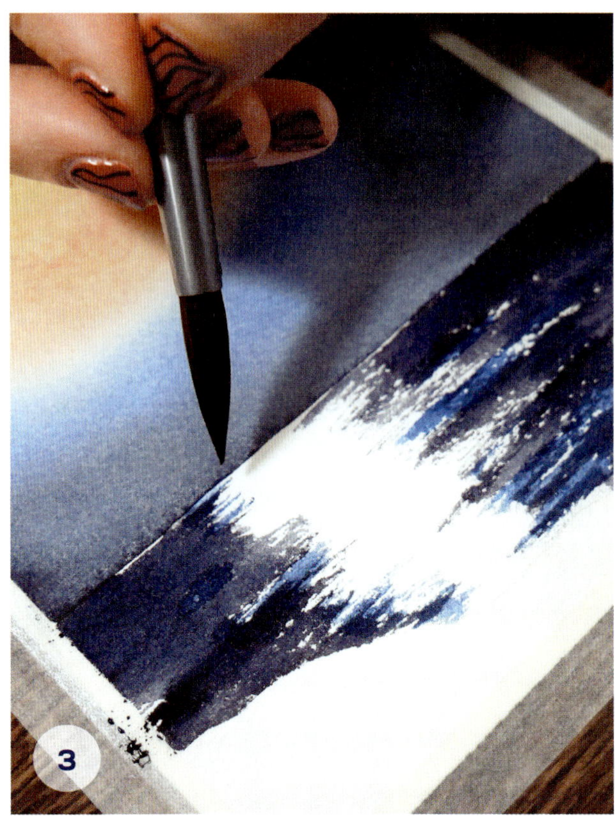

STEP 3: THE OCEAN

Unlike our glowing sky, the ocean in this painting is created via the dry-brushing technique (see page 46). Load up your size 10 round brush with dark-value indigo, and begin dry brushing in horizontal strokes. Because we want to add in the moon's glowing reflection in the water, we'll need to leave the portion below it white. This white portion should be uneven, with feathered edges, which is why the dry-brushing technique works so well for this.

For more color variety in the ocean, add in some additional dry brushstrokes of medium-value Prussian blue. Let the indigo and Prussian blue dry completely before moving on to the warmer colors.

Now, load up your brush with light-value yellow ochre, and fill in the white space you've created below the moon. Be careful not to touch the edges of your cool colors as you paint, otherwise they may reactivate and mix. It's okay to leave white space in between your colors because, in this case, the white sections will act as additional light reflections on the water's surface. Let the wash of yellow ochre dry, and then load up your brush with medium-value Pastel Orange. Apply this color in small, horizontal marks, mimicking the look of faraway waves. You can also add in small strokes of medium-value yellow ochre for additional variety.

Let dry.

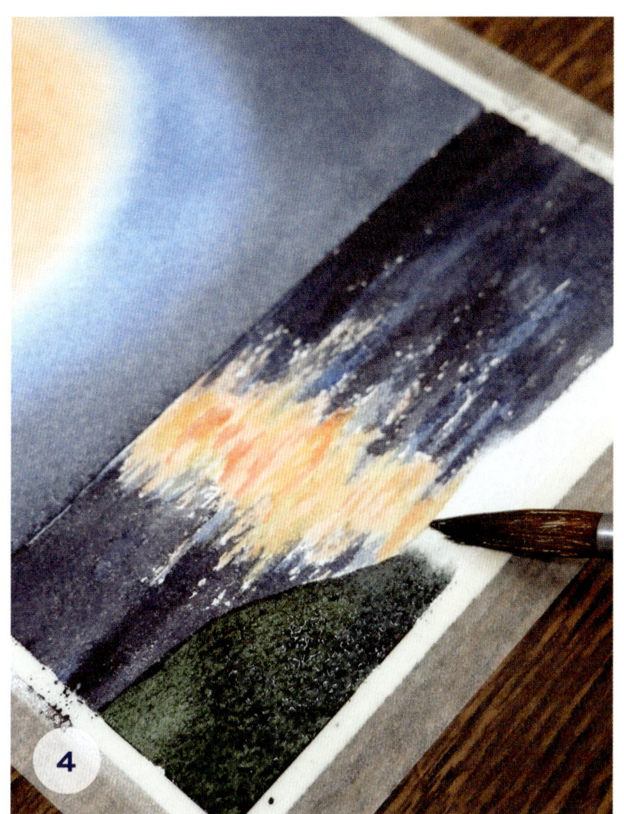

STEP 4: THE GRASSY HILL & SANDY PATH BASE WASH

Now, let's paint the grassy hill and sandy path down to the ocean, the foreground. Load up your brush with dark-value perylene green, and begin painting a wash of it, starting on the left-hand side of your paper. Once you reach approximately the middle, clean off your brush, and then apply clean water to the edge of your still-wet perylene green. This will soften the edge of the pigment, allowing us to then apply a wash of light-value yellow ochre without the pigments mixing too much.

Paint in the light-value yellow ochre in the middle section of the hilltop, and clean off your brush again. Then, pick up dark-value perylene green once more, this time painting it in from the right side until it once again touches the yellow ochre wash we just applied. Let these pigments naturally mix on the wet page. Now, there should be a wash of perylene green, with yellow ochre in the middle, depicting the sandy path in the middle of the grassy hill.

Let dry.

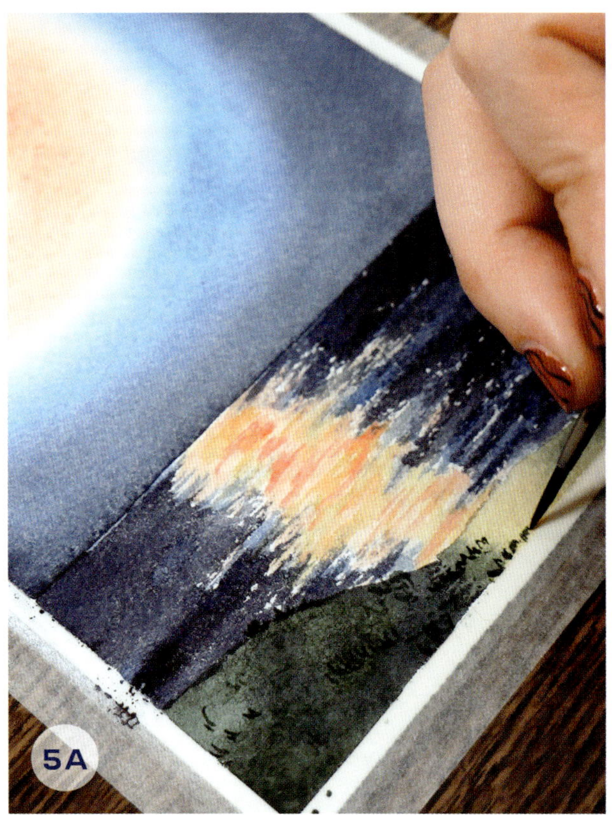

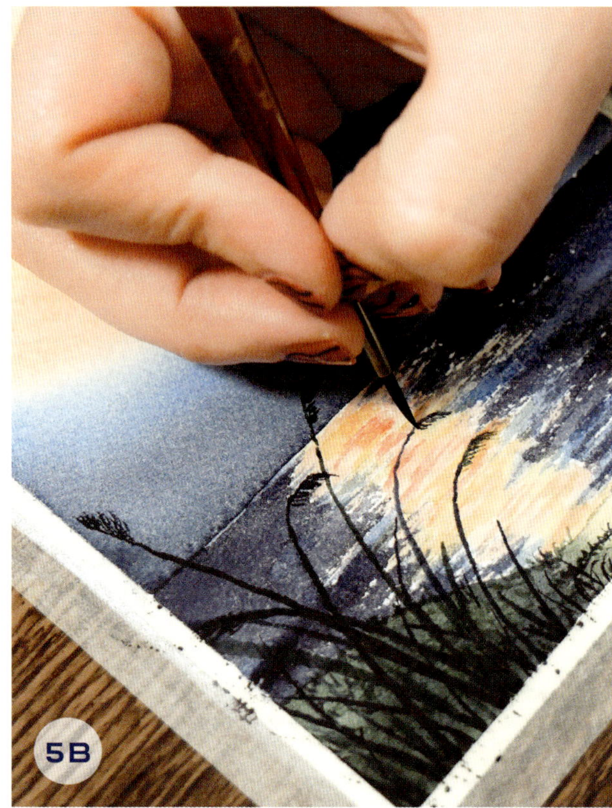

STEP 5: THE GRASSY HILL & SANDY PATH DETAILS

Now that your base wash is dry, it's time to add in some sprigs of grass. Grab your size 2 round brush, and load it up with dark-value perylene green. Paint in small sprigs of grass along both sides of the green hill. You can also paint some grass encroaching on the sandy path, as grass has a tendency to spread wherever it wants.

For the tall grass in the foreground, use both strokes of dark-value perylene green and dark-value indigo. I enjoy using this variety because dark-value indigo tends to be more opaque than perylene green—the difference in transparency adds to the illusion of depth on the paper.

To paint the tall grass, use a size 2 round brush or, if you have one, a small liner brush. For painting these long, skinny lines, make sure to use just the tip of your brush, applying more pressure to the brush bristles at the base of the grass and slowly lightening on the pressure as you move up the blade. This pressure difference will help you create long blades of grass that taper off at the end. Once you've created many overlapping pieces of grass, on a few of the taller ones, paint in small, short tufts at the tops. These are the seeds at the top of the grass stalk.

Let dry.

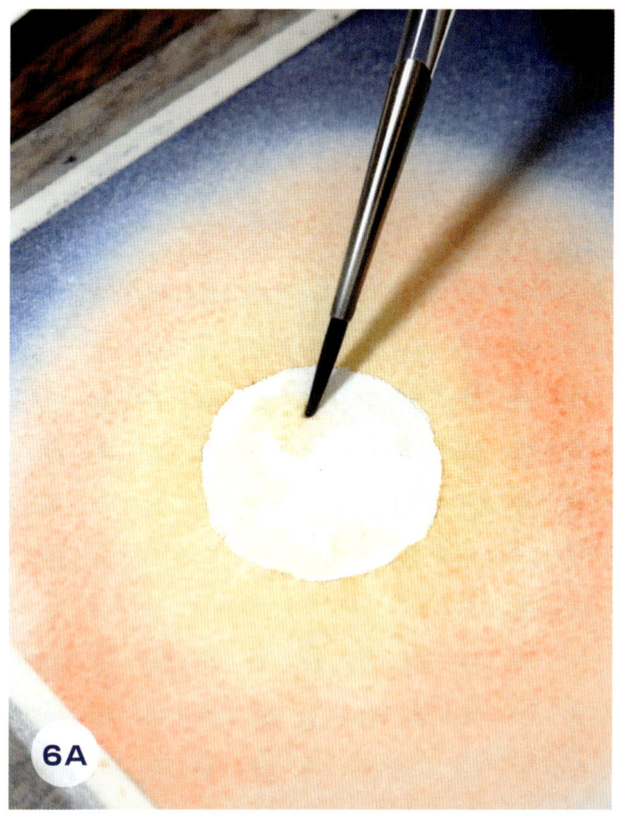

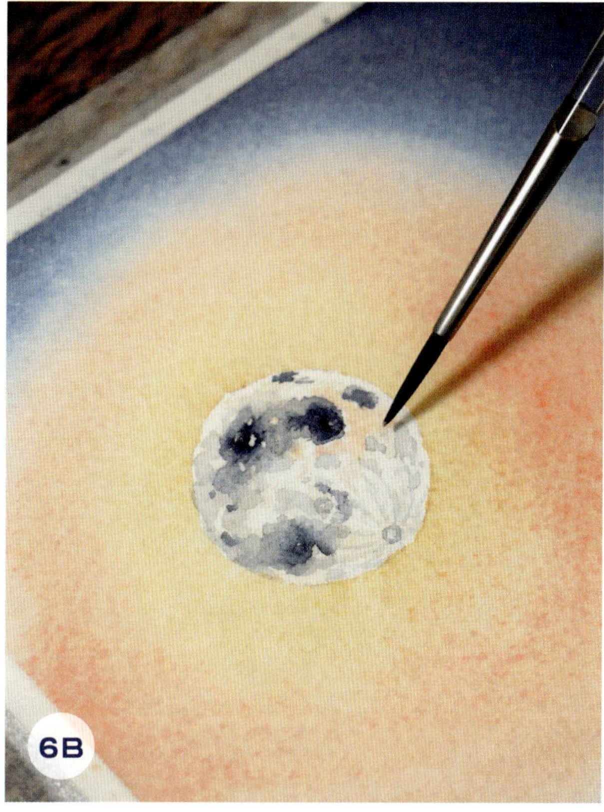

STEP 6: THE MOON

Carefully remove your masking fluid using the blunt end of a brush, your finger, a kneaded eraser or another gentle tool.

Once completely removed, we'll need to paint in the various craters on the moon. This will be accomplished in several layers. First, use a size 2 round brush to apply very light-value yellow ochre in varying shapes. Leave plenty of white space, as we're relying on the white of the paper to give the moon its dramatic glow.

Once the yellow ochre is dry, load up your brush with light-value indigo. Again, add in various round and blobby shapes, mimicking the texture of the many craters on the moon. At the bottom, paint a small circle surrounded by skinny lines in all directions—a distinct crater with blast marks. Your paint should be drying pretty quick, as we're painting in such a small space; therefore, you don't need to wait long before adding more indigo, this time in a darker value (medium or dark, your choice). Add in more splotches, some rounded, some blobby.

Lastly, let's add touches of Pastel Orange to give some warmth to the moon. Use your size 2 round brush to paint this color in and around the indigo craters. Let dry.

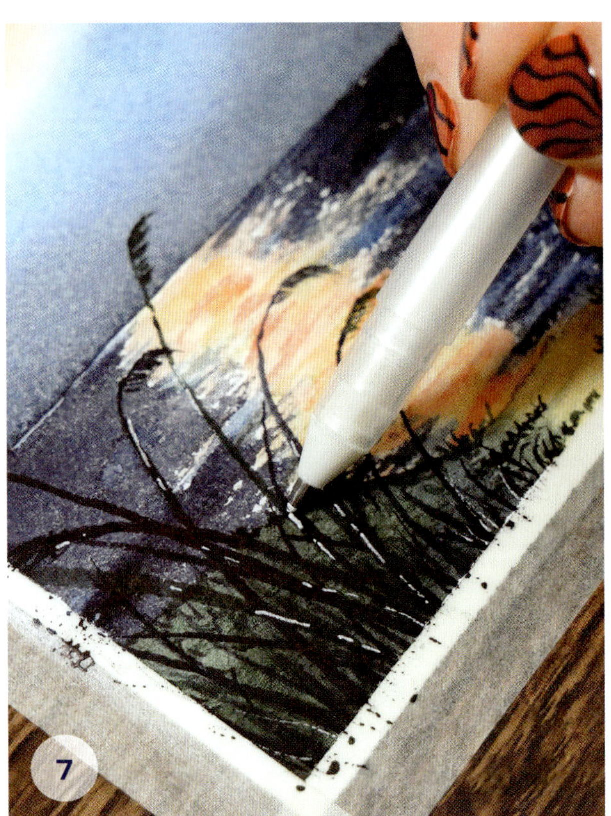

STEP 7: THE HIGHLIGHTS & STARS

For the finishing touches to our painting, grab your white gouache or white gel pen and a small detail brush. Add small white highlights along the blades of grasses to indicate light reflections. Additionally, draw/paint a multitude of stars in the sky. These stars won't be close to the moon because the moon's light would drown them out; therefore, only add these stars in the Prussian blue and indigo portions of the sky. Vary the size of these stars for variety and interest—and don't forget to add some that are twinkling!

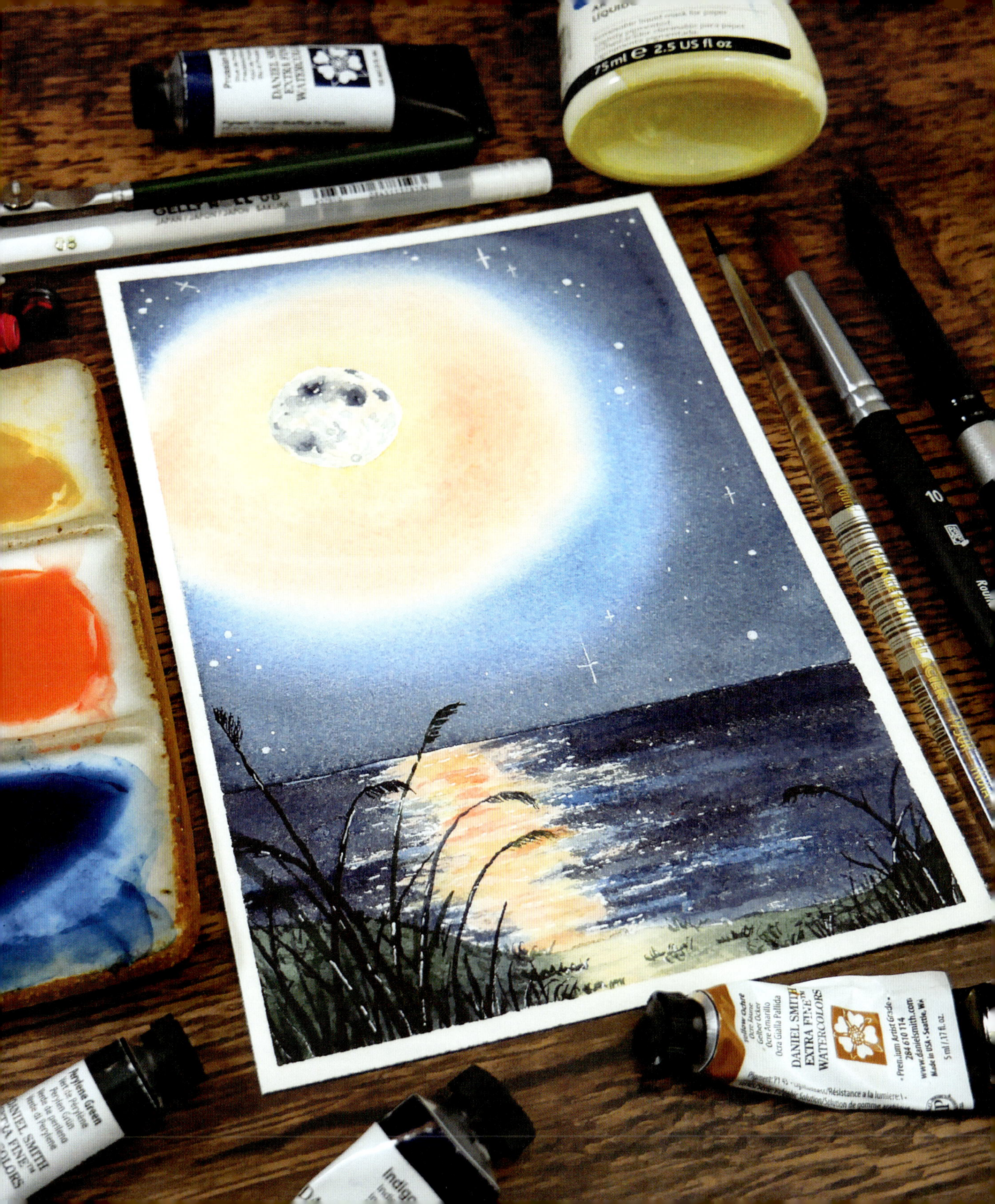
75ml ℮ 2.5 US fl oz
Yellow Ochre
DANIEL SMITH
EXTRA FINE™
WATERCOLORS
Perylene Green
Indigo

MOUNTAIN PATH TO THE GALAXY

Magic lights up the sky—a brilliant galaxy shining down on mountain peaks. There's a path that cuts across a grassy hill, disappearing into the pines in the distance. This seemingly daunting painting can be broken down piece by piece, section by section. Let's combine a vast majority of the skills we've learned in this book to create this magnificent scene.

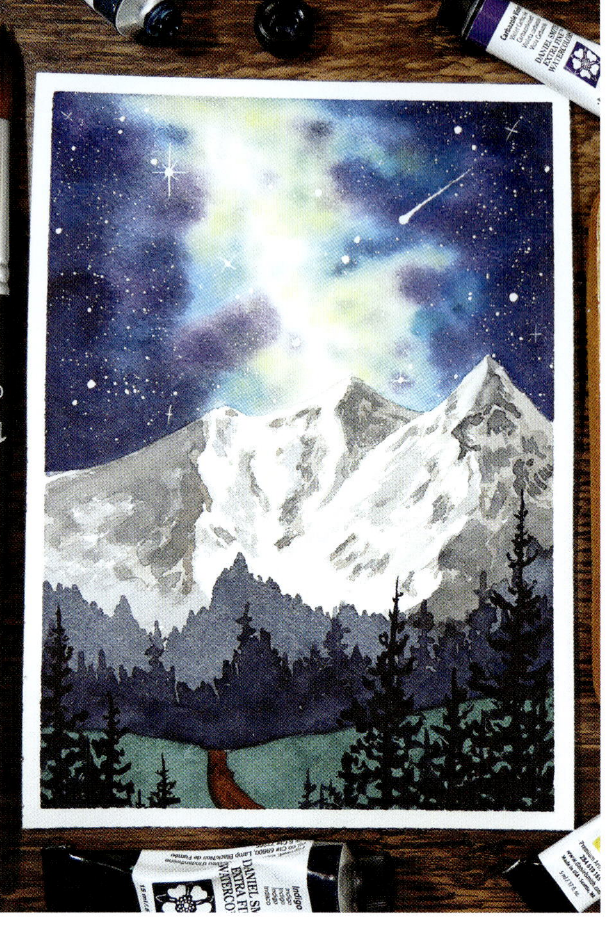

MATERIALS

Paints: lemon yellow, phthalo turquoise, carbazole violet, indigo, Neutral Gray (page 28), Payne's gray, Nighttime Grass (page 29) and burnt umber

Brushes: sizes 10, 6 and 2 round

Paper: 5 x 7-inch (13 x 18-cm) cold-pressed watercolor paper

Painter's tape (or washi tape)

Paper towels (or a rag)

Pencil and kneaded eraser

White gouache and/or white gel pen

SWATCHES

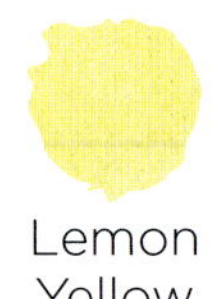

Lemon Yellow

Phthalo Turquoise

Carbazole Violet

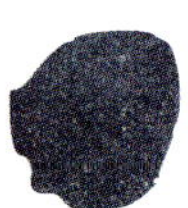

Indigo

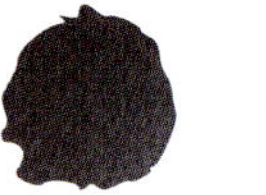

Neutral Gray (page 28)

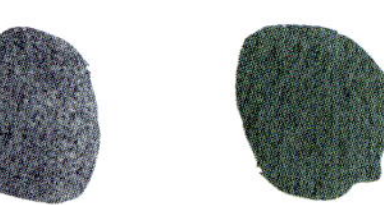

Payne's Gray

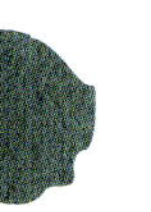

Nighttime Grass (page 29)

Burnt Umber

STEP 1: THE SKETCH

Like in previous projects, our sketch here is all about blocking out major shapes, not necessarily providing a ton of detail. Within the bottom one-third of your paper, draw your grassy hill with a path cutting across it. Above that, outline the shape of your distant forest and mountain peaks. On your mountain peaks, you can add in a few lines that detail where the shadows will fall. These shadow lines will roughly bisect each mountain. Then, take a ruler and create a few vertical lines at the bottom of the paper to outline where our foreground pine trees will go.

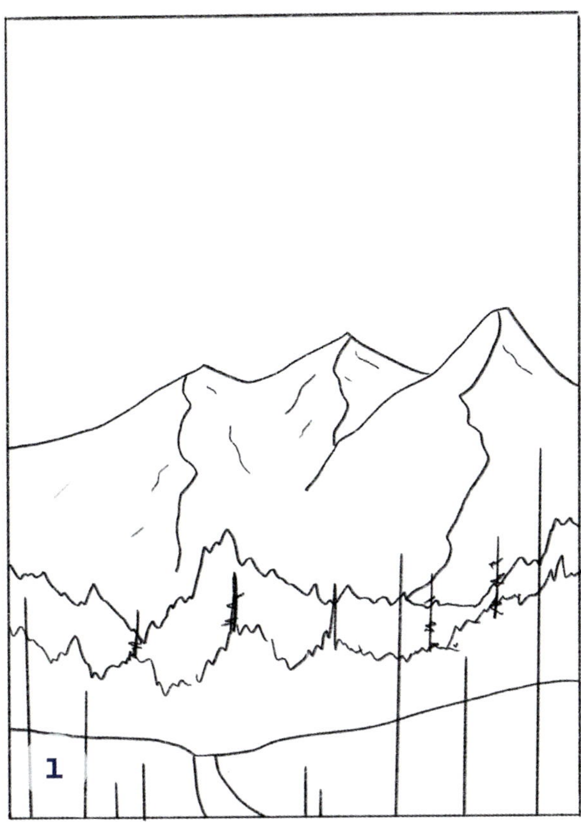

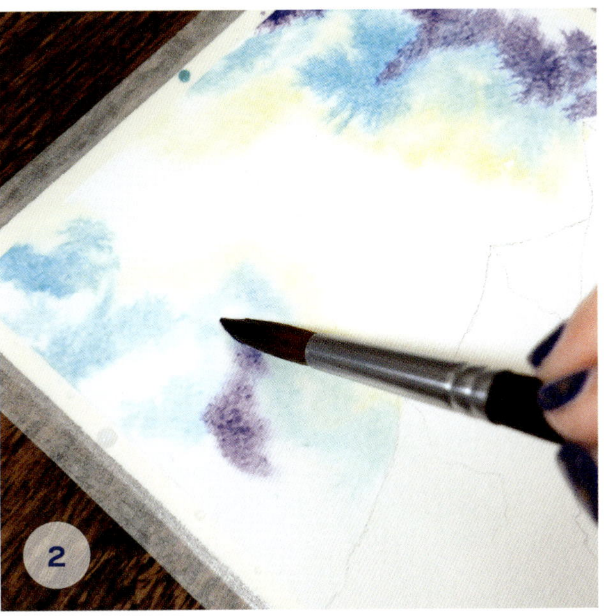

STEP 2: THE GALAXY (LAYER 1)

Unlike our previous galaxies (Milky Way Over the Desert, page 124, and Nighttime in the Towering Forest, page 132), we will be adding complementary colors to our sky to create a unique and powerful contrast. In order to do this, we'll need to avoid mixing lemon yellow and carbazole violet on the paper. We'll be tackling this task in two ways: We'll stick to mostly dropping color, rather than long and/or repetitive brushstrokes, and we'll buffer the lemon yellow and carbazole violet with a color that's in between them on the color wheel—phthalo turquoise.

With a size 10 round brush, wet only the sky with clean water. Carefully work your way around the tops of the mountains. We need our mountains to remain white, as they'll be covered in snow and rocky outcrops that we'll paint in future steps.

Once the sky portion is nice and glossy, pick up some light-value lemon yellow, and begin dropping in paint near the middle of the sky. Like before, we'll be leaving a portion of white in the middle. This white section creates luminosity and adds to the illusion of a million stars in the sky. After you've outlined your white middle section with lemon yellow, clean your brush, and begin to drop in light-value phthalo turquoise on either side of the yellow. As in the past, let these colors blend naturally on the wet page. Next, clean your brush, and load it up with medium-value carbazole violet, and repeat the steps you just completed with phthalo turquoise, dropping in the violet on the outside of the previous color.

Lastly, clean off your brush, and then pick up some medium-value indigo. Drop in the indigo outside of the carbazole violet, and fill in the rest of the paper up to the edges. As mentioned previously, the dark indigo color on the edges of your paper will help create depth.

Let dry.

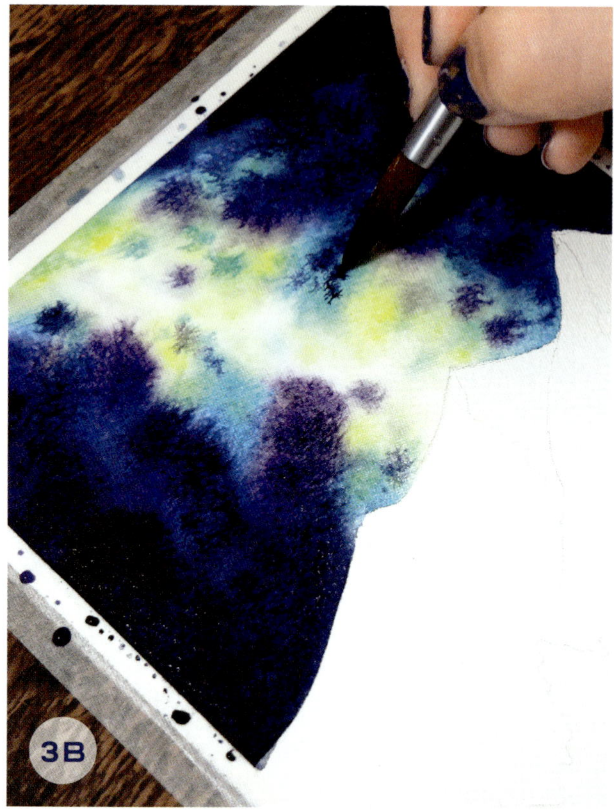

STEP 3: THE GALAXY (LAYERS 2 & 3)

Repeat the entire process from the previous step for a second and third layer. Each time, build up the color values of the lemon yellow, phthalo turquoise, carbazole violet and indigo. Additionally, allow the colors to exit their initial boundaries (for example, adding some phthalo turquoise to the carbazole violet area). To do this without muddying your colors, make sure to only drop in paint rather than stroke it in. Let the watercolor work its magic, dancing across the wet page to then dry in soft, blended edges.

For added texture to galaxies, I like to drop in darker pigments (for example, carbazole violet and indigo) within the lighter sections of the sky. This texture is akin to the space dust you can see in the Milky Way band (the darker sections among the brilliant starlight). Be careful not to go too overboard with this. If you drop in too much paint, you'll lose the glow from the white paper below, effectively canceling the contrast you've worked on over the course of a few layers of paint. If you drop in darker pigment and it spreads out too much, your paper is most likely too wet. Wait a few moments for the paper to begin to dry, and then try again.

Once you've painted a few layers and you're satisfied with your galaxy, let the entire layer dry before moving on to the mountaintops.

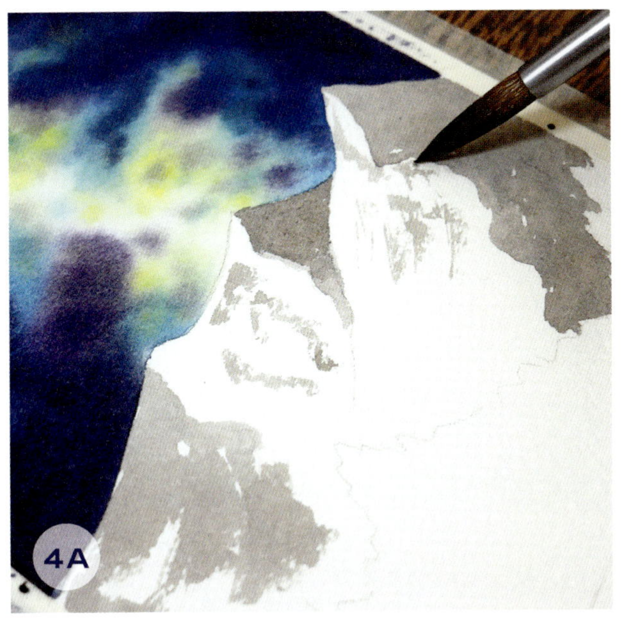

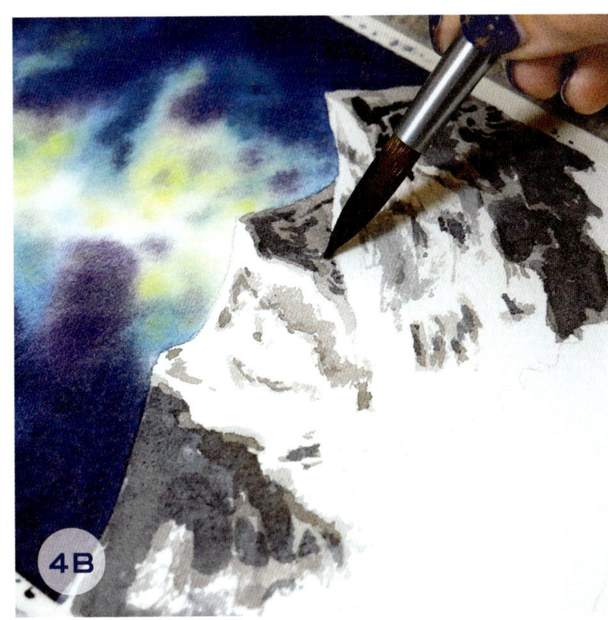

STEP 4: THE MOUNTAINTOPS

Like in the project Dancing Northern Lights (page 137), we're going to use multiple layers of paint to build up the details of our mountains. First, let's begin with painting the shadowed side of each peak.

The main source of light for this painting is the glowing galaxy sky; therefore, the shadows for the two mountain peaks on the right side of the paper will be on the right, and the mountain peak closer to the left side of the paper will have its shadow on the left. Load up your size 10 round brush with light-value Neutral Gray, and fill in the shadowed side of each peak. You don't need to extend these washes far down the paper, as we'll be adding in the silhouettes of forests in the middle ground. No worries if the wash isn't perfectly even; we'll be adding more details in the coming layers.

The dry-brushing technique (see page 46) always comes in handy for painting snowy mountaintops, so once you've painted in the mountain's shadows, feel free to dry brush in some additional details. Perhaps these are rocky sections where the snow can't stick or additional shadows created by the many dips and crevices in the mountain's side. That's for you to decide and interpret! A majority of painting mountains is simply making up textures and painting shapes as you go. Let this first light-value wash dry, and then pick up a slightly darker value of Payne's gray. Paint in additional shapes and shadows on each mountain, continuing to use the dry-brushing technique here and there, as well as various small washes. Let this layer of Payne's gray dry as well.

Next, load up your size 10 round brush with a light- to medium-value indigo, again repeating the same steps of adding various shapes, shadows and dry-brushed sections. Since our sky contains a lot of indigo, a fairly cool tone, it's important that we add that cool tone to our mountains as well. It will help the painting look cohesive. On that note, clean off your brush, and pick up some light-value lemon yellow, adding the color to some of the white sections of your mountains. Snow is very reflective, so it will reflect the color of the sky shining down on it.

Let your mountains dry before moving on.

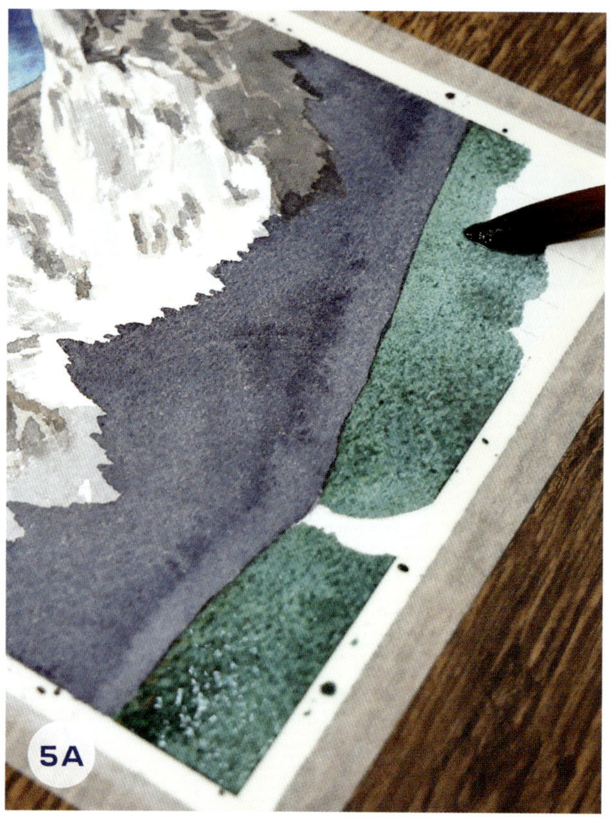

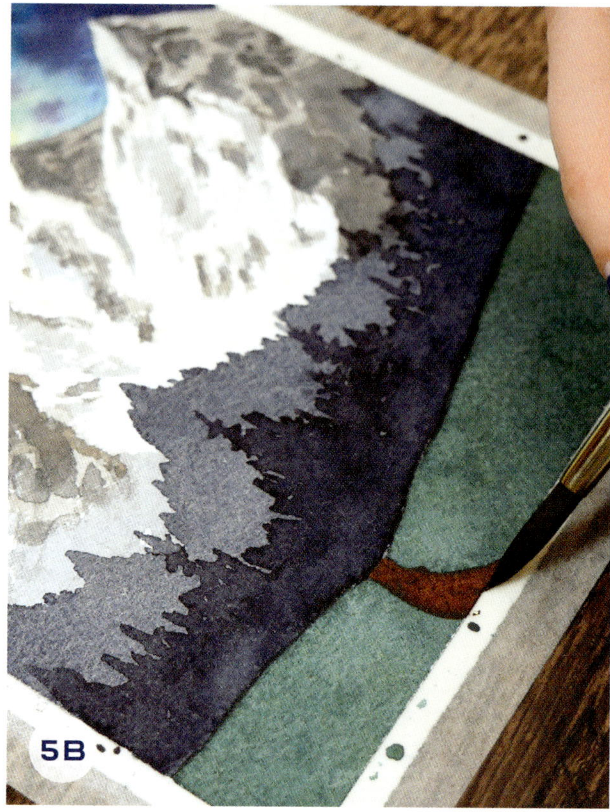

STEP 5: THE FOREST, PATH & GRASSY FIELD

Using your size 10 round brush, load it with light- to medium-value indigo, and begin filling in the sketch of your distant forest. Like in previous projects, the trees are too far away to see much detail, so we more or less just need to outline the tips of our trees. Use the pointed tip of the brush to achieve this effect. Let this first layer of indigo dry.

Clean off your brush, and then load it with medium-value Nighttime Grass, a color that works great for this piece due to it being mixed with pigments already contained within the painting. If possible, it's always better to use the same pigments already contained within your painting.

A painting created with a limited color palette will always look more cohesive than one with too many colors. That said, paint in the grassy field, avoiding painting over the path you sketched earlier. Leave this white, as we'll return to it momentarily to add in burnt umber. Let the grassy field dry.

Now, let's turn our attention back to the distant forest. It's looking a bit bare, so let's add in another layer of trees. Paint in these trees using a medium- to dark-value indigo, adding additional details like the tops of pines and more defined treetops. Let dry.

Finally, paint in the mountain path using a size 6 round brush loaded with dark-value burnt umber. Let dry.

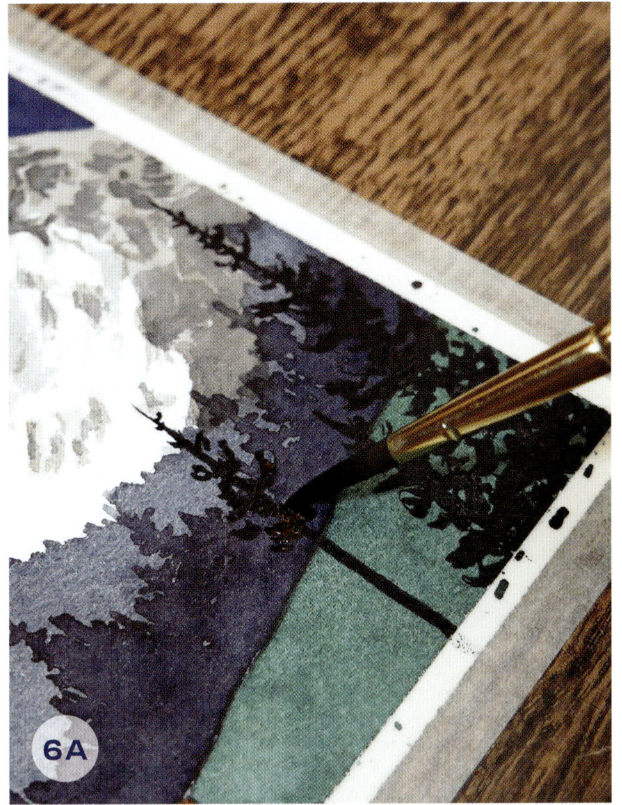

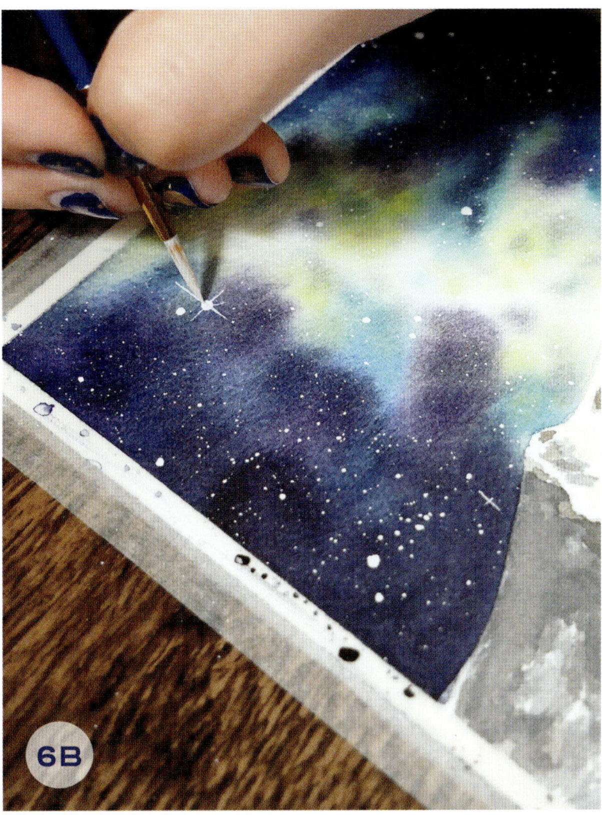

STEP 6: THE PINE TREES & STARS

Time to add in some foreground details and finishing touches! Using your size 6 round brush, paint some pine trees in the bottom right-hand and left-hand corners using a dark-value indigo. Let those dry, cover up the bottom portion of your painting with scrap sheets of paper and then use white gouache and the spatter technique to create stars in your galaxy sky (see page 58).

Lastly, with your white gouache, add in some stars of varying sizes with a small size 2 round brush, painting in some twinkling stars as well. For added magic, I used a white gel pen to create one falling star, shooting across the sky only to fade into the night (see page 130 for shooting stars).

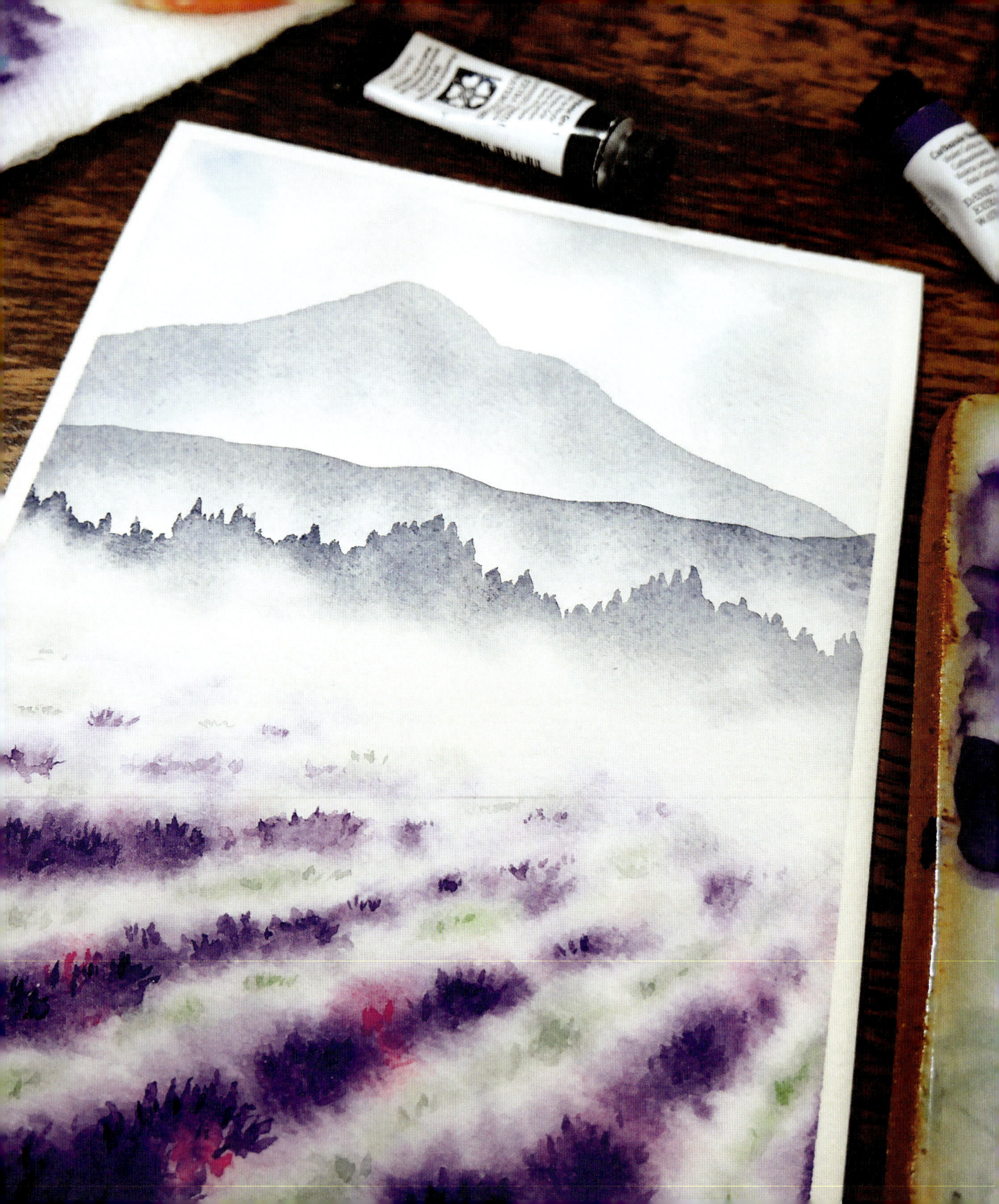

ACKNOWLEDGMENTS

Writing a book has always been a lifelong dream—who would've thought I would be writing one on watercolor painting? I certainly didn't. First and foremost, I need to thank my editors, Aïcha and Sarah, and to all those at Page Street, for taking a chance on me and making my dreams come true. Hilariously, when Aïcha first reached out to me through my Etsy shop, I initially thought it was a phishing attempt (perhaps my shock at being contacted for a book of all things also contributed to my disbelief). Needless to say, I'm so very glad that I reached back out. Aïcha, the amount of gratitude I feel cannot be fully expressed in words. Thank you for your endless kindness, patience and encouragement. Without you and the team, this book would not exist and I would still be dreaming.

Sarah, my best friend, and to whom this book is dedicated, was my constant consultant throughout the entire process. She provided me with guidance, gave me honest suggestions and helped me shape this book into what it is. I am a better person, artist and author because of her. Thank you, my friend. I don't know where I would be without your friendship.

Aunt Kathleen, you instilled in me a love of art from an early age. From gifting me my first sketchbook to our nature walks, you sowed the seeds of the nature lover, animal lover and art lover I am today. Thank you.

I also need to extend a huge thank you to my mom, dad and brother, who have always supported me through anything. Their excitement for me gave me encouragement and the fuel to continue on. My mom, especially, has heard many early drafts of chapters and seen many planning pieces, giving me advice and inspiration through it all.

For those curious about my various nail art throughout the book, I can thank my cousin Anna. Anna, thank you for your friendship and shared laughs—and for making my nails look fabulous!

I also need to thank my wonderful friends, Rachel and Arianna, for their time and help taking a wonderful About the Author photo. And Theresa, for lending us the use of the barn for photographs. It only seemed right that I include the place that is my second home.

To all of my friends and family—the buds, the barn family and more—thank you. You have lifted me up and encouraged me through every step of the process. This experience made me realize the incredible community I belong to and, for that, I am forever grateful.

Also, a BIG thank you to the incredible community of artists and other creatives on social media who have followed my journey, either joining from the beginning or somewhere along the way. I began posting my watercolor journey on Instagram on a whim, so it's incredible to believe where I am now. The sharing of art has brought an infinite amount of joy into my life, as I hope it does for you too. My biggest advice to any aspiring artist is to put yourself out there. You never know where you'll end up.

And, you, reader. Thank you for taking a chance on this book. I truly hope it brings a touch of magic into your life.

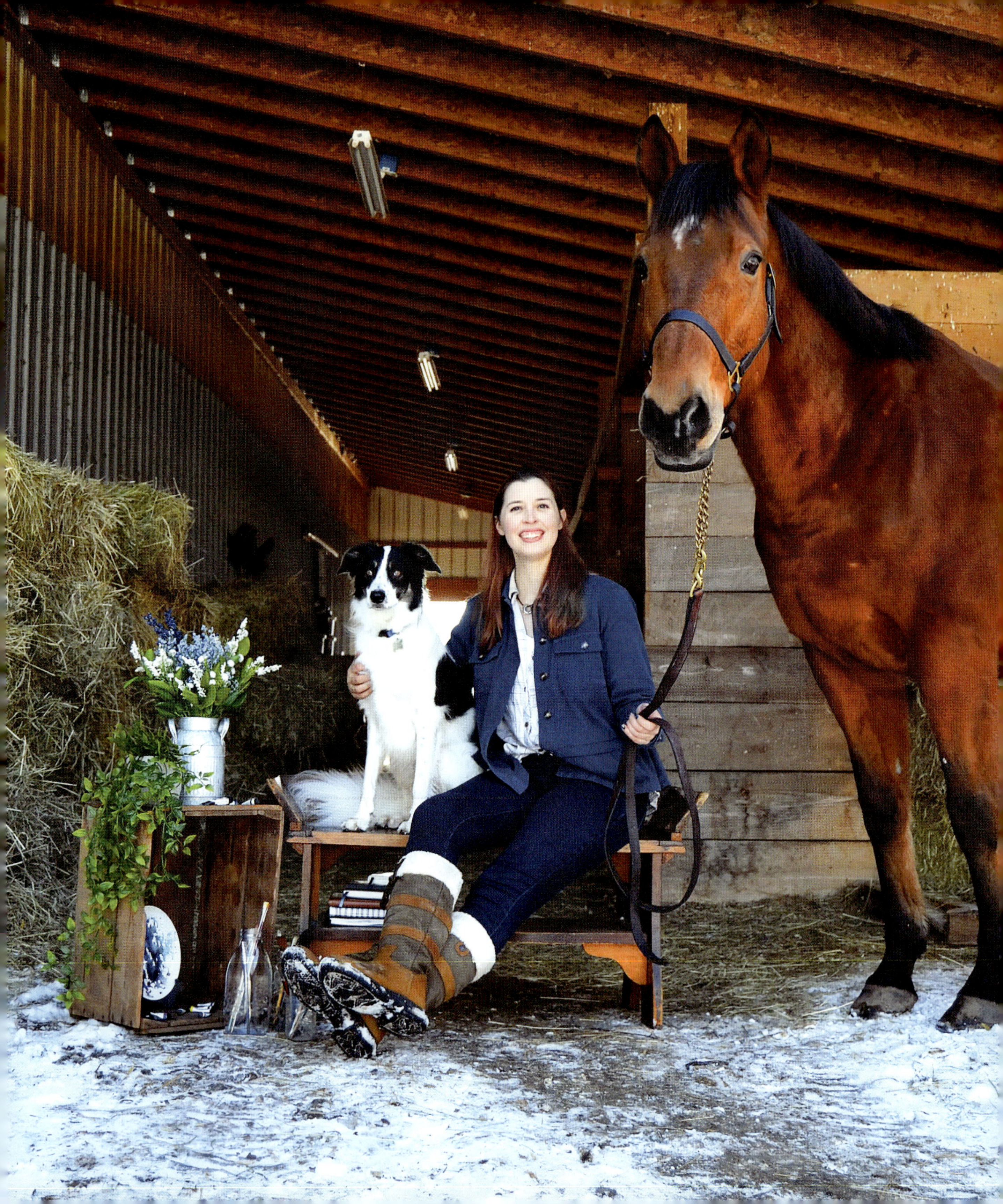

ABOUT THE AUTHOR

Rachael's love affair with watercolors began in 2018, right around the time she started an Instagram account called Rachy Sketches to document her journey attempting her first ever Inktober challenge. Initially, the account was a simple way to keep track of what she'd done, but it developed into something else entirely. Sketches turned into paintings—and her hobby turned into a business. Thus, Proximae Artistry was born, the name a combination of her favorite star, Proxima centauri, and her middle name, Mae.

Rachael is an environmental scientist by day, with a bachelor of science in toxicology and biology from Nazareth College and a master of science in sustainability from the University of Rochester, and an artist, an educator, a businesswoman and now an author by night. In addition to the painting tutorials and educational content she posts on Instagram, Rachael is also a Skillshare and Etchr teacher, with multiple online classes for artists to learn from—and she plans to develop more! She's also taught live demonstrations and classes out of her hometown in Rochester, New York.

You can learn more about Rachael by visiting her Instagram, @ProximaeArtistry, or Facebook page, Proximae Artistry. She also has an Etsy Shop, also called Proximae Artistry, where she sells stickers, bookmarks, art prints and originals of her work.

When Rachael isn't busy painting or trudging through wetlands, she loves to horseback ride; train her border collie, Finneas; read; play board games; and stare at the stars. She currently lives in the Rochester area with her three cats, Oliver, Pixie and Carney; two horses, Woody and Neuman; and dog, Finneas.

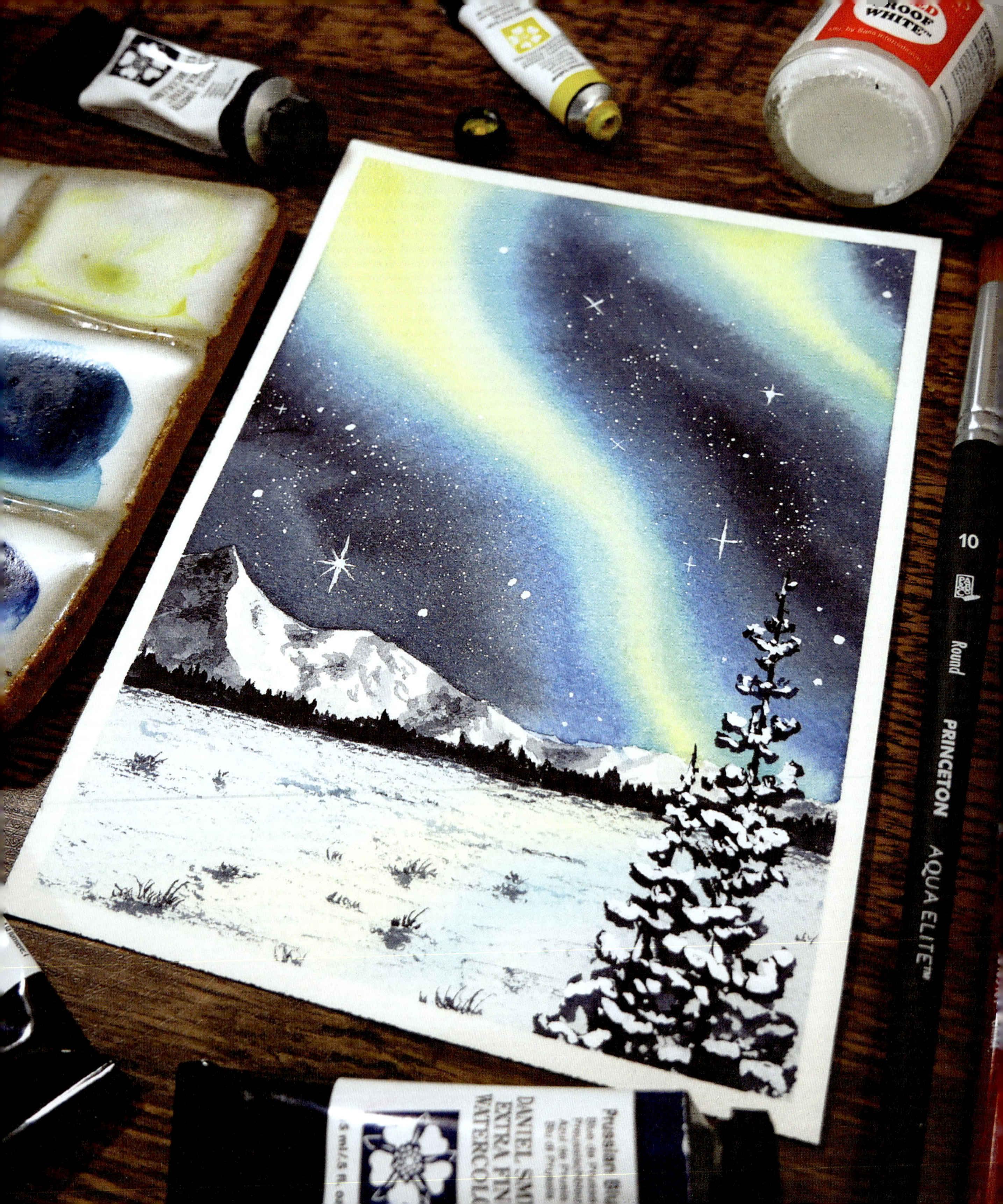
10
Round
PRINCETON
AQUA ELITE™

INDEX

E

F

G

H

I

J

K

L

R

S